Lecture Notes
in Business Information Processing

44

Series Editors

Wil van der Aalst
  Eindhoven Technical University

John Mylopoulos
  University of Trento, Italy

Michael Rosemann
  Queensland University of Technology, Brisbane, Qld, Australia

Michael J. Shaw
  University of Illinois, Urbana-Champaign, IL, USA

Clemens Szyperski
  Microsoft Research, Redmond, WA, USA

Wolfgang Ketter   Han La Poutré
Norman Sadeh   Onn Shehory
William Walsh (Eds.)

Agent-Mediated Electronic Commerce and Trading Agent Design and Analysis

AAMAS Workshop, AMEC 2008
Estoril, Portugal, May 12-16, 2008, and
AAAI Workshop, TADA 2008
Chicago, IL, USA, July 14, 2008
Revised Selected Papers

 Springer

Volume Editors

Wolfgang Ketter
RSM Erasmus University, Dept. of Decision and Information Sciences
Burgemeester Oudlaan 50, 3062 PA Rotterdam, The Netherlands
E-mail: wketter@rsm.nl

Han La Poutré
CWI – Centre for Mathematics and Computer Science
Sciencepark 123, 1098 XG Amsterdam, The Netherlands
E-mail: Han.La.Poutre@cwi.nl

Norman Sadeh
Carnegie Mellon University, ISR - School of Computer Science
5000 Forbes Avenue, Pittsburgh, PA 15213-3891, USA
E-mail: sadeh@cs.cmu.edu

Onn Shehory
IBM Haifa Research Lab
Haifa University Campus, Mount Carmel, Haifa 31905, Israel
E-mail: onn@il.ibm.com

William Walsh
CombineNet Inc.
Fifteen 27th Street, Pittsburgh, PA 15222, USA
E-mail: wwalsh@combinenet.com

Library of Congress Control Number: 2010932333

ACM Computing Classification (1998): K.4.4, J.1, I.2.11, H.3.5

ISSN   1865-1348
ISBN-10   3-642-15236-8 Springer Berlin Heidelberg New York
ISBN-13   978-3-642-15236-8 Springer Berlin Heidelberg New York

This work is subject to copyright. All rights are reserved, whether the whole or part of the material is concerned, specifically the rights of translation, reprinting, re-use of illustrations, recitation, broadcasting, reproduction on microfilms or in any other way, and storage in data banks. Duplication of this publication or parts thereof is permitted only under the provisions of the German Copyright Law of September 9, 1965, in its current version, and permission for use must always be obtained from Springer. Violations are liable to prosecution under the German Copyright Law.

springer.com

© Springer-Verlag Berlin Heidelberg 2010
Printed in Germany

Typesetting: Camera-ready by author, data conversion by Scientific Publishing Services, Chennai, India
Printed on acid-free paper   06/3180   5 4 3 2 1 0

Preface

The design and analysis of electronic commerce systems in which agents are deployed involves finding solutions to a large and diverse array of problems, concerning individual agent behaviors, interaction, and collective behavior. A wide variety of electronic commerce scenarios and systems, including agent approaches to these, have been studied in recent years. These studies suggest models that support the design and the analysis at both the level of the single agent and the level of the multiagent system.

This volume contains revised, selected papers from the 10th Workshop on Agent-Mediated Electronic Commerce (AMEC-X), co-located with the 7th International Joint Conference on Autonomous Agents and Multiagent Systems (AAMAS 2008), and from the 6th Workshop on Trading Agent Design and Analysis (TADA), co-located with the 23rd AAAI Conference on Artificial Intelligence (AAAI 2008). The primary, and complementary, goal of both workshops was to continue to bring together novel work from diverse fields that focus on modeling, implementation, and evaluation of computational trading institutions and/or agent strategies.

The papers in this volume that originated at AMEC address a variety of issues in the field of electronic commerce in general and agent and multiagent problems in the context of electronic commerce in particular. An interesting example of the diversity is a paper that suggests a test that can prevent a single user from creating multiple accounts. Some other papers in this volume focus on negotiation. For instance, in one study, preferences and reasoning are incorporated into a negotiation model to improve overall negotiation results. Another work facilitates the learning of preferences and their usage for negotiation. Automated bargaining is yet another aspect of negotiation addressed in this volume.

In addition to negotiation which is mostly two-sided, some studies in this volume address dynamic pricing and auctions, where multiple agents take part in the mechanism. For instance, one paper suggests the use of option pricing as a means to solving the exposure problem in sequential auctions. Another paper studies markets in which multiple double auctions are implemented and agents can select their auction of preference, thus introducing competition among the auctions. Dynamic pricing is also studied, where agents hold limited information regarding preferences and need to update prices of multiattribute goods dynamically.

In many cases, multiagent electronic commerce requires that agents be allocated tasks. The problem of task allocation is complex, and solutions depend on specific settings. In this volume, one study addresses task allocation in a social setting where agents attempt to under-report. The suggested solution devises means to prevent such under-reporting. In another study, task allocation is associated with a recommender system.

The papers in this volume that originated at TADA stem from the effort of the community to design scenarios where trading agent designers and market designers can be pitched against one another.

The Trading Agent Competition (TAC) has included several scenarios over the years, which have stimulated considerable research in autonomous economic behavior. The supply-chain management (TAC SCM) scenario placed six agents in the role of a PC manufacturer. Each agent had to procure raw materials and sell finished goods in competitive markets while managing inventory and production facilities. The supply-chain scenario included two side competitions. The first was a procurement challenge that allowed agents to balance risk and cost in the procurement market by providing both long-term and short-term contracts. The second was a prediction challenge designed to test price-prediction capabilities of competing agents in both procurement and sales markets. In contrast to the supply-chain scenario, which cast the competing agents as traders, the CAT scenario placed agents in the role of competing exchanges. The CAT competition was motivated by the rise of independent, for profit, stock and commodity exchanges that compete for the attention of traders. CAT agents competed by defining rules for matching buyers and sellers and by setting commission fees for their services. Profitability was the ultimate measure of performance in both the supply chain and CAT scenarios.

This volume includes two papers related to TAC SCM, one related to TAC Travel, and one related to the Market Design Competition (CAT). One of the papers focused on various aspects of performance analysis for the TAC SCM procurement and prediction challenges, giving an assessment of the agents' prediction performance in isolation of other decision components. The complexity and uncertainty in the baseline TAC SCM game scenario make it difficult to assess prediction accuracy, since the predictions of one agent affect another. One paper presented a survey of agent designs in TAC SCM. The survey showed that, in some areas such as modularity, there are common themes emerging in how to design a successful trading agent, while in other areas, such as coordination, there are strong differences in the designs. Another paper undertook an experimental study of bidding heuristics designed for the TAC Travel game, showing that using as much distributional information as possible is an effective approach for an agent in one-shot auctions settings. Another paper discussed how to classify bidding strategies in CAT, and found out that using a Hidden Markov Model yields the best results.

The decision on paper acceptance was not easy, as we had excellent submissions to select from. We believe that the resulting volume presents both quality and diversity. We have studies related to auctions and pricing; we have theoretical and experimental studies; we have research on automated negotiation and on market mechanism design; we have work on reputation; we also have work on trading agent design and dynamic market modeling and pricing.

The list of topics presented in this volume is diverse, but they all contribute to the theory and practice of agent electronic commerce. The papers included in this volume suggest models that support the design and the analysis at the level of the single agent and at the level of the multiagent system. Hence, this book addresses both the agent level and the system level, combining design and analysis aspects of electronic commerce. The primary goal of this volume is to continue to bring together novel work from diverse fields such as computer science, game theory, economics, artificial intelligence and distributed systems that focus on modeling, implementation and evaluation of computational trading agents and institutions. We hope that this collection indeed meets this goal.

Finally, we would like to conclude by thanking the members of the Program Committees of the AMEC and the TADA workshops. They were able to produce a large number of high-quality reviews in a very short time span. Furthermore, we would also like to thank the authors for submitting their papers to our workshops, as well as the active attendees and panelists for their valuable insights and discussions. These reviews helped the authors improve the revised papers published in this volume.

August 2008

Wolfgang Ketter
Han La Poutré
Norman Sadeh
Onn Shehory
William Walsh

Organization

AMEC Organizing Committee

Han La Poutré	CWI Amsterdam, The Netherlands
Onn Shehory	IBM Haifa Research Lab, Israel

TADA Organizing Committee

Wolfgang Ketter	Erasmus University, The Netherlands
Norman Sadeh	Carnegie Mellon University, USA
William Walsh	CombineNet Inc, USA

AMEC Program Committee

Chris Brooks	University of San Francisco, USA
Vincent Conitzer	Duke University, USA
John Debenham	University of Technology, Australia
Frank Dignum	Utrecht University, The Netherlands
Ulle Endriss	University of Amsterdam, The Netherlands
Shaheen Fatima	University of Liverpool, UK
Enrico Gerding	University of Southampton, UK
Amy Greenwald	Brown University, USA
Sverker Janson	Swedish Institute of Computer Science, Sweden
Kate Larson	University of Waterloo, Canada
Julian Padget	University of Bath, UK
David Pardoe	University of Texas at Austin, USA
Simon Parsons	Brooklyn College, City University of New York, USA
Juan Antonio Rodriguez-Aguilar	IIIA-CSIC, Catalonia, Spain
Jeffrey Rosenschein	Hebrew University of Jerusalem, Israel
Alberto Sardinha	Carnegie Mellon University, USA
William Walsh	CombineNet Inc, USA
Michael Wellman	University of Michigan, USA
Mike Wooldridge	University of Liverpool, UK

TADA Program Committee

Michael Benisch	Carnegie Mellon University, USA
Ken Brown	University College Cork, Ireland
John Collins	University of Minnesota, USA
Maria Fasli	Essex University, UK

Shaheen Fatima	University of Liverpool, UK
Enrico Gerding	University of Southampton, UK
Maria Gini	University of Minnesota, USA
Amy Greenwald	Brown University, USA
Sverker Janson	Swedish Institute of Computer Science, Sweden
Patrick Jordan	University of Michigan, USA
Kate Larson	University of Waterloo, Canada
Kevin Leyton-Brown	University of British Columbia, Canada
Peter McBurney	University of Liverpool, UK
Pericles A. Mitkas	Aristotle University of Thessaloniki, Greece
Tracy Mullen	Penn State University, USA
Benno Overeinder	Vrije Universiteit Amsterdam, The Netherlands
Julian Padget	University of Bath, UK
David Pardoe	University of Texas at Austin, USA
Simon Parsons	Brooklyn College, City University of New York, USA
Juan Antonio Rodriguez Aguilar	IIIA-CSIC, Catalonia, Spain
Jeffrey Rosenschein	Hebrew University of Jerusalem, Israel
Alberto Sardinha	Carnegie Mellon University, USA
Peter Stone	University of Texas at Austin, USA
Ioannis A. Vetsikas	University of Southampton, UK
Michael Wellman	University of Michigan, USA
Dongmo Zhang	University of Western Sydney, Australia
Haizheng Zhang	Penn State University, USA

Table of Contents

Preventing Under-Reporting in Social Task Allocation

Mathijs de Weerdt and Yingqian Zhang

Delft University of Technology
{M.M.deWeerdt,Yingqian.Zhang}@tudelft.nl

Abstract. In games where agents are asked to declare their available resources, they can also strategize over this declaration. Surprisingly, not in all such games a VCG payment can be applied to construct a truthful mechanism using an optimal algorithm, though such payments can prevent under-reporting of resources. We show this for the problem of allocating tasks in a social network (STAP).

Since STAP is NP-hard, we introduce an approximation algorithm as well. However for such an approximation, a VCG payment cannot prevent under-reporting anymore. Therefore we introduce an alternative payment function that motivates agents to fully declare their resources. We also demonstrate by experiments that the approximation algorithm works well in different types of social networks.

1   Introduction

In combinatorial auctions (CAs) agents try to buy sets (or bundles) of resources (or items) from an auctioneer preferably for less than what such a set is worth to them [1]. The values for these sets come for example from tasks that require these resources. In this paper we work towards a more general setting of such a resource allocation problem where the available resources have not just been trusted with a (central) auctioneer, but where these resources are owned by other agents.

In such a general resource allocation setting there are two classes of strategizing agents. On the one hand, there are agents that attach some value to specific sets of resources and construct bids based on this value (we call these the *managers*), and on the other hand there are agents that own resources and can decide to offer these resources to the others (we call these the *contractors*). In most current work on CAs [2] and resource allocation [3], agents are only allowed to strategize over the *value* of each bundle of resources. Here we consider the case where they may only strategize over the resources they have at their disposal.

As an application of the general resource allocation problem, consider a setting where a governmental institution would like to provide a platform to bring both suppliers and consumers together to form new contracts. In general, not all consumers (managers) want to buy services or resources from all suppliers (contractors), and not all contractors want to sell their resources to all managers.

W. Ketter et al. (Eds.): AMEC/TADA 2008, LNBIP 44, pp. 1–14, 2010.
© Springer-Verlag Berlin Heidelberg 2010

We therefore include such a setting of preferred partnerships in our model as a graph where the agents are nodes, and an edge between two nodes indicates the existence of a social relation between the agents concerned, meaning that these agents are prepared to exchange resources. We call this problem, where the contractor agents can strategize over the resources they declare to their neighboring managers, the social task allocation problem (STAP) [4].

From the perspective of the general resource allocation problem introduced above, this problem can be seen as a variant of reverse CAs where it is publicly known how valuations depend on allocated resources, but the resources available to each contractor are private. As we will see in Section 3, this means that lying agents can incur infeasible solutions, and Vickrey-Clarke-Groves (VCG) mechanisms [5,6,7] are no longer truthful.

In this paper we study the strategies of the contractors in STAP for two different mechanisms: for an optimal algorithm with a VCG payment, and for a greedy approximation with an alternative payment function. First we start with a formal introduction of STAP and the mechanism design problem for STAP (Section 2). There we distinguish between two types of strategic behavior for the contractor agents: they can declare resources they do not have (over-reporting), or they can omit resources they do have (under-reporting). Next we show in Section 3 that even an optimal algorithm with a VCG payment cannot make truth-telling incentive compatible regarding both under- and over-reporting. Knowing that an optimal algorithm cannot deal with larger instances since STAP is NP-complete, we introduce an approximation and an alternative payment function in Section 4 with similar truth-telling properties as the VCG payment (i.e., only preventing under-reporting). Finally, we analyze the quality of the heuristic experimentally, and draw our conclusions in Sections 5 and 6, respectively.

2   Preliminaries

In STAP, we start from a *social network* SN of a set of agents $\mathcal{A}$. This social network $SN = (\mathcal{A}, AE)$ is an undirected graph where vertices $\mathcal{A}$ are agents and each edge $(i,j) \in AE$ indicates the existence of a social connection between agents i and j. Some of the agents have a set of resources at their disposal. These are the *contractor* agents. Resources come in different types. The set of l resource types is R. The amount of resources of each type an agent $i \in \mathcal{A}$ has available is defined by the function $s_i : R \to \mathbb{N}$.

Some agents, called *managers*, have tasks they can perform to get some utility. The set of all n tasks is denoted by $\mathcal{T} = \{t_1, \ldots, t_n\}$. Each task t is defined by a tuple $\langle U(t), req(t), loc(t) \rangle$, where $U(t)$ is the utility gained if task t is accomplished, $req(t) : R \to \mathbb{N}$ is a function that specifies the resources required for the accomplishment of task t, and $loc(t) : \mathcal{A}$ defines the manager of task t.

The exact assignment of how many resources of which type from which agent are assigned to which tasks is defined by a *task allocation*, which is a mapping $o : \mathcal{T} \times \mathcal{A} \times R \to \mathbb{N}$. A task allocation must obey the social relationships—each agent's resources can only be allocated to tasks that are (direct) neighbors of this agent in the social network SN. A valid task allocation must also be: (1) correct—each agent cannot use more than its available resources; and (2) complete—each task is either not allocated or it receives all required resources. The set of all valid task allocations for a specific problem setting is denoted by $\mathcal{O}$. We write T_o to represent the tasks allocated in $o \in \mathcal{O}$. The utility of o is the sum of the utilities of each task in T_o, i.e., $U(T_o) = \sum_{t \in T_o} U(t)$. Note that we do not include costs for resources; we assume they are already owned by the contractor agents. The goal of the *social task allocation problem* (STAP) is to find an *optimal* task allocation o^*, such that o^* is valid and $U(T_{o^*})$ is maximal. STAP is NP-complete [4].

In this paper, we study the social task allocation problem in a *mechanism design* setting where the contractors can only strategize over the set of resources they declare. We give a brief summary of relevant mechanism design concepts below, but for a more elaborate introduction see e.g. [8]. In a mechanism design setting, we provide a method that determines an outcome, i.e., a valid task allocation $o \in \mathcal{O}$, given the inputs (called strategies) from in this case the contractor agents, and possibly some additional true (often public) information. In our case this is the social network and a set of tasks. We use Z to denote the space for this external information in STAP. Each $z \in Z$ is a tuple $(SN, \mathcal{T})$.

In the mechanism design setting we consider, each contractor is asked to declare its available resources, i.e., $s_i : R \to \mathbb{N}$. The set of all such functions is called its type space S. The type space of all m agents is defined by S^m. We use $\mathbf{s} = (s_1, \ldots, s_m) \in S^m$ to denote the *type profile* of the agents. We sometimes denote $\mathbf{s}$ by $(s_i, \mathbf{s}_{-i})$, where $\mathbf{s}_{-i}$ denotes the types of all agents except i. An agent can decide to declare another set of resources other than its true type. The set of all such choices is called its strategy space A. In our case $A = S$.

When the mechanism receives inputs $\mathbf{a} = (a_1, \ldots, a_m) \in A^m$ (called a *strategy profile*), it selects an allocation $o = O(z, \mathbf{a})$ with some allocation algorithm O. In addition, the mechanism computes payments $(p_1(z, \mathbf{a}), \ldots, p_m(z, \mathbf{a}))$ for all contractor agents. The result for agent i, called its *utility*, is the sum of the *valuation* v_i that i gets from the resulting allocation o with its type s_i and the payment it receives from the mechanism: $u_i(\mathbf{a}) = v_i(s_i, o) + p_i(z, \mathbf{a})$. This utility model is called *quasilinear*. This utility u_i is what agent i aims to maximize. In STAP, we define the valuation of a contractor agent i as its fair share of the utilities of the tasks it helped to fulfill. For this we define the *efficiency* e of a task t by dividing the utility of t by the total number of required resources for t: $e(t) = \frac{U(t)}{\sum_{r \in R} req(t)(r)}$. An agent then receives for each resource it is contributing the efficiency of the task it is allocated to, thus $v_i(a_i, o) = \sum_{t \in T_o} \sum_{r \in R} o(t, i, r) \cdot e(t)$. However, agent i may not be able to fully contribute to a given allocation $o = O(z, \mathbf{a})$ because it is asked for resources it does not own. Therefore we define the valuation $v_i(s_i, o)$ that agent i obtains based on its true type s_i as

$$v_i(s_i, o) = \sum_{t \in T'_{o,i}} \sum_{r \in R} o(t, i, r) \cdot e(t), \tag{1}$$

where $T'_{o,i} = \{t \in T_o \mid \forall_r o(t, i, r) \leq s_i(r)\}$ is the set of allocated tasks that are feasible regarding agent i's true type.

The *social welfare* $W(o)$ of the system is the sum of the valuations of the contractors in the allocation o, i.e., $W(o) = \sum_{i=1}^m v_i(s_i, o)$. We use this to define the mechanism design problem for STAP formally.

Definition 1 (Mechanism design for STAP). *Given the parameter space Z, the type space S, and the strategy space A, the* mechanism design problem for STAP *is to find a mechanism $\mathcal{M} = (O, p)$ that consists of an allocation function $O : Z \times A \to \mathcal{O}$, and a payment function $p : Z \times A \to \mathbb{R}$ such that the selected output $o \in \mathcal{O}$ maximizes the total social welfare $W(o)$.*

One of the most desirable properties of a mechanism is *truthfulness*.

Definition 2 (Truthful). *Given an output algorithm O, a mechanism is* truthful *if $A = S$, and for any parameter $z \in Z$, for any strategy profile $\mathbf{a_{-i}} \in A^{m-1}$, for any agent i with type $s_i \in S$, and for any other type $a_i \in A$, it holds that*

$$u_i(s_i, \mathbf{a}_{-i}) = v_i(s_i, O(z, s_i, \mathbf{a}_{-i})) + p_i(z, s_i, \mathbf{a}_{-i})$$
$$\geq u_i(a_i, \mathbf{a}_{-i}) = v_i(s_i, O(z, a_i, \mathbf{a}_{-i})) + p_i(z, a_i, \mathbf{a}_{-i}).$$

Informally, under a truthful mechanism, an agent i is never worse off by revealing its true private type s_i to the mechanism, no matter what strategies other agents play. In this paper, we study two types of lying by contractor agent i: (1) *under-reporting* its available resource types or amounts, i.e., $\exists_{r \in R} a_i(r) < s_i(r)$, denoted by $a_i < s_i$, and (2) *over-reporting* its available resource types or amounts, i.e., $\exists_{r \in R} a_i(r) > s_i(r)$, denoted by $a_i > s_i$.[1] We define *truthfulness with respect to under-reporting* and *truthfulness with respect to over-reporting* as follows.

Definition 3. *Given an output algorithm O, a mechanism is* truthful with respect to under-reporting *(or* with respect to over-reporting*) if $A = S$, and for any parameter $z \in Z$, for any strategy profile $\mathbf{a_{-i}} \in A^{m-1}$, for any agent i with type $s_i \in S$ and for any other type $a_i \in A$ and $a_i < s_i$ (or $a_i > s_i$), it holds that*

$$u_i(s_i, \mathbf{a}_{-i}) = v_i(s_i, O(z, s_i, \mathbf{a}_{-i})) + p_i(z, s_i, \mathbf{a}_{-i})$$
$$\geq u_i(a_i, \mathbf{a}_{-i}) = v_i(s_i, O(z, a_i, \mathbf{a}_{-i})) + p_i(z, a_i, \mathbf{a}_{-i}).$$

Proposition 1. *If a mechanism for STAP is truthful then it is both truthful with respect to under-reporting as well as truthful with respect to over-reporting.*

Proof. This follows immediately from Definition 2 and Definition 3.

A mechanism is *individually rational* (IR) when an agent never receives negative utility by declaring its true type. We are looking for a mechanism that is IR, because otherwise agents have no incentive to take part at all.

It is well known that truthful mechanisms can be achieved with carefully designed payment functions, such as VCG payments [5,6,7]. Nisan et al. [9] also

---

[1] Note that agents can in principle also under-report some and over-report some other resources. We will discuss this mixed lying type at the end of Section 3.

showed that truthfulness is guaranteed by a VCG payment if the mechanism outputs the optimal solution. However, in the next section, we show that VCG mechanisms with an optimal algorithm can only achieve truthfulness with respect to under-reporting, but not with respect to over-reporting. Consequently, it is impossible to have a truthful VCG mechanism for STAP.

3   An Exact VCG Mechanism for STAP

In this section, we first introduce an optimal allocation algorithm for STAP, and then a VCG mechanism to incentivize agents to report their true types with respect to under-reporting.

The optimal task allocation algorithm should deal with the restrictions posed by the social network. We translate this NP-complete problem to an integer linear programming (ILP) problem and use the GNU Linear Programming Kit [10] to solve this problem. For the ILP formulation we introduce two types of variables: the binary variables $y_j \in \{0, 1\}$ for $1 \leq j \leq n$ describe whether or not task j is allocated, and the integer variables $\forall_{1 \leq j \leq n, 1 \leq i \leq m, 1 \leq k \leq l} \; x_{ijk}$ denote the amount of resources of type k agent i supplies to task j. The ILP formulation then looks as follows: maxmize $\sum_{j=1}^{n} y_j \cdot U(t_j)$, subject to having sufficient resources of each type for each chosen task from the neighboring agents, and not using more resources than there are available, i.e.

$$\forall_{1 \leq j \leq n} \forall_{1 \leq k \leq l} \quad \sum_{\{i \in [1,m] | (i, loc(t_j)) \in AE\}} x_{ijk} \geq y_j \cdot req(t_j)(r_k), \text{ and}$$
$$\forall_{1 \leq i \leq m} \forall_{1 \leq k \leq l} \quad \sum_{j=1}^{n} x_{ijk} \leq rsc(i)(r_k).$$

This optimal algorithm (OPT) is in the worst case exponential in the number of variables, i.e., the number of tasks, agents, and resource types.

Our mechanism is then developed using OPT and a VCG payment scheme as follows.

Definition 4 ($\mathcal{M}_{\mathsf{OPT}}$ for STAP). *Let $z = (SN, \mathcal{T})$ be given. The **task allocation mechanism** $\mathcal{M}_{\mathsf{OPT}}$ is then defined as follows. First the mechanism center announces the set of tasks $\mathcal{T}$ that need to be allocated to all contractor agents. Next the contractors declare their types $\mathbf{a}$ to the center. The center then finds the efficient allocation $o = \mathsf{OPT}(z, \mathbf{a})$ using the ILP translation.*

*For the VCG **payment function** p^{OPT} we follow Clarke's rule, taking an agent's marginal contribution to the society [8]: $p_i^{\mathsf{OPT}}(z, a_i, \mathbf{a}_{-i}) = -v_i(a_i, o) + W(o) - W(o_{-i})$, where $o_{-i} = \mathsf{OPT}(z, \mathbf{a}_{-i})$ is the efficient allocation computed by OPT without i's participation.*

Proposition 2. *The mechanism $\mathcal{M}_{\mathsf{OPT}} = (\mathsf{OPT}, p^{\mathsf{OPT}})$ is individually rational.*

Proof. When agent i is truthful, its utility is computed by $u_i(s_i, \mathbf{a}_{-i}) = v_i(s_i, o) + p_i^{\mathsf{OPT}}(z, s_i, \mathbf{a}_{-i}) = W(o) - W(o_{-i})$. With agent i, the resulting allocation is never worse than that without i's participation, because of the additional resources i brings in. Therefore, $W(o) \geq W(o_{-i})$ and thus $u_i(s_i, \mathbf{a}_{-i}) \geq 0$, so i is guaranteed to receive non-negative utility when declaring its true type.   □

It seems that $\mathcal{M}_{\mathsf{OPT}}$ is both efficient and truthful, as its payment is VCG based and it uses an optimal allocation algorithm. Unfortunately, this is not always true. Before we show this, we discuss the relationship between the value $U(T_o)$ of the allocation o computed by any allocation algorithm O and the gained social welfare $W(o)$, since this relationship is important for the properties of the mechanism explained later. Consider the value of such an allocation o:

$$U(T_o) = \sum_{t \in T_o} U(t) = \sum_{t \in T_o} \sum_{r \in R} req(t)(r) \cdot e(t) = \sum_{i \in \mathcal{A}} \sum_{t \in T_o} \sum_{r \in R} o(t, i, r) \cdot e(t)$$

We distinguish two cases of a lying agent i: under-reporting and over-reporting.

- In the case of *under-reporting* ($a_i < s_i$), for each resource type $r \in R$, $o(t, i, r) \leq s_i(r)$, since the algorithm will not assign more resources than what i declares. Therefore, by Eq. 1, we have $v_i(s_i, o) = \sum_{t \in T_o} \sum_{r \in R} o(t, i, r)e(t)$ since $T'_{o,i} = T_o$. Hence, $U(T_o) = \sum_{i=1}^{m} v_i(s_i, o) = W(o)$, i.e., the utility of the allocation is *equal* to the social welfare.
- In the case of *over-reporting* ($a_i > s_i$), the algorithm may use i's non-existing but declared resources to allocate tasks. If so, the resulting allocation is *infeasible*, since agent i cannot actually deliver these resources. Furthermore, since there exist a resource r such that $o(t, i, r) > s_i(r)$, so by Eq. 1, we have $T'_{o,i} \subset T_o$. It follows that $U(T_o) \neq W(o)$, i.e. the utility of the allocation computed by the algorithm is *not* exactly the social welfare.

These results are used to show $\mathcal{M}_{\mathsf{OPT}}$ is only efficient and truthful with respect to under-reporting, but not with respect to over-reporting.

Theorem 1. $\mathcal{M}_{\mathsf{OPT}} = (\mathsf{OPT}, p^{\mathsf{OPT}})$ *is efficient and truthful with respect to under-reporting.*

Proof. Let s_i be the true type of agent i and a_i be any other type such that $a_i < s_i$. Given a problem instance z, let the resulting allocations be denoted by $o = \mathsf{OPT}(z, s_i, \mathbf{a}_{-i})$, and $\hat{o} = \mathsf{OPT}(z, a_i, \mathbf{a}_{-i})$, respectively, and let $o_{-i} = \mathsf{OPT}(z, \mathbf{a}_{-i})$ be the efficient allocation without i's participation. We have shown that when $a_i < s_i$, $W(o) = U(T_o)$. Since $U(T_o)$ is maximal, then $W(o)$ is maximal. That is, the mechanism is efficient.

We now prove that agent i never receives less utility by declaring its true type s_i instead of a_i. The difference δ is calculated as follows:

$$\delta = u_i(s_i, \mathbf{a}_{-i}) - u_i(a_i, \mathbf{a}_{-i})$$
$$= v_i(s_i, o) + p_i^{\mathsf{OPT}}(z, s_i, \mathbf{a}_{-i}) - v_i(a_i, \hat{o}) - p_i^{\mathsf{OPT}}(z, a_i, \mathbf{a}_{-i})$$
$$= W(o) - W(o_{-i}) - (W(\hat{o}) - W(o_{-i})) = W(o) - W(\hat{o}).$$

Since the optimal allocation will not get worse by adding more resources in the system, $U(T_o) - U(T_{\hat{o}}) \geq 0$, thus, $W(o) - W(\hat{o}) \geq 0$ and then $\delta \geq 0$.   □

Unfortunately, with $\mathcal{M}_{\mathsf{OPT}}$, agents do have an incentive to declare more resources than they actually have available.

Theorem 2. $\mathcal{M}_{\mathsf{OPT}} = (\mathsf{OPT}, p^{\mathsf{OPT}})$ *is not efficient and not truthful with respect to over-reporting.*

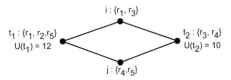

Fig. 1. Agent i is better off by over-reporting when a VCG payment is used

Proof. Consider the problem instance z with tasks t_1 and t_2 with $U(t_1) = 12$, $U(t_2) = 10$ (see Figure 1). Task t_1 requires resources $\{r_1, r_2, r_5\}$; task t_2 requires $\{r_3, r_4\}$. Both tasks are connected to contractor agents i and j, where i has got resources r_1 and r_3, and j owns r_4, r_5.

Suppose that agent j is truthfully reporting its resource r_4. If i also declares its type $\{r_1, r_3\}$ truthfully to the mechanism, the resulting optimal allocation $o_1 = \mathsf{OPT}(z, s_j, s_i)$ allocates $T_{o_1} = \{t_2\}$. So in this case, the utility that i receives by declaring truthfully is: $u_i(s_j, s_i) = v_i(s_i, o_1) + p_i^{\mathsf{OPT}}(z, s_j, s_i) = W(o_1) = U(t_2) = 10$. Consider now the case where i over-reports its resources, i.e., $a_i = \{r_1, r_2, r_3\}$. Then, both t_1 and t_2 are allocated, i.e. $T_{o_2} = \{t_1, t_2\}$. The utility of i then becomes: $u_i(s_j, a_i) = v_i(s_i, o_2) + p_i^{\mathsf{OPT}}(z, s_j, a_i) = v_i(s_i, o_2) - v_i(a_i, o_2) + W(o_2) = \frac{10}{2} - (\frac{12}{3} \cdot 2 + \frac{10}{2}) + 22 = 14$. Since $u_i(s_j, a_i) > u_i(s_j, s_i)$, agent i is better off by over-reporting its resources.

When i over-declares, the output of OPT is not exactly maximizing the social welfare. It is not efficient with respect to over-reporting.   □

The above example shows that $\mathcal{M}_{\mathsf{OPT}}$ is not truthful because an agent may declare a non-existing resource r_2 to improve its utility. In the example this results in an *infeasible* allocation, since t_1 cannot be executed successfully.[2] In general, it follows from Theorem 2 that no VCG mechanism for STAP can make the optimal algorithm truthful.

Corollary 1. *No VCG mechanism for STAP can make the optimal allocation algorithm OPT truthful.*

Proof. Consider the general description of a VCG payment for an agent i:

$$p_i(z, \mathbf{a}) = -v_i(a_i, \mathsf{OPT}(z, \mathbf{a})) + W(O(z, \mathbf{a})) + h^{\mathbf{a}-i}, \qquad (2)$$

where $h^{\mathbf{a}-i}$ is an arbitrary function that does not depend on i's truthfulness. We can therefore assume that $h^{\mathbf{a}-i} = 0$. Repeat the example in Theorem 2, we get the same result, i.e., agent i is better off by over-reporting its available type.   □

The results of [5,6,7,9] show that VCG mechanisms are truthful if the mechanism selects the optimal one among all allowable (or feasible) outputs. The private information of a player in [9] is a set of *values* of its types. Therefore given the type space of the players, the set of feasible outputs is *known* to the mechanism.

---

[2] Because this can be detected after the tasks have been executed, we may avoid over-reporting in some applications by transferring part of the payments afterwards.

Here the private information of a contractor is its available resources. As a consequence, over-reporting may lead to an infeasible allocation. In other words, the mechanism has no knowledge about the set of feasible outputs. Thus, the "optimal" output is not optimizing the true social welfare. This is exactly why the VCG mechanism cannot guarantee truthfulness in STAP.

In principle, an agent can have a mixed type of lying, i.e., under-reporting some resources and over-reporting some others. However, if VCG mechanisms are not able to prevent "pure" over-reporting as shown in Theorem 2, they cannot prevent the mixed type of lying either. Therefore, in the remainder of this paper, we only study the case of under-reporting.

One of the disadvantages of VCG mechanisms is that they are not *budget-balanced* (BB), i.e. $\sum_{i=1}^{m} p_i = 0$. However, it is still interesting to study the total payment of the mechanism $\mathcal{M}_{\mathsf{OPT}}$.

Proposition 3. *The total payment of the mechanism* $\mathcal{M}_{\mathsf{OPT}} = (\mathsf{OPT}, p^{\mathsf{OPT}})$ *to the contractors is:* $-W(o) \leq \sum_{i=1}^{m} p_i^{\mathsf{OPT}} \leq (m-1)W(o)$, *where* $W(o)$ *is the optimal social welfare and* m *is the number of contractor agents.*

4   A Greedy Mechanism for STAP

Often, we desire a polynomial-time mechanism where the allocation and the payments can both be computed in polynomial time. However, computing the efficient task allocation in a social network is NP-complete. Furthermore, when the number of neighbors of each agent is bounded by Δ for $\Delta \geq 3$, it is not approximable within Δ^{ε} for some $\varepsilon > 0$ (unless P = NP) [4]. This indicates that finding an approximation algorithm which has a non-trivial approximation ratio is difficult. Moreover, developing a payment function that makes such an approximation truthful is even more challenging. Still in this section, we work towards this by first introducing a greedy allocation approximation algorithm GTA. We show that VCG mechanisms for GTA cannot even make agents truthful with respect to under-reporting. We therefore propose a non-VCG mechanism that is truthful with respect to under-reporting.

4.1   A Greedy Allocation Algorithm

The idea for the greedy allocation algorithm is based on a greedy approximation for 0-1 knapsack [11]: first sort all items on their relative value, and then try to insert them in this order. If an item is inserted, it is never removed again.

In the greedy allocation algorithm (GTA) for STAP we consider the tasks in order of efficiency (the ratio between utility and required resources). If a task is feasible, it is inserted, if not, it is removed from the current selection of tasks. Feasibility of a selection of tasks is checked by translating the problem to a (polynomially solvable) network flow instance (see Algorithm 1).

Proposition 4. *The greedy allocation algorithm (GTA) is a* $K|R|$*-approximation algorithm for STAP, where* K *is the maximum number of resources of one type a task can require. The run time of GTA is* $\mathrm{O}(|R|n^2m)$.

Algorithm 1. Greedy centralized allocation algorithm (GTA)

---

1. Sort all tasks from all managers in descending order of their efficiencies $e(t)$. Denote the sorted tasks by $t'_1, t'_2, \ldots, t'_n$, and the current selection of tasks by $T' = \emptyset$.
2. For $i = 1, \ldots, n$ do:
   (a) Test if the selection of tasks $T' \leftarrow T' \cup \{t'_i\}$ is feasible:
   (b) Create a network flow problem for each resource type $r \in R$ (separately):
      i. Create a source s and a sink s'.
      ii. For each agent $j \in \mathcal{A}$, if $r \in a_j$ create an agent node and an edge from s to this node with capacity $a_j(r)$.
      iii. For each task $t \in T'$, if $r \in req(t)$ create a task node and an edge from this node to s' with capacity $req(t)(r)$.
      iv. For each agent $j \in \mathcal{A}$ connect its node to all nodes of neighboring tasks, i.e., $\{t \in T' \mid (j, loc(t)) \in AE\}$. Give this connection unlimited capacity.
   (c) Solve the maximum flow problem for the created flow networks. If the total maximum flow in all networks is equal to $\sum_{t \in T'} \sum_{r \in R} req(t)(r)$, the current combination of tasks is feasible. Otherwise remove task t'_i from T'.
3. Output the task set T' and the current allocation.

So, in the worst case, GTA may return quite bad solutions. Therefore, in Section 5 we study the average performance of GTA by a set of experiments.

Unfortunately, GTA cannot be made truthful even with respect to under-reporting by using a VCG payment function, in contrast to OPT.

Proposition 5. *No VCG payment function can make the greedy task allocation algorithm GTA a truthful mechanism with respect to under-reporting.*

Proof. In this proof we show that for a specific instance the VCG payment cannot incentivize a contractor to declare all its available resources truthfully. First consider the general description of a VCG payment for any agent i (see Equation 2), where without loss of generality we assume that $h^{\mathbf{a}-i} = 0$. Thus, $p_i(z, \mathbf{a}) = -v_i(a_i, \mathsf{GTA}(z, \mathbf{a})) + W(\mathsf{GTA}(z, \mathbf{a}))$.

Consider a problem instance with tasks t_1, t_2 and t_3. Task t_1 requires resources $\{r_1, r_2, r_3\}$; task t_2 requires $\{r_2, r_4\}$; and t_3 requires $\{r_3, r_5\}$. All three tasks are connected to contractors i and j, where i has resources $\{r_1, r_4, r_5\}$, and j owns $\{r_2, r_3\}$. Let the utilities of the tasks be $U(t_1) = 15$, $U(t_2) = 8$, and $U(t_3) = 8$. Thus the efficiencies are 5, 4, and 4, respectively. Suppose that agent j is truthfully reporting its resources $\{r_2, r_3\}$. We now compare two situations. When i also declares its type truthfully to the mechanism, i.e. $\{r_1, r_4, r_5\}$, then according to the greedy algorithm, the resulting allocation is $o_1 = \mathsf{GTA}(z, s_j, s_i)$ with $T_{o_1} = \{t_1\}$, because t_1 has the highest efficiency. The payment then is $p_i(z, s_j, s_i) = -v_i(s_i, o_1) + W(o_1)$. So in this case, the utility that i receives by declaring truthfully is $u_i(s_j, s_i) = v_i(s_i, o_1) + p_i(z, s_j, s_i) = W(o_1) = 15$.

Consider now a case where i under-reports $(a_i < s_i)$ its resources, i.e., $\{r_4, r_5\}$. In this case t_1 cannot be allocated. The greedy algorithm then outputs the allocation $o_2 = \mathsf{GTA}(z, s_j, a_i)$ and $T_{o_2} = \{t_2, t_3\}$. The utility of i then becomes $u_i(s_j, a_i) = v_i(s_i, o_2) - v_i(a_i, o_2) + W(o_2) = (4+4) - (4+4) + 16$. Since $u_i(s_j, a_i) >$

Algorithm 2. Greedy payment p^{GTA}

Inputs: a problem instance z, and the declared types **a**.
For each agent i, let $b_i = 0$, and do

1. For each resource type r declared by agent i in a_i, do
   (a) Sort tasks in T_i^r in descending order of their efficiencies $e(t)$. Let L denote this list of sorted tasks. Store the currently available resources of type r of agent i: $k_{i,r} = a_i(r)$, and initialize the set of assigned tasks: $T_{i,r} = \emptyset$.
   (b) For each task $t \in L$, if $k_{i,r} \geq req(t)(r)$, then
       i. assign the amount $req(t)(r)$ of agent i's resource r to t,
       ii. update i's available resource r: $k_{i,r} = k_{i,r} - req(t)(r)$; update the assigned task set: $T_{i,r} = T_{i,r} \cup \{t\}$.
   (c) For each task $t \in T_{i,r}$, if there exists no other agent j such that $t \in T_j^r$ and $a_j(r) > 0$, update $b_i = b_i + e(t) \cdot req(t)(r)$.
2. The payment to agent i is calculated by: $p_i^{\mathsf{GTA}}(z, a_i, \mathbf{a}_{-i}) = -v_i(a_i, o) + b_i$.

$u_i(s_j, s_i)$, agent i is better off by under-reporting its available resources. This mechanism is not truthful with respect to under-reporting. $\qquad\square$

4.2   A Mechanism That Is Truthful with Respect to Under-Reporting

Since we cannot make GTA truthful by a VCG payment, we propose a non-VCG payment function that pays agents for each resource that no other agent can provide. Consequently, agents will not benefit anymore from keeping essential resources from the mechanism to influence the selection of allocated tasks.

For this we introduce some notation and definitions. Given a strategy profile **a** and a set of tasks $\mathcal{T}$, let T_i denote the set of agent i's neighboring tasks to which it can contribute, and let T_i^r denote the set of tasks of i's neighbors to which agent i can contribute a resource r, i.e., $req(t)(r) > 0$ and $a_i(r) > 0$. Clearly, $\bigcup_{r \in R} T_i^r = T_i$. The payment is based on the allocation of each resource r of agent i to the most efficient task t such that the agent i's valuation for such an allocation is as high as possible. However, we pay agent i its contribution of resource r to t only if r is unique for t, that is, no other agent j connected to t has declared r. This greedy payment is described in Algorithm 2.

We now define the greedy mechanism $\mathcal{M}_{\mathsf{GTA}} = (\mathsf{GTA}, p^{\mathsf{GTA}})$ which uses the greedy allocation algorithm GTA to determine the task allocation, and uses the greedy payment function p^{GTA} defined above (in Algorithm 2) to calculate the payments to each participating agent.

We first show in the following lemma that given an outcome o based on an agent i's declared type a_i ($a_i \leq s_i$), i's valuation based on its true type s_i is equal to its valuation based on its declared type a_i.

Lemma 1. *Given any problem instance $z \in Z$, any algorithm O, strategy profile $\mathbf{a}_{-i} \in A^{m-1}$, and for any agent i its declared type a_i, if $a_i \leq s_i$, it holds that $v_i(a_i, o) = v_i(s_i, o)$ where $o = O(z, \mathbf{a})$.*

Theorem 3. *The greedy mechanism $\mathcal{M}_{\mathsf{GTA}} = (\mathsf{GTA}, p^{\mathsf{GTA}})$ is truthful with respect to under-reporting, individually rational, and runs in polynomial-time.*

Proof. Let a problem instance z, the declared types of others $\mathbf{a}_{-i}$, and the declaration $a_i \leq s_i$ be given. From this, the outcome $o = \mathsf{GTA}(z, a_i, \mathbf{a}_{-i})$ can be calculated. The utility of an agent i is then determined by $u_i(a_i, \mathbf{a}_{-i}) = v_i(s_i, o) + p_i^{\mathsf{GTA}}(z, a_i, \mathbf{a}_{-i}) = v_i(s_i, o) - v_i(a_i, o) + b_i$, where b_i is computed based on the greedy payment given in Algorithm 2. We know from Lemma 1 that $v_i(s_i, o) = v_i(a_i, o)$ for $a_i \leq s_i$. Thus the utility of i completely depends on the value of b_i, i.e. $u_i(a_i, \mathbf{a}_{-i}) = b_i$. According to the computation of b_i in Algorithm 2, for each resource type r, the value that i can get from the allocated tasks $T_{i,r}$ is maximal when i declares its full amount of resources, because in this way, more highly efficient tasks can be allocated, no matter whether its resource r is unique to tasks in $T_{i,r}$. Moreover, b_i is maximized when i declares every resource type r that it has. In other words, each agent's utility is *monotonically increasing* with its declared resources.

An agent i's utility for declaring its true type s_i is $u_i(s_i, \mathbf{a}_{-i}) = b_i \geq 0$. So, it is rational for agent i to participate.

In the greedy payment p^{GTA}, sorting the tasks takes $O(n \log(n))$, and determining the value and checking the unique for the resource of each contractor takes $O(|R|nm)$. Hence the total payment computation is $O(n \log(n) + |R|m^2 n)$. Since both GTA and p^{GTA} can be computed in polynomial time, the mechanism is a polynomial-time mechanism. $\qquad\square$

This result (and its proof) can be generalized for any mechanism for STAP as long as we can make the agent's utility function monotonically increasing with the declared resources.

Theorem 4. *Given any problem instance $z \in Z$, any allocation algorithm O, for any agent i with type $s_i \in S$ and for any other type $a_i \in A$ and $a_i \leq s_i$, a mechanism for STAP is truthful with respect to under-reporting if the payment to any agent i is of the form $p_i^{MON} = -v_i(a_i, O(z, \mathbf{a})) + h(a_i)$, where $h(a_i)$ is any function which is monotonically increasing with the declaration a_i.*

Proposition 6. *The total payment of the mechanism $\mathcal{M}_{\mathsf{GTA}} = (\mathsf{GTA}, p^{\mathsf{GTA}})$ to the contractors is: $-W(o) \leq \sum_{i=1}^{m} p_i^{\mathsf{GTA}} \leq U(\mathcal{T})$, where $W(o)$ is the social welfare and $U(\mathcal{T})$ is the total utility of all tasks.*

5   Experiments

The worst-case performance guarantee for the greedy heuristic presented in the previous section is based on a specific case where one task with a high efficiency blocks all other tasks. In practice, not all tasks are connected to the same agents and the average performance will be much better. To see how much better, we investigated the performance of this mechanism experimentally.

A problem instance in these experiments is defined by the number of agents, tasks, and resource types; the requirements, the utility and the location of each

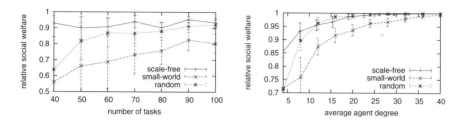

Fig. 2. These graphs show the relative social welfare of the greedy mechanism related to the number of tasks (left), and the degree of the networks (right), respectively

task; the available resources at each agent and the relations between the agents. In our case these relations are defined by the type of social network. The types we consider in our experiments are: (i) random networks, where agents are connected completely at random until the desired degree has been reached, (ii) small-world networks [12], where most agents are connected locally (to the neighbors of their neighbors), but have a fixed "rewiring" probability of 0.05 to connected to any other agent, and (iii) scale-free networks, where agents have a higher probability to get connected to agents with more neighbors [13].

First we investigated each parameter separately using default settings for the other parameters such that the optimal solution can still be calculated in at most 10 minutes. These defaults were: 200 contractors, 100 tasks, 20 resource types, 20 resources per task on average, 10 resources on average per agent, a uniformly random distribution of resources and tasks to agents, and the value of a task drawn from a normal distribution around two times the number of resources with a standard deviation of one time this number (with a minimal value of 1). We kept the total number of resources required by the tasks and the total available resources in the network the same, and equal to each other. In a fully connected network this would mean that all tasks can be allocated. However, in the networks we consider they generally cannot. For each experiment with the parameter settings described above, we generated 20 instances of each of the three types of networks. In the plots we only showed the average and the standard deviation over these 20 instances for each setting.

When we varied the problem size by increasing the number of tasks from 40 to 100, we noticed (see the first graph in Figure 2) an increase of the quality of the greedy mechanism from about 0.55 up to about 0.8 in the small-world network setting, and about 0.9 in the random and scale-free setting. Interestingly, it seems that the greedy algorithm works better on structures like scale-free networks where some tasks (managers) are very well connected, while some others are (almost) not connected at all, than on more uniform structures like small-world networks, where each task has about the same number of connections.

Next we show the results for problem instances with a degree of the social network varying from 4 to 40. The greedy mechanism performed extremely well for networks with a large degree showing a relative social welfare of about 0.99.

In such a setting most tasks can be allocated, because they end up in very well-connected nodes, having many alternative contractor agents.

A more important observation is that the performance over all these instances (about 200 per figure) was between 0.55 and 0.99, and on average around 0.85 of the optimal outcome. This is a much better result than the worst-case theoretical bound of $K|R|$ (in this case K was 8) presented in Section 4.1.

6   Discussion and Conclusions

This paper started with a very general resource allocation problem where both the agents providing the resources (contractors) as well as the agents having some utility for bundles of resources (managers) can be strategizing. When the contractors are trusted, and only the managers are allowed to strategize over their value for each bundle, we end up with the well-studied CA problem. However, in this paper we consider a mechanism design setting which differs in an important way from most of the studied situations, such as CAs [2], single-parameter and single-value domains [14,15], because the contractors are not strategizing about the valuation they declare, but about the resources they have available. When agents lie about their valuation, the output of a mechanism can be inefficient, but is always feasible. However, when agents lie about such things as their available resources, the mechanism can come up with an infeasible outcome.

We showed that in such a setting a VCG payment with an optimal algorithm cannot guarantee a truthful mechanism, but it can realize a mechanism that is truthful with respect to under-reporting. Moreover, since the problem is NP-hard, we can only expect to find optimal algorithms that run in time exponential in the size of the input.

In this paper we therefore proposed a polynomial-time approximation. We first showed that using this approximation, VCG mechanisms cannot be used to create similar truth-telling properties as for the optimal mechanism. However, we then proposed another payment function that actually could realize these properties. In general, we showed that this is because the utility of agents is monotonically increasing in the number of declared resources. Our experimental results show that the overall quality of the solutions using this mechanism is quite good. Since STAP is NP-complete, we conclude that this heuristic is more useful than the optimal mechanism in many practical situations with a moderate or larger problem size.

The fact that agents have an incentive to over-report is very severe, because it could lead to infeasible solutions. However, we believe that this consequence may also imply a solution, because lying agents can thus be detected and punished. This is an important topic in our current work.

Furthermore, we will consider the general resource allocation problem where not only the contractor agents, but also the managers can strategize. Our goal is to also incentivize the managers to truthfully declare their tasks and the attached utilities. It is relatively straightforward to see that a VCG payment can achieve this if an optimal algorithm is used. How to achieve this using an approximation algorithm is still an open question.

With the proposed greedy payment algorithm an agent may receive zero utility if its contribution (i.e. resource) is not unique to the task. Moreover, additional funding is required to incentivize the agents. To avoid these undesirable situations, we are interested in developing a dynamic payment scheme which adapts the payments based on (i) the specific instance, e.g. the resource distribution, and (ii) the generated social welfare, while maintaining the truthfulness property.

As a final remark, we believe that the results in this paper generalize to other (NP-hard) problem domains where a wrong input to the mechanism by the agents can lead to infeasible outcomes, such as in multiagent planning. We intend to show in the future that alternative payment functions such as the one proposed here can be applied to those settings as well.

Acknowledgments

This work is partially supported by the Technology Foundation STW, applied science division of NWO, and the Ministry of Economic Affairs of the Netherlands.

References

1. de Vries, S., Vohra, R.: Combinatorial Auctions: A Survey. INFORMS Journal on Computing 15(3), 284–309 (2003)
2. Blumrosen, L., Nisan, N.: Combinatorial auctions. In: Algorithmic Game Theory, pp. 209–242. Cambridge University Press, Cambridge (2007)
3. Chevaleyre, Y., Dunne, P.E., Endriss, U., Lang, J., Lemaitre, M., Maudet, N., Padget, J., Phelps, S., Rodriguez-Aguilar, J.A., Sousa, P.: Issues in multiagent resource allocation. Informatica 30, 3–31 (2006)
4. de Weerdt, M., Zhang, Y., Klos, T.B.: Distributed task allocation in social networks. In: Proc. of 6th Int. Conf. on AAMAS, pp. 17–24. ACM, New York (2007)
5. Vickrey, W.: Counterspeculation, auctions, and competitive sealed tenders. The Journal of Finance 16(1), 8–37 (1961)
6. Clarke, E.H.: Multipart pricing of public goods. Public Choice 11(1) (1971)
7. Groves, T.: Incentives in teams. Econometrica 41(4), 617–631 (1973)
8. Nisan, N.: Introduction to mechanism design (for computer scientists). In: Algorithmic Game Theory, pp. 209–242. Cambridge University Press, Cambridge (2007)
9. Nisan, N., Ronen, A.: Algorithmic mechanism design (extended abstract). In: Proc. of 31th ACM Symposium on Theory of Computing, pp. 129–140. ACM, New York (1999)
10. Makhorin, A.: GLPK. GNU Linear Programming Kit (2004)
11. Dantzig, G.: Discrete variable problems. Operations Research 5, 266–277 (1957)
12. Watts, D.J., Strogatz, S.H.: Collective dynamics of 'small world' networks. Nature 393, 440–442 (1998)
13. Barabási, A.L., Albert, R.: Emergence of scaling in random networks. Science 286(5439), 509–512 (1999)
14. Archer, A., Tardos, E.: Truthful mechanisms for one-parameter agents. In: Proc. of 42nd IEEE Symposium on FOCS, pp. 482–491 (2001)
15. Babaioff, M., Lavi, R., Pavlov, E.: Mechanism design for single-value domains. In: Proc. of 20th Nat. Conf. on Artificial intelligence, pp. 241–247. AAAI, Menlo Park (2005)

Reasoning and Negotiating with Complex Preferences Using CP-Nets*

Reyhan Aydoğan, Nuri Taşdemir, and Pınar Yolum

Department of Computer Engineering
Boğaziçi University
34342 Bebek, Istanbul, Turkey
{reyhan.aydogan,nuri.tasdemir,pinar.yolum}@boun.edu.tr

Abstract. Automated negotiation is important for carrying out flexible transactions. Agents that take part in automated negotiation need to have a concise representation of their user's preferences and should be able to reason on these preferences effectively. We develop an automated negotiation platform wherein consumer agents negotiate with producer agents about services. A consumer agent represents its user's preferences in a compact way using a CP-net, which is a structure that allows users to order their preferences based on the different value combinations of attributes. Acquiring user's preferences in a compact way is crucial since it significantly decreases the number of questions to be asked to the user by the consumer agent. We design strategies for consumer agents to reason on and negotiate effectively with the preference graph induced from a CP-net. These strategies are designed to generate deals that are acceptable by the provider and the consumer. We compare our proposed strategies in terms of how well and how quickly they can find desirable deals for the consumer.

1 Introduction

Automated negotiation is a key problem in agent-mediated e-commerce [1]. Negotiation is a process in which participants deviate from their most desired offerings to the extent that is acceptable. In order to engage in an automated negotiation, participants should know and reason about their *preferences*. Preferences represent the desired and acceptable alternatives for the services being negotiated. In order to decide if an offer is acceptable, an agent needs to consult its user's preferences, decide which offer is more preferable, and generate possible counter-offers based on this. Hence, representation and reasoning of preferences constitutes an irreplaceable part of automated negotiation. Whereas the preferences should be simple to represent and manipulate, they should also be represented expressively.

Preferences can be considered as the choice of the user when there exist more than one alternative for a particular issue. Preferences can be represented quantitatively or

---

* Reyhan Aydoğan is the primary contact author. Phone: +90-212-359-7095, Fax: +90-212-287-2461. This research has been partially supported by Boğaziçi University Research Fund under grant BAP07A102 and the Scientific and Technological Research Council of Turkey by a CAREER Award under grant 105E073. We thank the anonymous reviewers for helpful comments.

W. Ketter et al. (Eds.): AMEC/TADA 2008, LNBIP 44, pp. 15–28, 2010.
© Springer-Verlag Berlin Heidelberg 2010

qualitatively. Quantitative representations require the users to associate numerical values to denote the extent of their preferences. However, obtaining these values are difficult. Further, representing and quantifying conditional preferences is cumbersome. Contrary to quantitative representations of preferences, qualitative representations are mostly in the form of comparatives and conditionals. For example, a user may prefer *Rose* wine to *White* wine (comparative) or may prefer *Rose* wine to *White* wine only if the region is *French* (conditional).

Since expressing preference in a compact way decreases the required time for preference elicitation, it is preferred to use a compact representation while taking the preferences from the user. There are several compact representations such as GAI-nets [2] and CP-nets [3]. Whereas the GAI-nets are utility-based quantitative preference model, CP-nets are qualitative models. Since it is hard to obtain numerical utility values for subset of attributes, we prefer to use CP-nets as our preference representation model. This paper studies the following questions about preferences:

– How can the preferences be taken efficiently from the user?
– How can the user preferences be represented in a compact way?
– How will the consumer agent generate its request in accordance with its preferences in an automatic way?
– When should the consumer agent accept the counter offer of the producer (in the light of its preferences)?
– According to the request, which service content should be offered by the producer?

The rest of this paper is organized as follows. Section 2 describes our general architecture, discusses representations for preferences and provides a background on CP-nets. Section 3 introduces novel strategies with which CP-nets can be used. The producer strategy for generating its counter offer is explained in Section 4. Section 5 evaluates these strategies experimentally and compares their benefits. Finally, Section 6 reviews our work in relation to existing literature and gives directions for further research.

2 Representing and Ordering Preferences

We consider the negotiation between a consumer and a producer agent, which communicate with each other in order to reach a mutual agreement on the service. As is commonly the case, the producer agent cannot provide all possible services requested by the consumer. Hence, both the consumer and the producer need to reach a consensus on an acceptable service. To reach a consensus, the agents negotiate the content of the service in an iterative way so that if either agent does not accept the proposal of the other, it makes a counter offer. In principle, the negotiation can continue until either a consensus is found, or the producer runs out of services it can offer [4]. However, to be more realistic, we are interested in negotiations that have a deadline; i.e., the negotiation is expected to end in a fixed number of iterations or in a fixed amount of time.

In this automated negotiation, common understanding between the agents are provided via a shared ontology that can be used to specify information on service description, features constructing the service, the domain information for each feature and so on. In our experiments, we prefer to use a modified version of *Wine* ontology, since this ontology is well-known and publicly used for test purposes. Thus, the service that is being negotiated between consumer and producer is that of selling wine.

2.1 Ceteris Paribus Nets (CP-Nets)

From our point of view, complexity of a preference can be investigated in two ways. Firstly, a preference may have a simple structure such as the customer prefers red wine, which means any red wine is an acceptable offer. Here, the boundary of the preferences is explicitly specified. There is no information about how much the consumer prefers red wine. We just know that red wine is preferred. In our previous study [4], we assume that the preferences are in the form of disjunctions and conjunctions of the attributes. For instance, a customer may prefer rose or red dry wine (($Color = (Red \vee Rose)$) and ($Sugar = Dry$)). The consumer agent accepts any wine compatible with this preference. Secondly, we can represent preferences in a more sophisticated way. Some constraints can be defined over the preferences such as if the region is *FrenchRegion*, the red wine is better than rose wine. Here, it does not mean only red wine is acceptable. It just gives the preference ordering. CP-nets can also represent conditional preference. Such preference structures enable more flexible negotiation interaction among agents. In contrast to our previous work, this study deals with more flexible preferences instead of strict ones.

CP-net is a tool for representing qualitative preferences in a compact way [3]. Even though they are compact, they can represent most practical preference orderings. Preference statement such as *Rose* wine is better than *White* wine, means that any *Rose* wine is better than any *White* wine when all the other features such as grape, region have the same value. For example, when both wine has made from the same grape type in the same region and all other wine features except color are same, *Rose* wine is better than *White* wine for the user. Such statement is called the preference ceteris paribus, "everything else being equal" [5].

A CP-net is composed of a dependency graph of features showing child-parent relations and a set of conditional preference tables (CPT) including preference statements. A ceteris paribus preference statement indicates which feature value is dominant over others. For example, $White \succ Red$ means that *White* is preferred to *Red*. Further, $(FrenchRegion \wedge Dry) : Red \succ White$ means that if the region is *FrenchRegion* and the sweetness degree of the wine is *Dry*, then *Red* color is preferable to *White* color.

In CP-net terminology, a feature may have parent feature(s). This parent-child relation of features depends on the preferential dependency. The value of parent feature affects the user preferences over the values of child feature. By this way, we can express the conditional preferences. For instance, we can express if the color is *Red*, then we prefer *Dry* wine to *Sweet* wine. Here, the parent feature can be thought as color and preference of the sweetness degree attribute of wine depend on the wine color attribute value. Example 1 explains CP-net representation in depth.

We can see a preference as an ordering of instances. The problem is the number of instances is exponentially many with respect to the number of features. Asking a user for a complete definition of her preferences is cumbersome. Therefore, tools like CP-nets representing preferences with asking proportionally fewer questions are crucial. That is, all potential orderings cannot be captured by CP-net but mostly necessary partial information can acquired.

Example 1. Assume that we have only two features: *Flavor* and *Color*. Figure 1 depicts a sample CP-net. In this example, *Flavor* is the parent of *Color* attribute. According to the CP-net terminology, the *Flavor* and *Color* are variables. And, *Color* may take one of the values: *Red*, *White* and *Rose* whereas the domain of *Flavor* includes *Delicate*, *Moderate* and *Strong*. A CPT involves the preference statements related to the values of the variables. We can infer some conclusions from these statements such as when the flavor is *Delicate*, then the user prefers *Red* wine to *White* wine and to *Rose* wine.

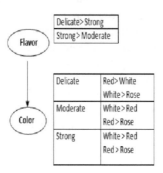

Fig. 1. Sample CP-net

The preference ordering specified on a particular variable is transitive such that if $X \succ Y$ and $Y \succ Z$ then we can say that $X \succ Z$. As seen in Figure 1, we know that $Delicate \succ Strong$ and $Strong \succ Moderate$. Because of transitivity, it can be said that $Delicate \succ Moderate$.

Furthermore, we can induce a preference graph from a given CP-net. The nodes of this preference graph represent the decision choices such as $(Rose \wedge Moderate)$ meaning that a wine whose color is rose and flavor is moderate. The edges of the induced preference graph can be established via *improving flips* on a given CP-net. An improving flip is changing the value of a single attribute with a more desired value by using the CPT of the attribute. Therefore, the instance obtained via this method is more desirable. The preference graph of the sample CP-net in Figure 1 is drawn in Figure 2. Every edge is obtained by an improving flip. Example 2 explains the improving flipping for the given sample CP-net. The root element(s) of the induced graph represents the worst choice whereas the leaf node(s) expresses the best one. From top to bottom, the choice becomes more desired. For instance, there is an edge from $(Rose \wedge Moderate)$ to $(Rose \wedge Strong)$. It can be inferred that rose and strong wine is more preferable than rose and moderate wine.

Example 2. Let's start with the choice node $(Rose \wedge Moderate)$. From the CPT table of *Flavor*, we know the fact of $Strong \succ Moderate$. By using this fact, $Moderate$ is changed with $Strong$. By this improving flip, an edge is established between the first

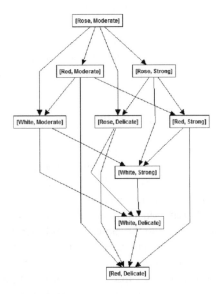

Fig. 2. The induced preference graph from the sample CP-net in Figure 1

node and the new node ($Rose \wedge Strong$). Afterwards, $Rose$ is replaced by Red because of the fact $Red \succ Rose$ in CPT of *Color*. Now, we draw an edge from ($Rose \wedge Strong$) to ($Red \wedge Strong$). By a sequence of improving flips, the induced preference graph is generated. We can make a comparison between some choices by investigating this graph. For example, the fact that red and strong wine is more preferable than rose and moderate wine, can be inferred from this graph.

As a result, CP-nets are very convenient model to get user preferences in a compact way. From this compact representation, we can induce a preference graph showing the degree of the user preferences. According to the graph shown in Figure 2, the most preferable wine is *Red* and *Delicate*.

2.2   Obtaining Preferences

Getting all possible preference orderings from the user is an expensive task so we need to take these preferences in a more efficient way. At this point, using the CP-net construction seems an efficient way to get the preferences from the user. To accomplish this, there are two subtasks: taking the dependency among features and getting preference ordering of for possible values of these features based on the dependency.

The consumer agent has only one interaction with the user to obtain the user preferences, before starting the negotiation. These preferences are taken by using the CP-net as follows. First, the dependency among features are obtained. As we explained before, the ordering of preferences for a particular attribute (child attribute) may depend on the values of other attributes (parent attributes). Thus, the user is asked firstly for child-parent relations of the features, which constitute a service. For example, according to the user, the preference ordering for color attribute may depend on the flavor attribute. Afterwards, the order of preferences is taken. Every combination of parent attribute values form the conditional part of the ceteris paribus statements. For instance, for each value of flavor, the preference ordering is asked for wine color. And for the attributes not having any parent attributes such as flavor, the preference ordering is asked unconditionally. As a result, the user preferences are elicited easily by this way.

3   Strategies for Generating Requests

The consumer agent keeps the preferences in a CP-net form constructed by the given dependency graph of features and a set of conditional ceteris paribus preference statements. Then, a preference graph is induced from this CP-net structure. This preference graph is used by the consumer agent to generate a request for the desired service.

In this graph, each node represents a possible service. The direction of the edges is from the less preferable service to the more preferable service. In order to compare these services, making some assumptions is required for comparison of the services since less information is taken to construct the CP-net from the user compared to the complete preference information. Therefore, we assume that the depth of service plays a determinative role in comparison of the services. According to our approach, the higher depth a service has, the more likely to be preferred by the user. Thus, determining the depth of each node is necessary when comparing two services in terms of which service is more preferable by the user. One node may be pointed by more than one node. Thus, we start assigning depth to each node from the root node(s). The depth of root node(s) is equal to zero. Then, we increment the depth by one and assign one to the depth of all child nodes of the root node(s). Afterwards, the same process is applied to all child nodes of the child nodes of root node(s) in a recursive way. By this way, a parent node may have child nodes at different depths.

To illustrate this, consider the graph in Figure 2. Here, the root node is ($Rose \land Moderate$) with depth zero. It has three child nodes: ($White \land Moderate$), ($Red \land Moderate$) and ($Rose \land Strong$). Their depths are initially assigned one. Afterwards, the incrementing the child node process continues for these three child nodes in a recursive way. Since ($White \land Moderate$) is child of ($Red \land Moderate$), its depth is incremented by one again. At the end, the depth of ($White \land Moderate$) becomes equal to two whereas that of other child node of the root node ($Red \land Moderate$) is one. From the point of consumer agent, the depth is a measure of preference. That is the services at higher depths are more preferable than the lower ones. The nodes at the highest depth are the most preferable by the user. For instance, in the previous example, the user prefers mostly red and delicate wine.

Using this preference graph, requests can be generated in several ways. Here, we develop and analyze four types of strategies for generating the requests: (1) Sequential Search Strategy (Section 3.1), (2) Depth Limited Search Strategy (Section 3.2), (3) Binary Search Strategy (Section 3.3), and Upper Random Strategy (Section 3.4).

The producer agent in this architecture provides the service if it is available in his stock. Otherwise, the most similar service to the last request of the consumer is offered to the consumer. This simplistic approach is chosen deliberately for the producer to enable us to focus on the customer strategies.

3.1 Sequential Search Strategy

From the preference graph, we obtain a hierarchy of nodes based on their depths. According to sequential search strategy, the consumer generates a request with the highest possible depth. Note that the node having the highest depth means the service that the user prefers the most. The intuition here is that if the consumer requests the most desired services and if a service can be provided by the provider, the consumer will end up with the most desired outcome. In order to get the most desired service that is available, consumer requests services in descending order with respect to their depth over time.

The aim of consumer agent is to complete the negotiation as soon as possible in addition to taking the best service it can gain. Thus, a heuristic for deciding when the consumer should accept the producer's offer is required. For this reason, the consumer agent keeps the best service offered by the producer. At each interaction with the producer, he updates the best offer if the current offer is better than the best offer. There is no need to investigate other services at the current depth if the current depth is less than or equal to the best offer. In this case, the consumer requests the best offer. This request is met by the producer and the negotiation is completed successfully.

The performance of the strategies depends on the available services in the producer's stock. According to our expectation, if the services are spread on the higher depths, the agents will negotiate quickly. On the other hand, this strategy may not give a good performance if the producer only has the services that are mostly less desired by the user. In this case, the time for consensus may increase.

Assume that the producer has four services, which are less desired by the consumer: $(Rose \wedge Moderate)$, $(Red \wedge Moderate)$, $(Rose \wedge Strong)$ and $(White \wedge Moderate)$. According to this strategy, the consumer first request $(Red \wedge Delicate)$, whose depth is five. The producer offers an alternative service, which is most similar to the request, $(Red \wedge Moderate)$. This offer is kept as best offer whose depth is one but the consumer does not accept it because its depth is lower than five. Next, the consumer requests $(White \wedge Delicate)$ of depth four and the producer offers $(White \wedge Moderate)$. Because its depth is two, the consumer updates its best offer with this new offer. Afterward, the consumer asks for $(White \wedge Strong)$. Now, the producer offers $(Rose \wedge Strong)$ of depth one. The consumer does not accept it and now the current depth is equal to two for the consumer. Thus, it asks for the best offer that he got before, $(White \wedge Moderate)$. Hopefully, the producer provides this service and negotiation is completed successfully with four interactions. If the producer has services whose depth is higher, the agents have a consensus sooner. For example, if the producer has $(White \wedge Delicate)$, the agents interact with each other twice.

3.2 Depth Limited Search Strategy

In this strategy, the consumer applies depth limited search technique in order to generate a request. Here, the consumer starts his request with the most desired service and decreases his ambition level on the service up to an acceptable degree. After reaching this limit, he starts to ask for higher preferred services. Initially the limit is predefined as the half of the highest depth of the preference graph and it is updated during the negotiation with the depth of the producer's best offer plus one since it is unnecessary to ask for services whose depth is less than or equal to the depth of producer's best offer.

To make the clear understanding of depth limited approach, an example is explained where in the best offer proposed by the producer does not make the limit be updated. After this example, we will deal with another example demonstrating the case that the limit is updated according to the producer's best offer.

As the first example, consider the preference graph in Figure 2. According to the preference graph, the highest depth is equal to five so the limit is equal to two. The consumer generates his first request by starting at the leaf node, which holds the most desired service ($Red \wedge Delicate$). In the second iteration, he chooses one parent of this node as a request. For example, he may select ($White \wedge Delicate$) of depth four. Afterwards, the consumer selects the parent of that node, ($White \wedge Strong$). It goes on until the depth of the parent is less than the limit, two. Search will go on by backtracking to the leaf node step by step. At each step, all the parents of the current service are checked for being a possible request. For instance, after requesting ($Red \wedge Strong$), consumer backtracks to the node ($White \wedge Strong$). Whether the depth of the other parents of this node is equal to or greater than the limit is investigated. If there are such nodes, these nodes are chosen for the request one by one. In our example, ($White \wedge Strong$) has three parents: ($Red \wedge Strong$) is asked before, the depth of ($Rose \wedge Strong$) is less than limit and ($White \wedge Moderate$) is a suitable candidate for being a request. Since a particular node may be parents of more than one, it is required to check whether the service node is used as request before in order to prevent the duplication in request.

Second example differs from the first one in the response of the producer to the request of ($Red \wedge Strong$). In this example, producer offers ($Rose \wedge Delicate$) whose depth is equal to two. Afterwards, the limit is updated as three (= 2+1). This situation results a change in the suitability of the next candidate. For example, namely ($White \wedge Moderate$) of depth two will not be requested.

In this approach, the consumer does not always generate the request having highest depth but it also considers the request from the nodes having lower depth. If the producer has services in between the most preferred services and moderately preferred services, this strategy may lead the consumer to a consensus in a short time compared to sequential strategy. Technically, such kind of strategy may be beneficial when the services in the stock of producer are at any depth between limit and highest depth.

3.3   Binary Search Strategy

The consumer generates the requests using binary search over the preference graph. Algorithm 1 explains binary search procedure for this task. According to the algorithm, two boundaries are defined for the depth hierarchy: lower and upper. At the beginning, upper boundary is equal to the highest depth whereas the lower boundary is equal to zero. The consumer uses a service node in the graph whose depth is equal to half of the sum of these two boundaries ($(upper + low)/2$). To speed up the negotiation process, lower boundary is updated after each interaction with the producer. After the producer offers an alternative service whose depth is higher than the lower, it would be irrational for the consumer to request a service less desired than the previously offered service by the producer. For instance, assume that the producer offers a service of depth three. From the consumer point of view, it does not make sense to ask for a service whose depth is less than three.

Algorithm 1. Generating Request with Binary Search Strategy

```
 1: control ← False
 2: while control==False do
 3:     curDepth ← (upper + lower)/2
 4:     if index[curDepth] < hierarchy.at(curDepth).size then
 5:         control ← True
 6:     else
 7:         hierarchy.remove(curDepth)
 8:         index.remove(curDepth)
 9:         depthIndex.remove(curDepth)
10:         if lower < upper then
11:             upper ← (upper − 1)
12:         else
13:             negotiated ← True
14:             return best
15:         end if
16:     end if
17: end while
18: value ← index[curDepth]
19: index[curDepth] ← (value + 1)
20: return hierarchy.at(curDepth).at(value)
```

In the given algorithm, $upper$ represents the upper depth and $lower$ represents the lower depth (initially zero). The consumer first asks for any service whose depth is equal to $curDepth = (upper + lower)/2$. According to the algorithm, firstly whether there exists any service node that was not be used previously at the $curDepth$ is checked (Lines 1-5). If such a node exists, it returns it as a potential request (Line 20). For each depth, $index$ holds the number of service that has been used as a request by the consumer. After each request, this value for the current depth is updated by increasing it by one (Lines 18-19).

If there are no remaining services at the current depth ($curDepth$), the current depth may be eliminated from the hierarchy. In this case, the next depth is chosen as the current depth (Lines 7-9). To illustrate this, assume all the services of depth two are requested before. In this case, the current depth is removed from the hierarchy and the new current depth becomes third depth in the previous hierarchy. Also the upper depth is now equal to upper depth minus one (Line 11). In this case, the lower depth may not be higher than the upper depth. At this time, negotiation is completed with the best offer done by producer (Line 14).

3.4 Upper Random Strategy

The consumer chooses his request randomly from the preference graph. To improve the negotiation, the consumer selects the service randomly whose depth is higher than the depth of service offered by producer. For instance, in the second interaction with the producer the consumer selects a service randomly whose depth is higher than two if the producer has offered a service of depth two in the previous interaction. The negotiation continues until there is no unrequested service whose depth is higher than that of the best offer. In this case, the best offer proposed by the producer is requested by the consumer.

4   Producer's Strategy for Counter Offer

Unless the producer does not own the requested services, it has a tendency to offer a service from its stock, which is most similar to the last request of the consumer. To estimate the similarity, Tversky's similarity measure [6] comparing two vectors in terms of the number of exactly matching features is used. The formula for this similarity metric is shown in Equation (1) [6]. Here, *common* represents the number of matched attributes whereas *different* represents the number of the different attributes. We assume that α and β is equal to each other.

$$SM_{pq} = \frac{\alpha(common)}{\alpha(common) + \beta(different)} \tag{1}$$

5   Experiments

To evaluate our proposed strategies, we construct a system including one producer and one consumer agent that are negotiating a wine service automatically. This system is implemented in Java. The shared ontology describing the wine service is a modified version of the Wine Ontology [7]. OWL [8] is used as the ontology language and Jena2 [9] is used as the ontology reasoner. In the modified wine ontology, the wine service is described as a concept including six properties: grape, sugar, flavor, color, region and winery.

To start the negotiation, first the user's preferences are taken using the CP-net interface application. Based on the dependencies of the features, the user is asked to order her preferences. The obtained CP-net is kept in a file that can be reached only by the consumer agent. Note that the producer does not know the user's preferences. The producer agent has a service stock consisting of 20 wine services. These services are not known by the consumer.

We evaluate the performance of the strategies that are used by the consumer in order to generate requests. Intuitively, the customer prefers to get the best offer as soon as possible. Thus, the performance criterion is taken as the number of interactions with the producer to take the best service in terms of consumer preferences available on the producer side.

The experiments are conducted using two different customer preference profiles. The induced preference graph for the first customer profile has a depth of 18, whereas the second graph has a depth of 25. For each customer profile, four strategies explained in Section 3 are tested separately. These strategies are: sequential, depth limited, binary and upper random. To observe the performance of the strategies for generating a request, 20 different service stocks are constructed. Half of these service stocks (Stock1A ... Stock10A) are used for the first customer profile and remaining (Stock1B ... Stock10B) are used for the second profile. Since the available services in the stock

Table 1. Information about datasets in according to pattern and preference profile

Pattern	Preference	Max Depth	Information
First	First	14	11 of depth 8, 8 of depth 9 and 1 of depth 14
First	Second	20	11 of depth 12, 8 of depth 13 and 1 of depth 20
Second	First	17	5 of depth 8, 5 of depth 9, 5 of depth 16 and 5 of depth 17
Second	Second	24	5 of depth 12, 5 of depth 13, 5 of depth 23 and 5 of depth 24

may influence the negotiation process, we study two patterns for service stocks. The stock information for each pattern and preference profile is given in Table 1.

First pattern includes services of moderately desired level and one highly desired level service. In order to observe the behavior of the consumer's strategy, the stock has 11 services of depth eight, eight services of depth nine and one service of depth 14 as far as the first preference graph is concerned. To be fair, we use five different service stocks in this pattern for the first customer profile: Stock1A ... Stock5A. The second preference profile is composed of 11 services of depth 12, eight services of depth 13 and one service of depth 20. Similarly, we use five different stocks in this pattern for the second customer profile: Stock1B ... Stock5B. Different from other strategies, upper random strategy is run at five times and the average value is used for the evaluation.

Table 2 and Table 3 show the number of interactions with the producer for each strategy to obtain the producer's best offer for the first preference profile and second preference profile respectively. As seen from the results, the consumer using sequential strategy for generating requests takes the producer's best offer sooner than using binary or upper random strategies. The performance of the depth limited strategy is similar to that of sequential strategy but it gets worse compared to the sequential strategy for two of the five stocks for each preference.

Since the producer offers the most similar service to the request, the available services existing in producer's stock influence the negotiation direction. For some particular stocks, the similarity between the best service that the producer can offer and the consumer request inevitably causes the depth limited strategy to take longer then the sequential strategy. Consider Stock1A in which the best offer is similar to second service of depth 17. After requesting the first service of depth 17, consumer asks for a lower depth when the depth limited strategy is used. In this case, the consumer's next requests become far away from the best offer that can be proposed by the producer. Therefore, it takes more time to reach the best offer.

Table 2. Number of interactions to get the best offer (first preference profile, first pattern)

Strategy	Stock 1A	Stock 2A	Stock 3A	Stock 4A	Stock 5A
Sequential	3	1	1	1	3
Depth Limited	14	1	1	1	6
Binary	9	2	2	6	13
Upper Random	12.8	8.6	8	9.8	6

Table 3. Number of interactions to get the best offer (second preference profile, first pattern)

Strategy	Stock 1B	Stock 2B	Stock 3B	Stock 4B	Stock 5B
Sequential	1	1	3	2	1
Depth Limited	1	1	11	15	1
Binary	4	3	4	4	5
Upper Random	6.8	4	12.8	4.8	13.8

The second pattern that we investigated in our experiments involves same numbers of services of moderately desired level and highly desired level. For first preference profile, the stock has five services of depth eight, five services of depth nine , five services of depth 16 and five services of depth 17. Five different service stocks having these features are Stock6A … Stock10A. The pattern of the stock for the second preference profile consists of five services of depth 12, five services of depth 13, five services of depth 23 and five services of depth 24 as far as the preference graph is concerned. Half of the services are highly desired whereas other half is desired moderately. We use different stocks having these features: Stock6B … Stock10B.

Table 4 shows the number of interaction with the producer for each strategy to obtain the producer's best offer for the first preference profile whereas Table 5 indicates the same for the second preference profile. According to the results, the sequential and depth limited strategies gives the best results for both preference profiles. The performance of the binary and upper random strategies is better for the second stock pattern than for the first pattern. Since the number of highly desired services in the second pattern is larger than that in the first pattern, the probability to reach the best offer is high in the second pattern. Therefore, the performance of binary strategy as well as the upper random strategy increases implicitly.

As a summary, the consumer using sequential strategy receives the producer's best offer sooner than those using other strategies. The consumer using depth limited strategy achieves the second high performance but in some cases binary strategy works better than depth limited. This stems from the fact that the performance of the strategies are affected by the content distribution of the stocks. That is, the producer offers the most similar service which does not necessarily correspond to services that are of the same or consecutive depths. Therefore the producer may offer a service of unexpected depth. As a result, the strategies may give different performance for different stocks in the same pattern.

Table 4. Number of interactions to get the best offer (first preference profile, second pattern)

Strategy	Stock 6A	Stock 7A	Stock 8A	Stock 9A	Stock 10A
Sequential	1	1	1	1	1
Depth Limited	1	1	1	1	1
Binary	3	2	2	3	3
Upper Random	2	1.8	2.6	2.4	2.8

Table 5. Number of interactions to get the best offer (second preference profile, second pattern)

Strategy	Stock 6B	Stock 7B	Stock 8B	Stock 9B	Stock 10B
Sequential	1	1	1	1	1
Depth Limited	1	1	1	1	1
Binary	2	3	2	2	3
Upper Random	2.6	2.8	2.6	2.4	3

6 Discussion

Tykhonov and Hindriks propose to learn the opponent's preferences using Bayesian learning in order to improve the performance of the negotiation process [10]. They study learning opponent's preferences from bid exchanges in automated multi-issue negotiation. Whereas Tykhonov and Hindriks assume issues to be independent, we also consider dependent issues in our model. Under this setting, we do not learn the opponent's preferences but develop strategies to negotiate with preferences. In this respect, our work is complementary.

Dastani *et al.* study mediating agents and modeling user preferences in e-commerce [11]. They argue that preferences can be modeled automatically. In order to induce the preferences, they suggest applying inductive logic programming in that mediating agent finds out the regularities in the behavior of the participants. By this way, it induces hypotheses about their preferences. Instead of learning preferences, we take the preferences in the form of CP-net and provide strategies to propose offers.

Faratin *et al.* propose a multi-issue negotiation mechanism based on trade-offs [1]. The service variables for the negotiation process such as price, quality, and so on are considered trade-offs against each other (i.e., higher price for earlier delivery). They generate a heuristic model for trade-offs including fuzzy similarity estimation and a hill-climbing exploration for possibly acceptable offers. A possible offer having the same score value for the agent with its previous offer, which approximates the opponent's last offer is proposed by the agent. In our study, the consumer generates its requests via the proposed strategies explained in Section 3. These strategies use the preference graph induced by the CP-net.

Lue *et al.* study gaining user trade-off strategies and preferences to improve the efficiency of the negotiation [12]. They propose a default-then-adjust method for this. According to their approach, system first makes an interview with the user about the possible trade-off strategies. Then, the user can alter the default suggested trade-off strategies and also the default preferences on the trade-off alternatives. Compared to that approach, we deal with taking consumer preferences in order to generate requests rather than trade-off preferences.

Present work only focuses on the consumer's strategies for generating requests. In the future, we plan to incorporate mechanisms such as learning preferences to improve negotiation capabilities of the producer. Further, we plan to study the trade-offs of strategies under different patterns of service distributions.

References

1. Faratin, P., Sierra, C., Jennings, N.R.: Using Similarity Criteria to Make Issue Trade-offs in Automated Negotiations. Artificial Intelligence 142(2), 205–237 (2002)
2. Gonzales, C., Perny, P.: GAI networks for utility elicitation. In: KR 2004 (2004)
3. Boutilier, C., Brafman, R.I., Domshlak, C., Hoos, H.H., Poole, D.: CP-nets: A Tool for Representing and Reasoning with Conditional Ceteris Paribus Preference Statements. Journal of Artificial Intelligence Research (JAIR), 135–191 (2004)
4. Aydoğan, R., Yolum, P.: Learning Consumer Preferences Using Semantic Similarity. In: 6th International Joint Conference on Autonomous Agents and Multiagent Systems (AAMAS), Hawaii, USA, May 2007, pp. 1293–1300 (2007)
5. Hansson, S.O.: What is ceteris paribus preference? Journal of Philosophical Logic 25(3), 307–332 (1996)
6. Tversky, A.: Features of Similarity. Psychological Review 84(4), 327–352 (1977)
7. Wine Ontology (2003),
   http://www.w3.org/TR/2003/CR-owl-guide-20030818/wine.rdf
8. OWL Web Ontology Language Guide (2004), http://www.w3.org/TR/owl-guide
9. Jena (2006), http://jena.sourceforge.net/
10. Tykhonov, D., Hindriks, K.: Opponent Modelling in Automated Multi-Issue Negotiation Using Bayesian Learning. In: 7th International Joint Conference on Autonomous Agents and Multiagent Systems (AAMAS), Estorial, Portugal (May 2008)
11. Dastani, M., Jacobs, N., Jonker, C.M., Treur, J.: Modelling user preferences and mediating agents in electronic commerce. Knowledge-based systems 18(7), 335–352 (2005)
12. Luo, X., Jennings, N.R., Shadbolt, N.: Acquiring user strategies and preferences for negotiating agents: a default then adjust method. Int J. of Human Computer Studies 64(4), 304–321 (2006)

Using Priced Options to Solve the Exposure Problem in Sequential Auctions

Lonneke Mous[1,2], Valentin Robu[1], and Han La Poutré[1]

[1] CWI, Dutch National Center for Mathematics and Computer Science
Kruislaan 413, NL-1098 SJ Amsterdam, The Netherlands
[2] Erasmus University Rotterdam, Econometrics Institute
P.O. Box 1738, 3000 DR Rotterdam, The Netherlands
{mous,robu,hlp}@cwi.nl

Abstract. This paper studies the benefits of using priced options for solving the exposure problem that bidders with valuation synergies face when participating in multiple, sequential auctions. We consider a model in which complementary-valued items are auctioned sequentially by different sellers, who have the choice of either selling their good directly or through a priced option, after fixing its exercise price. We analyze this model from a decision-theoretic perspective and we show, for a setting where the competition is formed by local bidders, that using options can increase the expected profit for both buyers and sellers. Furthermore, we derive the equations that provide minimum and maximum bounds between which a synergy buyer's bids should fall in order for both sides to have an incentive to use the options mechanism. Next, we perform an experimental analysis of a market in which multiple synergy bidders are active simultaneously.

1 Introduction

The exposure problem appears whenever a bidder with complementary valuations (i.e. synergies) tries to acquire a bundle of goods sold through sequential auctions. Informally, the problem occurs whenever an agent may buy a single good at a price higher than what it is worth to her, in the hope of obtaining extra value through synergy with another good, which is sold in a later auction. However, if she then fails to buy this other good at a profitable price, she is exposed to the risk of a potential loss. In the analysis presented in this paper, we call such a global bidder a *synergy bidder*.

The exposure problem is well known in auction theory and multi-agent systems research. The usual way to tackle this problem in the mechanism design community is to replace sequential allocation with a one-shot mechanism, such as a combinatorial auction [4]. However, this approach has the disadvantage of typically requiring a central point of authority, which handles all the sales. Moreover, many allocation problems occurring in practice are inherently decentralized and sequential. Possible examples range from items sold on Ebay by different sellers, loads appearing over time in distributed transportation logistics, dynamic resource allocation in hospitals, etc.

In this paper, we consider a different approach to handle the exposure problem, and propose a mechanism which involves auctioning *priced options* for the goods, instead of the goods themselves.

W. Ketter et al. (Eds.): AMEC/TADA 2008, LNBIP 44, pp. 29–45, 2010.
© Springer-Verlag Berlin Heidelberg 2010

1.1 Options: Basic Definition

An option can be seen as a contract between the buyer and the seller of a good, subject to the following rules:

- The writer or seller of the option has the *obligation* to sell the good for the *exercise price*, but not the right.
- The holder or buyer of the option has the *right* to buy the good for the *exercise price*, but not the obligation.

Since the buyer gains the right to choose in the future whether or not she wants to buy the good, an option comes with an *option price*, which she has to pay regardless of whether she chooses to exercise the option or not. Options can thus help a synergy buyer reduce the exposure problem she faces. She still has to pay the option price, but if she fails to complete her desired bundle, then she does not have to pay the exercise price as well and thus she limits her loss. So part of the uncertainty of not winning subsequent auctions is transferred to the seller, who may now miss out on the exercise price if the buyer fails to acquire the desired bundle. At the same time, the seller can also benefit indirectly, from the additional participation in the market by additional synergy buyers, who would have otherwise stayed out, because of the exposure to a potential loss.

1.2 Related Work

The first work to introduce an explicit option-based mechanism for sequential-auction allocation of goods to the MAS community is Juda & Parkes [2,3]. They create a market design in which global bidders are awarded free (i.e. zero-priced) options, in order to cover their exposure problem and, for this setting, they propose truth-telling as a dominant strategy. In their case, the exposure problem is entirely solved for the synergy bidders, because they do not even have a possible loss consisting of the option price. However, this approach also introduces some limitations. Because the options are assumed to be offered free (zero-priced), there may be cases in which sellers do not have a sufficient incentive to offer free options, because of the risk of remaining with their items unsold. The sellers could, however, demand a premium (in the form of the option price) to cover their risk. In such cases, only positively-priced options can provide sufficient incentive for for both sides to use the mechanism. Furthermore, the mechanism proposed by Juda & Parkes requires sellers to be more patient than all synergy bidders present in the market.

Priced options have a long history of research in finance (see [1] for an overview). However, the underlying assumption for all financial option pricing models is their dependence on an underlying asset, which has a known public value that moves independently of the actions of individual agents. This type of assumption does not hold for the private values, sequential auctions setting we consider.

Finally, there is a connection between options and leveled commitment mechanisms (Sandholm & Lesser [5] 't Hoen et. al. [6]). In leveled commitment, both parties have the possibility to decommit (i.e. unilaterally break a contract), against paying a pre-agreed decommitment penalty. This differs from option contracts, where the right to exercise the option is paid by one party in advance.

1.3   Outline and Contribution of Our Approach

The goal of this paper is to study the use of priced options to solve the exposure problem and to identify the settings in which using priced options benefits both the synergy buyer and the seller. An option consists out of two prices, so an adjustment needs to be made to the standard auction with bids of a single price. The essence of options, in our model, is that bidders obtain the right to buy the good for a certain exercise price in the future. The value of such an option may be different for different market participants at different times. Throughout this study, in order to make the analysis tractable, we have a fixed exercise price and a flexible option price. The seller determines the exercise price of an option for the good she has for sale and then sells this option through a first price auction. Bidders bid for the right to buy this option, i.e. they bid on the option price.

Note that, in this model, direct auctioning of the items appears as a particular sub-case of the proposed mechanism, assuming free disposal on the part of the buyers. If the seller fixes the future exercise price for the option at zero, then a buyer basically bids for the right to get the item for free. Since such an option is always exercised (assuming free disposal), this is basically equivalent to auctioning the item itself. Our analysis of the problem can be characterized as decision-theoretic, meaning both buyer and seller reason with respect to expected future price. To summarize, our contribution to the literature can be characterized as being twofold:

First, we consider a setting in which n complementary-valued goods (or options for them) are auctioned sequentially, assuming there is only one synergy bidder or global bidder (the rest of the competition is formed by local bidders desiring only one good). For this setting, we show analytically (under some assumptions), that using priced options can increase the expected profit for both the synergy bidder and the seller, compared to the case when the goods are auctioned directly. Furthermore, we derive the equations that provide minimum and maximum bounds between which the bids of the synergy bidder should fall in order for both sides to have an incentive to use options.

In the second part of the paper, we consider market settings in which multiple synergy bidders (global bidders) are active simultaneously, and study it through experimental simulations. We show that, while some synergy bidders lose because of the extra competition, other synergy bidders may actually benefit, because sellers are forced to fix exercise prices for options at levels which encourages participation of all bidders.

2   Expected Profit for a Sequence of n Auctions and 1 Synergy Bidder

Section 3 will analytically prove, that options can be profitable to both synergy bidder and seller. In order to do that, this section derives the expected profit functions for the synergy bidder and the seller. Throughout this study it is assumed that both sellers and bidders are risk neutral and that they want to maximize their expected profit.

2.1   Profit with n Unique Goods without Options

This section describes the expected profit of the synergy bidder and the sellers as a function of the synergy bidder's bids for a market with n unique, complementary goods, which are sold without options.

Let G be the set of n goods for sale in a temporal sequence of auctions and $v_{syn}(G_{sub})$ be the valuation the synergy bidder has for $G_{sub} \subseteq G$. Then assume that $v_{syn}(G) > 0$ and $\forall G_{sub} \subsetneq G$, $v_{syn}(G_{sub}) = 0$. In other words, the synergy bidder only desires a bundle of all the goods considered in the model.

The goods $G_1..G_n \in G$ are sold individually through sequential, first-price, sealed-bid auctions. Here we choose the auctions to be first price, as they are more tractable to study using game-theoretic analysis. Furthermore, in a sequential setting with valuation complementarities of the bidders, second-price auctions do not have the nice dominant strategies properties, described by Vickrey. Furthermore, in many settings where such a model could be used in practice, such as request-for-quotes (RFQ) auctions in logistics or supply chains, first-price auctioning is often used.

The time these auctions take place in is $t = 1 \ldots n$, such that at time t good $G_t \in G$ is auctioned. The above assumptions mean that if the synergy bidder has failed to obtain G_t, then she cannot achieve a bundle for which she has a positive valuation. If the synergy bidder fails to obtain G_t, then it is rational for her to not place bids in subsequent auctions. The bids of the synergy bidder are $\boldsymbol{B} = (b_1, \ldots, b_n)$, where b_t is the bid the synergy bidder will place for good G_t, conditional on having won the previous auctions. Because of the first-price auction format, b_t is also the price the synergy bidder has to pay if she has won the auction.

Throughout this analysis, we assume the competition the synergy bidder faces for each good G_t (sold at time t) is formed by local bidders that only require the good G_t. We further assume that these local bidders are myopic, i.e. the bids placed by the synergy bidder have no effect on their bidding behaviour. Therefore, from the perspective of the synergy bidder, the competition can be modeled as a distribution over the expected closing prices at each time point t, more precisely as a distribution over a value bm_t, which is the maximal bid placed by the competition not counting b_t.

Denote by $F_t(b_t)$ the probability that the synergy bidder wins good G_t with bid b_t - where $F_t(b_t)$ depends on whether b_t can outbid the maximal bid bm_t placed by the competition, excluding b_t. For each good G_t, there exists a strictly positive reserve price of $b_{t,res}$, which is the seller's own valuation for that good. Then bm_t is the highest bid of the local bidders (who only want G_t), if that bid is higher than $b_{t,res}$. Otherwise bm_t equals $b_{t,res}$. To deal with ties, we assume the synergy bidder only wins G_t if $b_t > bm_t$ and not if the bids are equal. Then $F_t(b_t)$ can be defined as follows:

$$F_t(b_t) = Prob(b_t > bm_t) \tag{1}$$

The synergy bidder only has a strictly positive valuation for the bundle of goods G, which includes all the goods G_t, sold at times $t = 1..n$. Therefore, in a market without options, the a-priori expected profit π_{syn}^{dir} of the synergy bidder is:

$$E(\pi_{syn}^{dir}) = \left[v_{syn}(G) \prod_{i=1}^{n} F_i(b_i) \right] + \left[\sum_{j=1}^{n} (-b_j) \prod_{k=1}^{j} F_k(b_k) \right] \tag{2}$$

The synergy bidder wants to maximize her expected profit. So her optimal bids $\boldsymbol{B}^* = (b_1^*, \ldots, b_n^*)$ maximize equation 2:

$$\boldsymbol{B}^* = argmax_{\boldsymbol{B}^*} E(\pi_{syn}^{dir}) \tag{3}$$

Next the profit of the sellers are examined. It is assumed that all sellers have their own valuation for the good that they sell and that they set their reserve price of $b_{t,res}$ equal to this private valuation. So when the good is sold for b_t, the seller of G_t has a profit π_t^{dir} of $b_t - b_{t,res}$. As previously shown, the synergy bidder only participates when she has won the previous auctions; otherwise bm_t is the maximal placed bid. The expected profit of the seller of the good G_t sold at time t is:

$$E(\pi_t^{dir}) = (E(bm_t) - b_{t,res})(1 - \prod_{i=1}^{t-1} F_i(b_i)) + \left(F_t(b_t)(b_t - b_{t,res}) \right.$$

$$+ (1 - F_t(b_t))(E(bm_t|bm_t \geq b_t) - b_{t,res})) \prod_{i=1}^{t-1} F_i(b_i) \tag{4}$$

2.2 Profit with n Unique Goods with Options

Next, we derive the expected profits for the synergy bidder and the sellers for a market with options. This section has the same setting as the general model with n goods being sold, only now an option on G_t is auctioned at time t. Therefore, all the sellers in the market will sell options for their goods, instead of directly the goods themselves. After the n auctions have taken place, the bidders need to determine whether or not they will exercise their option. It is assumed that an option is only exercised if a bidder has obtained her entire, desired bundle. The local bidders are only interested in G_t, so they will always exercise an option on G_t should they have one. The synergy bidder is only interested in a bundle of all goods, so she will only exercise an option (and pay the corresponding exercise price) if she has options on all the goods required.

The option exists out of a fixed exercise price K_t and the synergy bidder's bids on the option price are $\boldsymbol{OP} = (op_1, \ldots, op_n)$. The maximal bid without the synergy bidder was bm_t, but now opm_t is the maximal placed option price.

Since the competition only wants one good, they do not benefit from having an option and they will always exercise any option they acquire. Therefore the competition's best policy is to keep bidding the same total price, which is the bid without options minus the exercise price. Thus the distribution of the competition is only shifted horizontally to the left, by the reduction of the exercise price: $opm_t = bm_t - K_t$. Thus, if the synergy bidder bids the same total price (option + exercise), then she has the same probability of winning the auction in both models. Let $F_t^o(op_t)$ be the probability that op_t wins the auction for the option on G_t. So if $op_t + K_t = b_t$, then $F_t^o(op_t) = F_t^o(b_t - K_t) = F_t(b_t)$.

The synergy bidder's expected profit with options then is:

$$E(\pi_{syn}^{op}) = \left[(v_{syn}(G) - \left[\sum_{h=1}^n K_h \right] \right] \prod_{i=1}^n F_i^o(op_i) + \left[\sum_{j=1}^n (-op_j) \prod_{k=1}^j F_k^o(op_k) \right] \tag{5}$$

So her optimal bids $\boldsymbol{OP}^* = (op_1^*, \ldots, op_n^*)$ maximize the profit equation 5:

$$\boldsymbol{OP}^* = argmax_{\boldsymbol{OP}^*} E(\pi_{syn}^{op})) \tag{6}$$

The main difference for the seller of G_t, is that if the synergy bidder wins, then she only earns $K_t - b_{t,res}$ when the option is exercised. She then gains the exercise price, but loses the value the good has to her, which is the reserve price. And the probability of exercise is the probability that the synergy bidder wins all the other auctions. Therefore, the total expected profit of the seller at time t is:

$$E(\pi_t^{op}) = (E(opm_t) + K_t - b_{t,res})(1 - \prod_{i=1}^{t-1} F_i^o(op_i))$$

$$+ \left(F_t^o(op_t)(op_t + \left[(K_t - b_{t,res}) \prod_{h=t+1}^{n} F_h^o(op_h) \right] \right)$$

$$+ (1 - F_t^o(op_t))(E(opm_t | opm_t \geq op_t) + K_t - b_{t,res}) \prod_{i=1}^{t-1} F_i^o(op_i) \qquad (7)$$

3   When Options Can Benefit Both Synergy Bidder and Seller

Section 2 resulted in the a-priori, expected profit for the synergy bidder and the sellers as a function of the synergy bidder's bids for a market with and without options. This section uses these functions to determine the difference in profit between the two markets, which is $\pi_{\delta t}$ and $\pi_{\delta syn}$ for the seller of good G_t and the synergy bidder respectively.

$$\pi_{\delta t} = \pi_t^{op} - \pi_t^{dir},$$

$$\pi_{\delta syn} = \pi_{syn}^{op} - \pi_{syn}^{dir}$$

So if $\pi_{\delta t}$ and $\pi_{\delta syn}$ are positive, then both agents are better off with options.

3.1   The Case When Agents Are Better Off with Options

Let B^* denote the synergy bidder's optimal bidding policy in a market where goods are sold directly (without options). We assume for the rest of Sect. 3 that for $1 \leq t \leq n$, $F_t(b_t^*) > 0$ and $F_t(b_t^*) < 1$. So she may complete her bundle, but may also end up paying for a worthless subset of goods. Thus she faces an exposure problem. For the market with options, we define a benchmark strategy OP' for the synergy bidder, so that the two markets can easily be compared.

Definition 1. *The benchmark of the synergy bidder's bids with options* $OP' = (op'_1,$ $\ldots, op'_n)$ *is that for* $1 \leq t \leq n$:

$$op'_t = b_t^* - K_t$$

In other words, the benchmark strategy implies that the synergy bidder will bid the same total amount for the good, as if she used her optimal bidding policy in a direct sale market. Clearly this does not have to be her profit-maximizing bid in a market where priced options are used. In fact, it is almost always the case that the synergy bidder will bid a different value in a market in with priced options. This deviance from the benchmark is denoted by λ_t:

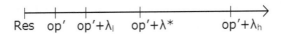

Fig. 1. A possible situation in which options are desirable for both the synergy bidder and seller

Definition 2. *Let λ_t denote the deviation in the bid of the synergy bidder on the item G_t sold at time t, in a model with options, with respect to her profit-maximizing bid b_t^* in a model without options. So her bid on an option for G_t will be $op_t' + \lambda_t$.*

These definitions enable us to rigorously define the bounds within which the use of options (with a given exercise price) are desirable for both the synergy bidder and the seller. Figure 1 gives the visual description of a generic setting in which options are beneficial for both sides. It shows the possible bids a synergy bidder can place for an option. First, valid bids have to be bigger than the reserve price Res, for each good in the sequence. The point op' is where the synergy bidder keeps bidding the same total price as in a market without options, c.f. Definition 1.

The deviations, in an option model, from the benchmark bid op' is measured by three levels, all denoted with λ: λ_l is the minimal risk premium the seller requires to benefit from using options, λ_h is the maximal extra amount the synergy bidder is willing to pay for an option and $op^* = op' + \lambda^*$ is the synergy bidder's profit-maximizing bid. So, if it were rational for the synergy bidder to bid an additional quantity between λ_l and λ_h (as shown in Fig. 1), then both she and the seller are better off with options.

In the rest of Sect. 3, we derive the analytical expressions which can be used to determine the values for λ_l, λ_h and λ^* and compare them. Before this, however, we describe an important assumption behind the proofs in the remainder of this section.

Assumption on the proof structure. Performing an exhaustive theoretical analysis of the minimum, maximum and optimal bidding levels of the λ-s for all auctions in a sequence would not be tractable, as they all influence each other. Therefore, we simplify our proof structure by focusing only on one of the λ parameters: the one corresponding to the first good. This is possible since, as explained in the introduction, each seller sells one good and is only interested in maximizing the expected profit from that sale. The decision of using options contract or a direct sale is a decision taken bilaterally by each seller and the synergy bidder, thus has to benefit both of them. The reason why we focus on the first good in the sequence is that, for this good, the bidder's probability of not completing her desired bundle, hence her exposure problem, is the greatest. Our proof structure could be generalized as a recursive procedure: if one shows that options are beneficial to use for the first item in a sequence, given a remaining [non-empty] sequence of auctions, this can be generalized to all remaining sub-sequences (except the last item, for which options would be always exercised, thus they are not needed).

In order to analytically examine the benefits of deviating from the benchmark strategy op_1' in the first auction, the proofs in this paper use the additional assumption that the synergy bidder will use the benchmark strategy from Def. 1 for all remaining goods in the sequence. This is a reasonable assumption for this model (as defined above), as sellers of items in subsequent auctions can only benefit from (or are indifferent to) the fact that items sold earlier in the sequence were sold through options, rather than directly. To explain, if there are no complementarities between the earlier items and the good they are currently selling, then sellers are indifferent to the use of options in earlier sales. If there are such complementarities however, subsequent sellers also benefit, because the synergy bidder has a higher chance of acquiring the first good, she also has a higher probability of participating in subsequent auctions.

When synergy bidder is better off with options. This part of Section 3.1 examines for which bids the synergy bidder is better off with options. This is done by determining the maximal amount she is willing to pay for options.

Lemma 1. *Let $B^* =< b_t >$ for $1 \leq t \leq n$ be the vector of optimal bids of the synergy bidder in the model without options, and $op'_t + \lambda_t$ be the bids in a model with options. The expected gain (i.e. difference in expected profit) from using options $E(\pi_{\delta syn})$ is:*

$$E(\pi_{\delta syn}) = \left[v_{syn}(G)(\prod_{i=1}^{n} F_i(b_i^* + \lambda_i) - \prod_{i=1}^{n} F_i(b_i^*)) \right] + \left[\sum_{j=1}^{n} K_j(\prod_{k=1}^{j} F_k(b_k^* + \lambda_k) - \right.$$

$$\left. \prod_{i=1}^{n} F_i(b_i^* + \lambda_i)) + \sum_{j=1}^{n}(-\lambda_j) \prod_{k=1}^{j} F_k(b_k^* + \lambda_k) + \left[\sum_{j=1}^{n}(-b_j^*)(\prod_{k=1}^{j} F_k(b_k^* + \lambda_k) - \prod_{k=1}^{j} F_k(b_k^*)) \right] \right]$$

Proof. The proof is omitted due to lack of space. In short, the expression from Lemma 1 can be obtained by deducting the profit without options from Eq. (2) from the profit with options in Eq. (5), and using $F_{ot}(op'_t + \lambda_t) = F_t(b_t^* + \lambda_t)$.

Intuitively, if λ_t is positive for all G_t, then the difference is formed by a summation of 4 terms: 1) the synergy bidder bids more with options, so she has a higher probability of obtaining her desired bundle 2) with options she does not have to pay the exercise price right away, but only when she completes her bundle 3) she bids more, so she pays a higher price and 4) since she bids more in previous auctions, there is a higher chance that she wins the current one and pays for the good.

Next, we provide the equations that allow us to deduce the λ parameters that give the synergy bidder an incentive to use options. As explained in Sect. 3.1, we simplify the proof structure by only focusing on the most important option for the synergy bidder: the one on the first good (when bidding for this good, the probability of not completing her entire bundle is the greatest). This is done under the assumption that for the goods in the sequence, we assume the benchmark strategy is used (i.e. $\lambda_t = 0$ for $t > 1$). For the rest of the items in the sequence, the same proof technique can be applied recursively.

Theorem 1. *Let λ_1 be the deviation in the bidding strategy, compared to the benchmark strategy op'_1, as defined in Def. 1. If $\lambda_t = 0$ for $1 < t \leq n$, then $E(\pi_{\delta syn}) >= 0$ if $0 \leq \lambda_1 < \lambda_h$. The value of λ_h (corresponding to $E(\pi_{\delta syn}) = 0$) can be determined as the numerical solution of the following equation:*

$$F_1(b_1^* + \lambda_h)\lambda_h = F_1(b_1^* + \lambda_h) \left[\sum_{j=1}^{n} K_j(\prod_{k=2}^{j} F_k(b_k^*) - \prod_{i=2}^{n} F_i(b_i^*)) \right]$$

$$+ (F_1(b_1^* + \lambda_h) - F_1(b_1^*)) \left[v_{syn}(G) \prod_{i=2}^{n} F_i(b_i^*) - \sum_{j=1}^{n}(b_j^*) \prod_{k=2}^{j} F_k(b_k^*) \right]$$

Proof. The proof is based on the difference in profit function derived in Lemma 1, using the assumption that $\lambda_t = 0$ for $1 < t \leq n$. As the expectation function of the synergy bidder is descending in the value of λ, we determine when $E(\pi_{\delta syn}) = 0$.

$$\left[v_{syn}(G)(F_1(b_1^* + \lambda_h) - F_1(b_1^*)) \prod_{i=2}^{n} F_i(b_i^*) \right]$$

$$+ \left[\sum_{j=1}^{n} K_j(F_1(b_1^* + \lambda_h) \prod_{k=2}^{j} F_k(b_k^*)) - (F_1(b_1^* + \lambda_h) \prod_{i=2}^{n} F_i(b_i^*)) \right]$$

$$+ (-\lambda_h)F_1(b_1^* + \lambda_h) + \left[\sum_{j=1}^{n} (-b_j^*)(F_1(b_1^* + \lambda_h) - F_1(b_1^*)) \prod_{k=2}^{j} F_k(b_k^*) \right] = 0$$

Isolating the values of λ_h yields the formula in Th. 1.

When the first seller is better off with options. We now determine the minimum or lower bound λ_l (the level of λ that, according to Def. 2, keeps the seller of G_1 indifferent about options). In order to compare this bid with the λ_h from the previous section, it is again assumed that $\lambda_t = 0$ for $1 < t \leq n$.

Theorem 2. *If without options the synergy bidder bids B^* and with options $op_1' + \lambda_1$ for G_1 and op_t' for $1 < t \leq n$, then $E(\pi_{\delta 1})$ for the seller of G_1 is:*

$$E(\pi_{\delta 1}) = F_1(b_1^*)(\lambda_1 + (b_{1,res} - K_1)\left[1 - \prod_{h=2}^{n} F_h(b_h^*)\right]) + (F_1(b_1^* + \lambda_1) - F_1(b_1^*))(b_1^* + \lambda_1$$

$$- E(bm_1 | b_1^* + \lambda_1 \geq bm_1 > b_1^*) + (b_{1,res} - K_1)\left[1 - \prod_{h=2}^{n} F_h(b_h^*)\right])$$

By definition, λ_1 is the lower bound for λ_l that guarantees that the expected profit of the seller $E(\pi_{\delta 1}) > 0$. The value of λ_l can be obtained as the solution to the equation $E(\pi_{\delta 1}) = 0$, which using the equation above gives:

$$F_1(b_1^* + \lambda_l)(-\lambda_l) = F_1(b_1^* + \lambda_l)((b_{1,res} - K_1)\left[1 - \prod_{h=2}^{n} F_h(b_h^*)\right])$$

$$+ (F_1(b_1^* + \lambda_l) - F_1(b_1^*))(b_1^* - E(bm_1 | b_1^* + \lambda_l \geq bm_1 > b_1^*))$$

Proof. The proof is derived by taking the difference in profits between Eq. (7) and Eq. (4), and replacing op_1' with its definition, as follows: $op_1 = op_1' + \lambda_1 = b_1^* - K_1 + \lambda_1$ and $F_1^o(op_1) = F_1^o(op_1' + \lambda_1) = F_1(b_1^* + \lambda_1)$:

$$E(\pi_{\delta 1}) = F_1(b_1^* + \lambda_1)(b_1^* - K_1 + \lambda_1 + \left[(K_1 - b_{1,res}) \prod_{h=2}^{n} F_{oh}(op_h')\right])$$

$$+ (F_1(b_1^* + \lambda_1) - F_1(b_1^*))(-E(bm_1 | b_1^* + \lambda_1 \geq bm_1 > b_1^*) + b_{1,res})$$

$$- F_1(b_1^*)(b_1^* - b_{1,res})$$

Splitting $F_1(b_1^* + \lambda_1)$ into $F_1(b_1^*)$ and $F_1(b_1^* + \lambda_1) - F_1(b_1^*)$, and combining some K_1 and $b_{1,res}$ leads to the equation in Theorem 2. The optimal λ_l can then be determined by solving the equation $E(\pi_{\delta 1}) = 0$, from the expression in Theorem 2.

Intuitively, the difference in profit has two parts: the cases where the synergy bidder wins the auction in both markets and the ones where she only wins with options. With the first, the synergy bidder pays more than she used to and with the second, the synergy bidder pays more than the local bidders, who used to win if $\lambda_1 < \lambda_l$. But both cases have the downside for the seller that the synergy bidder may now not exercise her option.

Both agents can be better off with options

Theorem 3. *If synergy bidder bids λ_x extra for an option on G_1, where $\lambda_l < \lambda_x < \lambda_h$, then both the seller of G_1 and the synergy bidder have a higher expected profit in a market with only options compared to one without options.*

Proof. The proof for this follows immediately from the definition of λ_l and λ_h, and from Theorems 1 and 2.

3.2   Synergy Bidder's Profit-Maximizing Bid

In Section 3.1, we derived the equations for the bounds λ_l and λ_h between which the additional bids of the synergy bidder have to fall in order for both parties to be incentivised to use options. In this section, we look at the synergy bidder's profit-maximizing bids op^*, but with the added assumption that $F_1(b_1)$ follows a uniform distribution in the range of the possible bids. We do this by using the same framework introduced in Definition 2 and Figure 1 above. That means, we compute the deviation λ^* between the optimal bid in a model with options and the optimal bid in a model without options, i.e. the difference $\lambda^* = (K_1 + op_1^*) - b_1^*$.

If the profit-maximizing bid $op_1^* > op_1' + \lambda_l$, then according to Theorem 2 the seller of G_1 is better off with options. Therefore, it is in the rational interest of the seller to set the exercise price for selling her good such that the expected optimal bid of her bidders, in a model with options, will provide sufficient incentive for the seller to also use options, and thus the following condition holds: $op_1^* > op_1' + \lambda_l$. Note that in order to use Theorem 2, the bids for the other goods are set at op_t'.

Lemma 2. *If $F_1(b_1)$ follows a uniform distribution between two values $ua, ub \in \mathbb{R}$ (such that $ua < ub$), then $op_1^* + K_1 - b_1^* = \lambda^*$, where:*

$$\lambda^* = 0.5(K_1(1 - \prod_{i=2}^{n} F_i(b_i^*)) + \sum_{j=2}^{n} K_j(\prod_{k=2}^{j} F_k(b_k^*) - \prod_{i=2}^{n} F_i(b_i^*)))$$

While the lower bound λ_l is:

$$\lambda_l = -(b_1^* - ua + \left[1 - \prod_{h=2}^{n} F_h(b_h^*)\right](b_{1,res} - K_1))$$

$$+\sqrt{(b_1^* - ua + \left[1 - \prod_{h=2}^{n} F_h(b_h^*)\right](b_{1,res} - K_1))^2 - 2(b_1^* - ua)\left[1 - \prod_{h=2}^{n} F_h(b_h^*)\right](b_{1,res} - K_1)}$$

Proof. The proof for Lemma 2 had to be omitted due to lack of space. Basically, the partial derivatives are taken from the expected profit equations (Equations 2 and 5), using the uniform distribution $F_1(b_1)$ between the values ua and ub. For deriving λ_l, we used the equation from Theorem 2, with the added assumption of a uniform distribution.

The seller then can set K_1 at a value for which $\lambda_l < \lambda^*$ holds. We found that deriving a closed-form solution for this condition is not possible analytically. However, the framework developed above is sufficient to enable the seller to solve this condition numerically using a standard solver and, choose the optimal level for exercise price K_1.

4   Simulation of a Market with a Single Synergy Bidder

This section presents an experimental examination of a market with one synergy bidder. It introduces the market entry effects in the synergy bidder's behaviour, as well as the threshold effects that may determine which exercise prices the seller chooses for her options. Section 5 considers a market with multiple synergy bidders.

The experimental setting is as follows: we consider a simulation where two goods A and B are auctioned n_A and n_B times respectively. The synergy bidder desires one copy of both goods and has zero valuation for the individual goods. That is, each synergy (or global) bidder requires exactly one bundle of $\{A, B\}$.In the setting considered in this section, local bidders only want one good and participate in one auction, thus their bids can be modeled as a distribution.

Furthermore, in order to simplify the simulation we assume there is a single seller who auctions all the goods. This is actually equivalent to studying whether *on average* sellers have an incentive to use options. To explain, on any single sequence of auctions, the sellers of different items may have diverging incentives to use options, based on their position in the auction queue. However, in a large, open setting, where bidders enter the market randomly, it is difficult for any individual seller to strategise about her particular place in the sequence. Our goal is to study under which conditions, on average, sellers benefit from using options if there are synergy bidders in the market.

Note that, typically a seller has a resale value of for the goods that remain unsold, which is typically lower that the value at the start of the auction sequence. The reason for this may be that there is some time discounting associated with waiting for a sequence of auctions to resell her items, or even a listing cost, which is paid per auction (such as in the Ebay case). In this paper, we do not explicitly simulate resale, but we use a reservation value, which represents the expected resale value the seller expects to get, if she is forced to resell her items.

For each auction, in each simulation run, there is a set of local bidders, assumed to be myopic. The bids of these local bidders are therefore, assumed to follow a normal price distribution, with the parameters $n, mean, std$ and res consisting out of two values: one for good A and one for good B. For each simulation run, the synergy bidder(s) compute their profit-maximizing bid for that setting, as described in Section 4.1.

Since there may be considerable variance in the bids of the local bidders, each possible auction sequence is run k times (typically, we had $k > 10000$). The average profit of the seller and the synergy bidder which are reported here, for both the case of with and without options, are averages over all these k simulations and also over all possible auction orders of items A and B in the sequence.

4.1 Synergy Bidder's Strategy

Let $Q(z_A, z_B, X, I_t, b_t)$ be the expected profit of the synergy bidder when bidding b_t at each time step t. Here, z_A and z_B are the number of remaining auctions for A and B respectively ($z_A \leq n_A$, $z_B \leq n_B$), while X_t is the current endowment of the agent (i.e. items it already acquired) at time t. The profit-maximizing bid b_t^* is computed as:

$$b_t^* = argmax_{b_t}\ Q(z_A, z_B, X, I_t, b_t) \tag{8}$$

This value can be computed through standard dynamic programming. Exact search for b_t^* is computationally feasible for the experiments reported in this paper (as the size of the desired bundle and the length of the auction sequence are limited). For larger domains, solving this MDP may be more involved, however.

4.2 Experimental Results: Market Entry Effect for One Synergy Bidder

First, we study experimentally the incentives to use options for the sellers and bidders, in the case there is just one synergy bidder present in the market. The experimental setting presented in this paper involves 2 auctions for each type of item, i.e. $n_A = 2$ and $n_B = 2$. As mentioned above, the local bidders are considered myopic and only bid in one local auction. Therefore, their bids can be modeled as a distribution $\sim N(10, 4)$ for both goods. Thus, the goods A and B are, in this model, of equal rarity and attract an equal amount of independent competition during bidding. We made this choice because having a certain degree of symmetry in the experimental model allows us to reduce the number of parameter settings we need to consider. More specifically, we can assume the same exercise prices are set for both goods of type A and B.

Furthermore, for each good, the seller has a reservation value $res = 8$, which gives its estimate resell value in the case the synergy bidder acquires an option for the item, but fails to exercise it. The value of a bundle of {A,B} which the synergy bidder requires, is $v(A, B) = 21$, which is, on average, 5% more than the local competition.

Results for this setting are shown in Fig. 2. There are two main effects to be observed. First, the synergy bidder in such a market always prefers *higher* exercise prices. If the option for an item is sold with a higher exercise price, then the synergy bidder can bid more aggressively on the option price to get the item, since she is "covered" for the loss represented by the exercise price. The myopic bidders extract no advantage from being offered the good as an options vs. a direct sale, because, if they acquire the option, they would always exercise it, regardless of the exercise price.

Second, the expected profit of the seller seems to decrease if she has to sell the option with a higher exercise price. However, an important effect to note are the participation thresholds (that appear as "peaks" in the picture). These can be explained by the synergy bidder joining the market, as the expected profit becomes non-negative. For the settings used in Fig. 2, the synergy bidder will only bid on a good if there are two remaining auctions for the other good. So she places a bid for A if the auctions are $[A, B, B]$, but not if they are $[A, B]$. This is because with a single auction for B, the risk of ending up with a only a worthless A is too great. But in a market with exercise prices of at least 2.5, the risk is reduced and one remaining auction is already enough for the synergy bidder to stay in the market. So a higher exercise price enables the synergy bidder to

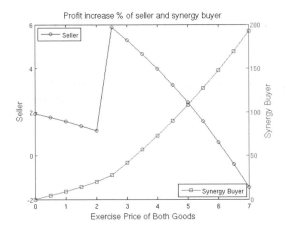

Fig. 2. Percentage increase in profit for a model using options wrt. direct sale, for the case there is one synergy bidder is present in the market. Note the threshold effect in the profit increase for the seller when the exercise price $K \geq 2.5$.

stay the market, even if she owns nothing and there are only a few auctions left, which increases the seller's expected profit. This increase in participation is beneficial to the seller, who thus has an incentive to fix the exercise prices $K_A = K_B = 2.5$.

5   Multiple Synergy Bidders

Next, we considered market settings in which multiple synergy bidders are active simultaneously. The experimental set-up and parameter choices are the same as for the case of one for the single synergy bidder. The only difference is that now multiple synergy bidders may enter and leave the market at different times and they have different valuations for the combination of A and B.

The results from this setting are based on the assumption that the synergy bidders have some prior expectations about the closing prices in future auctions and compute their optimal strategy w.r.t. these expectations. In the tests performed here, these expectations were assumed to be the same for all synergy bidders, which is a reasonable choice in comparing their strategies. In a more realistic market, however, synergy bidders could be expected to be able to learn and adjust their expectations based on past interactions, as well as reason game-theoretically about the fact that another synergy bidder may present in the market. At this point, these more sophisticated forms of reasoning are left to future work.

As in the previous section all simulations of this section have reserve prices of 8 and local bidders following $\sim N(10, 2.5)$. The first two experiments also have two synergy bidders syn_1 and syn_2 with valuations for both goods of 21.5 and 22.5 respectively. The order the synergy bidders enter the market (and the number of auctions they can stay in) are given in Figure 3, while results for these settings are shown in Fig. 4. In the following, we discuss these in separate subsections.

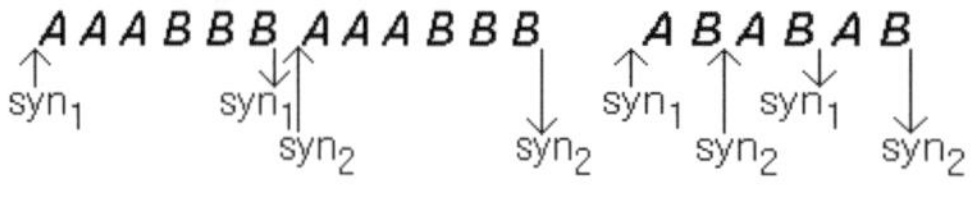

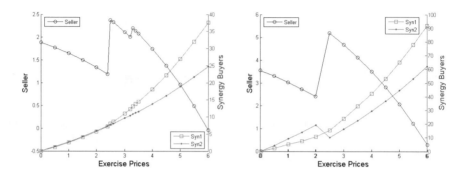

Fig. 3. Illustration of market entry order for two synergy bidders: 1. Interacting only through the exercise price level (left), 2. Directly competing in the same auctions (right).

Fig. 4. Percentage increase in profits for a market with with 2 synergy bidders. The length of the auction sequence and the entry points of the synergy bidders into the market correspond to the two cases shown in Fig. 3: 1. Interacting only through the exercise price level (left side), 2. Directly competing in the same auctions (right side).

5.1 Two Synergy Bidders Interacting Indirectly through the Exercise Price Level

In the setting examined here, the two synergy bidders each have $n_A = 3$ and $n_B = 3$, without the other agent participating in these auctions. An example of such an auction sequence is shown in Fig. 3 (left). However, these two synergy bidders do interact indirectly as follows. Since options are sold through open auctions based on the option price, the seller has to fix the exercise prices for the whole market. So while synergy bidders may not participate in the same auctions, their presence does influence the competition through the exercise prices set by the seller.

This effect can be seen in Fig. 4 (left), in which the seller maximizes her expected profit at $K = K_A = K_B = 2.4$. In this case syn_2 is better off, because without the presence of syn_1 she would be offered options with lower exercise prices. But syn_1 is worse off, because if she were alone in the market the seller would choose $K = 3.2$, which gives her a higher expected profit. Yet, due to syn_2, the seller sets $K = 2.4$. In this case, due to the seller's choice of exercise prices, one synergy bidder (syn_1) gains, while syn_2 loses.

5.2 Direct Synergy Bidder Competition in the Same Auctions

Next, we considered a setting in which synergy bidders compete directly for some of the goods. The entry points for such a setting are shown in Fig. 3 (right), while simulation results for this setting are given in Figure 4 (right).

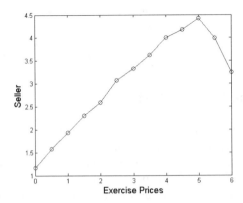

Fig. 5. Percentage increase in seller's profits in a larger experimental setting, with synergy bidders randomly entering the market with a probability of 25% at each time step

As can be seen from the right-hand side graph in Fig. 4, the profit of syn_2 drops at 2.5. In Fig. 4 (left), the synergy bidders' profits were monotonically increasing in the exercise prices, because they then have a smaller loss when they fail to complete their bundle. But now this effect cannot immediately compensate the extra competition coming from syn_1, who participates in the same auctions more often after this threshold at 2.5. So, in this case, both synergy bidders lose, in expectation, from the presence of additional synergy bidders. While one synergy bidder (i.e. syn_2) should benefit because she is offered better (higher) exercise prices than if she were alone in the market, this effect cannot immediately compensate the additional competition.

5.3   Larger Simulation with Random Synergy Bidders' Market Entry

Finally, we conducted a larger scale simulation with multiple synergy bidders, which can enter the market randomly, with a certain probability.

The experimental setup implies that each sequence of auctions (forming a test case) has 10 items of each type (i.e. $n_A = 10$ and $n_B = 10$). What differs from previous settings is the random entry of synergy bidders. For each auction, there is a 25% chance that a synergy bidder will enter the market. If she does, then her valuation is drawn from a uniform distribution between 20 and 22 and she will stay in the market for exactly four auctions. To simplify matters, the auction sequence is fixed at first selling A, then B, then A etc. so that each synergy bidder will face exactly two auctions for an item of type A and two for an item of type B. However, the general result of this section is also true for a random auction sequence, since the basic effects remain the same.

As shown in Figure 5, the seller's profit now only has one maximum at 5, because initially each increase in exercise prices causes, with some probability, a synergy bidder to participate more often. So each point is a threshold and the profit graph smooths out over those many local maxima, corresponding to a steady increase (on average) of the expected profit. This result shows why it can be rational for the seller to have the same exercise prices for all goods of the same type (e.g. the same K_A). In a market with random entry of synergy bidders, the seller does not know which bidders are participating in any particular auction. Her optimal policy is to set her exercise prices which maximize her overall expected profit (in this case, $K = 5$).

6   Discussion and Further Work

This paper examined, from a decision-theoretic perspective, the use of priced options as a solution to the exposure problem in sequential auctions. We consider a model in which the seller is free to fix the exercise price for options on the goods she has to offer, and then sell these options through an open auction.

For this setting, we derived analytically, for a market with a synergy bidder and under some assumptions, the expressions that provide the bounds on the option prices between which both synergy buyers and sellers have an incentive to use an option contract over direct auctions. Next, we performed an experimental analyses of several settings, where either one or multiple synergy bidders are active simultaneously in the market.

The overall conclusion of our study is that the proposed priced options mechanism can considerably reduce the exposure problem that synergy bidders face when taking part in sequential auctions. Furthermore, and most important, *both* parties in the market have an incentive to prefer and use such a mechanism. We show that in many realistic market scenarios, sellers can fix the exercise prices at a level that both provides sufficient incentive for bidders to take part in the auctions, as well as cover their risk of remaining with the items unsold.

Finally, while this paper provides an analysis and results for several realistic cases, it leaves several issues to future work. These include more sophisticated reasoning abilities on the part of participating synergy bidders and sellers, as well as markets where bidders have asymmetric or imperfect information or different attitudes to risk.

To conclude, sequential auction bidding with complementary valuations is a problem that appears in many real-life settings, although participating synergy bidders face a severe exposure problem. The main intuition of this work is that a simple options mechanism, where sellers auction options for their goods (with a pre-set exercise price), instead of the goods themselves can go a long way in solving the exposure problem, and can be beneficial to both sides of such a market.

References

1. Hull, J.C.: Options, Futures, and Other Derivatives, 5th edn. Prentice-Hall, Englewood Cliffs (2003)
2. Juda, A.I., Parkes, D.C.: An options-based method to solve the composability problem in sequential auctions. In: Faratin, P., Rodríguez-Aguilar, J.-A. (eds.) AMEC 2004. LNCS (LNAI), vol. 3435, pp. 44–58. Springer, Heidelberg (2006)
3. Juda, A.I., Parkes, D.C.: The sequential auction problem on ebay: An empirical analysis and a solution. In: Proc. of the 7th ACM Conf. on Electronic commerce, June 2006, pp. 180–189. ACM Press, New York (2006)

4. Sandholm, T.: Algorithm for optimal winner determination in combinatorial auctions. Artificial Intelligence 135(1-2), 1–54 (2002)
5. Sandholm, T., Lesser, V.: Leveled-commitment contracting: a backtracking instrument for multiagent systems. AI Magazine 23(3), 89–100 (Fall 2002)
6. 't Hoen, P.J., Redekar, G., Robu, V., Poutré, J.A.L.: chapter Decommitment in a Competitive Multi-Agent Transportation Setting. In: Whitestein Series in Software Agent Technologies, pp.409–433. Birkhäuser, Basel (2005)

Towards a Quality Assessment Method for Learning Preference Profiles in Negotiation

Koen V. Hindriks and Dmytro Tykhonov

EEMCS, Delft University of Technology, Delft, The Netherlands
{k.v.hindriks,d.tykhonov}@tudelft.nl

Abstract. In automated negotiation, information gained about an opponent's preference profile by means of learning techniques may significantly improve an agent's negotiation performance. It therefore is useful to gain a better understanding of how various negotiation factors influence the quality of learning. The quality of learning techniques in negotiation are typically assessed indirectly by means of comparing the utility levels of agreed outcomes and other more global negotiation parameters. An evaluation of learning based on such general criteria, however, does not provide any insight into the influence of various aspects of negotiation on the quality of the learned model itself. The quality may depend on such aspects as the domain of negotiation, the structure of the preference profiles, the negotiation strategies used by the parties, and others. To gain a better understanding of the performance of proposed learning techniques in the context of negotiation and to be able to assess the potential to improve the performance of such techniques a more systematic assessment method is needed. In this paper we propose such a systematic method to analyse the quality of the information gained about opponent preferences by learning in single-instance negotiations. The method includes measures to assess the quality of a learned preference profile and proposes an experimental setup to analyse the influence of various negotiation aspects on the quality of learning. We apply the method to a Bayesian learning approach for learning an opponent's preference profile and discuss our findings.

1   Introduction

In the area of learning in negotiation, the benefits of the application of learning techniques are often measured with respect to the final outcome or other generally relevant parameters of negotiation such as number of rounds to reach an agreement. The quality of the model of what has to be learned thus is often not directly analyzed but a more indirect method is used to assess these benefits. One of the problems with this indirect method of measuring the benefits of learning in negotiation is that it does not provide any tools to analyse the performance of the learning mechanism itself nor does it provide insight into the factors influencing the quality of learning in negotiation.

To gain a better understanding of the performance of proposed learning techniques and the potential to improve the performance of such techniques in the

W. Ketter et al. (Eds.): AMEC/TADA 2008, LNBIP 44, pp. 46–59, 2010.
© Springer-Verlag Berlin Heidelberg 2010

context of automated negotiation a more systematic assessment method for the quality of learning is needed. Such a method should provide the technical tools for analysis, identify the key factors that need to be taken into account and propose an experimental setup to evaluate the quality of learning. In this paper we present a method that can be used to assess the quality of a learning of an opponent's preference profile. Useful technical tools as well as an approach for analysis are discussed. We apply the method to illustrate its value for the analysis of opponent preferences learning techniques, and we present some of the insights that may be gained.

The paper is organized as follows. In Section 2 we briefly discuss learning in negotiation and introduce the problem concerning the quality of learning in negotiation that we address in this paper. In Section 3 a method is proposed and the various components of the proposed method are discussed. In Section 4 the proposed method is applied to the Bayesian learning approach proposed in [8] and results are presented. In Section 5 conclusions and several directions for future research are outlined.

2 Related Work and Problem Description

Learning in automated negotiation is an important topic since it has been shown that it can significantly improve the performance of a negotiating agent. Work in the area of opponent modelling in negotiation has resulted in a variety of approaches that usually focus on learning one aspect of the negotiation process. The range of negotiation aspects that are learned includes reservation values [21], issue priorities (or weights associated with negotiated issues modelling the relative importance of each issue; [2,9]), and negotiation strategies [12,14].

In [11] an opponent's preference profile is learned in a qualitative negotiation setting. It is assumed that a fixed set of possible profile types is given. Bayesian learning then is used to determine the likelihood that an opponent has one of these given profiles. In [4] a model is presented that incorporates domain knowledge for deciding on a negotiation move, which is extended in [2] with a learning technique based on on kernel density estimation (KDE) to learn the issue priorities of an opponent. [9] proposes an alternative method for learning issue priorities. In [8] a Bayesian learning technique is presented to learn an opponent's preference profile including both issue priorities as well as the ranking of issue alternatives. The evaluation method that has been used to assess the quality of learning in each of these approaches has been indirect, e.g. by evaluating the improvement of the outcome that is reached with respect to standard notions such as Pareto efficiency. An exception is the work reported in [17] where the quality of learning is discussed on the basis of statistical analysis, and the work reported in [1] that presents quantitative results on a Bayesian classifier to classify the type of profile of an opponent. However, it is not clear from [1,17] how various factors determine the quality of learning.

In order to define a quality assessment method that provides insight into the contribution of various factors to the learning quality, we first introduce the model of negotiation that we use. Negotiation is a form of decision-making where two or more parties jointly search a space of possible outcomes Ω with the goal of reaching a consensus [18]. In this paper, we only consider *bilateral* negotiation, i.e. negotiation between two parties. We further assume that both parties are able to express their preferences over possible outcomes $\omega \in \Omega$ and that these preferences can be modelled by means of a utility function U that maps a possible outcome ω to a real-valued number in the range $[0; 1]$ (cf. [20]). A utility function will also be referred to as a *preference profile*.

Possible outcomes of a negotiation may have additional structure and consist of a package-deal of several *issues* or attributes. Each issue has an associated range of alternatives one of which for each issue needs to be agreed upon to reach a final outcome. The space of possible outcomes each of which consists of values assigned to a number of issues is also called the *negotiation domain*.

It is often assumed that a preference profile can be defined as a function of the evaluation functions associated with individual issues and we do so as well here. More specifically, we assume that utility functions are linearly additive [16]. That is, in a domain with n issues and outcomes that consist of one alternative x_i for each of the n issues, we assume that a utility function can be defined by:

$$U(\omega) = \sum_{i=1}^{n} w_i e_i(x_i \in \omega) \tag{1}$$

where the w_i are normalized weights that sum to 1 and the $e_i(x_i \in \omega)$ are evaluation functions with range $[0; 1]$ which model preferences for issue alternatives. An important reason that justifies this restriction is that most existing negotiation strategies can handle linearly additive utility functions but cannot (efficiently) handle more complex utility functions.

In order to obtain an advantageous negotiation outcome, i.e. to reach an agreement as best as possible, it is useful to have as much information about the preference profile of an opponent as is possible. In a closed negotiation the negotiating parties however do not exchange information about the preferences of each other. In single-instance negotiations a negotiating agent may then try to obtain a model of the preference profile of its opponent by means of learning [2,8,9,11]. The goal of applying learning techniques here is to construct a function $\tilde{U}$ that is similar to the actual utility function U of the opponent. The problem that we address in this paper is how to assess the quality of a learning technique in this context, that is, which tools can be used to assess the similarity of the learned preference profile with the actual profile and which factors influence the similarity. The method proposed aims at a direct assessment of the quality of a learned preference profile instead of indirect evaluations based on results that indicate comparative utility increases of negotiation outcomes, reaching agreements in fewer negotiation rounds, or outcomes closer to the Pareto frontier or fair outcomes such as the Nash **solution**. One of our objectives is to be able to analyze the influence of various negotiation aspects on the learning quality.

3   Quality Assessment Method

The method we propose has three components: (i) quality measures to estimate the learning performance, (ii) criteria for selecting a diverse range of negotiation domains and preference profiles on these domains, and (iii) criteria for selecting a number of negotiation strategies of the opponent. These components then are used to define an experimental setup to obtain data to analyze learning quality by means of a negotiation tournament.

The first component consists of several similarity measures that provide a metric for assessing the accuracy of the learned preference profile with respect to the actual preference profile. We discuss several measures that can be used to assess the quality of the learned preference profile. Apart from the restriction on utility functions which need to be linearly additive, the second component of the method consists of several additional criteria for selecting negotiation domains such as size and complexity of the domain, and the similarity of the preference profiles of the negotiating parties. These criteria are used to define the experimental setup of the negotiation tournament. The third component provides criteria for selecting negotiation strategies that should be used by negotiating agents in the tournament. Since learning of an opponent's preference profile in single-instance negotiations has to be accomplished with only the observations of the opponent's negotiation moves [8,12,17,22], typically such learning algorithms use assumptions about an opponent's behaviour. For instance, in [1,8,22] a concession assumption is used which states that negotiators on average decrease the utilities of offers as time passes in order to find a deal. Although this assumption is reasonable and can be applied in typical negotiation settings, it is important to assess the robustness of a learning technique also when negotiating against agents that use strategies that do not comply with this assumption. It thus is important to incorporate a diverse range of negotiation strategies in any experimental setup to evaluate learning quality.

3.1   Quality Measures

In this Section we discuss two quality measures to assess learning quality that are based on two metrics to measure the distance between the actual preference profile of an opponent and the learned preference profile. These quality measures are applied to both the complete preference profiles or utility functions, as well as to the issue priorities or weights.

The learning task of learning an opponent's preference profile clearly is an approximation problem. The task is to re-constructs the actual utility function U of the opponent by means of a learning technique resulting in an approximate function $\tilde{U}$. A quality measure with respect to learning preference profiles therefore can be defined as a distance metric of two utility functions, and can be formally represented as $d(U, \tilde{U})$.

Ideally, the approximation $\tilde{U}$ of an opponent's utility function would provide an accurate prediction of the exact utility value an opponent associates with an outcome. Some strategies like the Tit-for-Tat-based strategy introduced in [3] depend on the accuracy of cardinal values of the utility function of the opponent since a negotiation move is chosen based on an estimate of the concession the other party made in the previous move. It therefore is important to have a distance metric that can be used to measure the accuracy of the cardinal values predicted by the learned profile. Here we use Pearson's correlation coefficient for that purpose. This coefficient represents the degree of linear relationship between two variables and is defined as follows:

$$d_{pearson}(U, \tilde{U}) = \frac{\sum\limits_{\omega \in \Omega} (U(\omega) - \langle U \rangle)(\tilde{U}(\omega) - \langle \tilde{U} \rangle)}{\sqrt{\sum\limits_{\omega \in \Omega} (U(\omega) - \langle U \rangle)^2 \sum\limits_{\omega \in \Omega} (\tilde{U}(\omega) - \langle \tilde{U} \rangle)^2}} \qquad (2)$$

where $\langle U \rangle$ (respectively $\langle \tilde{U} \rangle$) denotes the average utility over the outcome space defined by utility function U ($\tilde{U}$). The Pearson's correlation coefficient takes a real value from the interval $[-1; 1]$. A value of $+1$ means that there is a perfect positive linear relationship between variables, whereas a value of -1 means that there is a perfect negative linear relationship between variables. A value of 0 means that there is no linear relationship between the two variables.

Although a perfect match of cardinal values of the actual and learned utility function would be ideal, in practice it may be sufficient and more important to approximate the preference ranking of outcomes by an opponent (cf. [4]). For example, negotiation strategies that aim at maximizing an opponent's utility by means of walking on an utility iso-curve in one's own preference profile only need adequate information about an opponent's ranking of outcomes. It is sufficient when using such strategies to possess accurate ordinal ranking information.

To estimate the distance between the rankings of the bids given the actual utility function of the opponent and the learned utility function, a metric is introduced that compares all outcomes in the outcome space pairwise. In order to do so, a ranking relation $\prec_U$ is defined as follows: $\forall \omega_i, \omega_j \in \Omega, \omega_i \prec_U \omega_j \Leftrightarrow U(\omega_i) < U(\omega_j)$. Using this ranking relation, we can define a conflict indicator function adapted from [6] to measure conflicting rankings given arbitrary utility functions u and $\tilde{u}$. The conflict indicator function is defined as follows:

$$c_{\prec_u, \prec_{\tilde{u}}}(\omega_i, \omega_j) = \begin{cases} 1 & \text{if } (\omega_i \preceq_u \omega_j \wedge \omega_j \prec_{\tilde{u}} \omega_i) \vee (\omega_i \prec_u \omega_j \wedge \omega_j \preceq_{\tilde{u}} \omega_i) \\ & \vee (\omega_i \preceq_{\tilde{u}} \omega_j \wedge \omega_j \prec_u \omega_i) \vee (\omega_i \prec_{\tilde{u}} \omega_j \wedge \omega_j \preceq_u \omega_i), \\ 0 & \text{otherwise.} \end{cases} \qquad (3)$$

The conflict indicator function yields 1 when the ranking relation of two arbitrary outcomes ω, ω' based on the learned utility space $\tilde{U}$ is not the same as the ranking relation based on the actual utility space of the opponent U; if the rankings based on both utility functions match the conflict indicator takes the value of 0.

Using the conflict indicator c, we can define a metric called the *ranking distance* of two utility functions. The ranking distance is the calculated average of the number of conflicts between two utility functions given c:

$$d_{ranking}(U, \tilde{U}) = \frac{1}{|\Omega|^2} \sum_{\omega \in \Omega, \omega' \in \Omega} c_{\prec_U, \prec_{\tilde{U}}}(\omega, \omega') \qquad (4)$$

In [6] various properties of this distance measure are proved, including e.g. reflexivity, symmetry and the triangle inequality property.

It is useful to not only apply the distance measures to complete preference profiles but also to apply it to the issue priorities or weights in such a profile. In Section 4 we apply the assessment method to the learning approach for automated closed negotiation based on Bayesian learning proposed in [8]. In this learning approach the different components of a linearly additive utility function, i.e. weights and evaluation functions, are learned in a different way. In order to obtain experimental data about these different learning processes we therefore also define similar distance measures to those discussed above for measuring distance of actual and learned issues weights.

The set of weights can be represented as a weight vector, and it is not hard to define the Pearson correlation coefficient for the vectors of weights. The coefficient is defined as follows:

$$d_{pearson}(W, \tilde{W}) = \frac{\sum_{i=1}^{n}(w_i - \langle w \rangle) * (\tilde{w}_i - \langle \tilde{w} \rangle)}{\sqrt{\sum_{i=1}^{n}(w_i - \langle w \rangle)^2 \sum_{i=1}^{n}(\tilde{w}_i - \langle \tilde{w} \rangle)^2}} \tag{5}$$

To calculate the ranking distance between the two weight vectors W and $\tilde{W}$ a ranking relation is constructed on the weights of the corresponding vector as follows: $i = 1 \ldots n, j = 1 \ldots n, i \prec j \Leftrightarrow w(i) < w(j)$, where $w(i) = w_i$. Then, the conflict indicator $c_{\prec_W, \prec_{\tilde{W}}}(i, j)$ can be defined in the same way as for utility functions. The ranking distance of two weight vectors is defined as follows:

$$d_{ranking}(W, \tilde{W}) = \frac{1}{n^2} \sum_{i=1}^{n} \sum_{j=1}^{n} c_{\prec_W, \prec_{\tilde{W}}}(i, j) \tag{6}$$

3.2 Negotiation Domains and Profiles

Whereas precise mathematical metrics can be defined for measuring distance of preference profiles, for the selection of an adequate set of domains to be used in the experimental setup less formal criteria are proposed here. The main reason is that it is impossible to assess a learning technique on the space of all negotiation domains and associated preference profile. Ideally, then, one would use an experimental setup based on random sampling of the domains and profiles in order to deal with this problem. However, it is not clear how to setup such a sampling procedure.[1] Instead, we therefore discuss and propose to use three factors for selecting domains that are relevant in testing the learning quality.

Size of the negotiation domain. The amount of information exchanged during the negotiation is limited in a closed negotiation since we can rely only on observed

---

[1] As an example, we found that the predictability of issue preferences (see below) may influence the outcomes of negotiation strategies. It is not particularly clear, however, how to obtain a random sample which would be an adequate representation of domains with and without predictable issues.

negotiation moves of an opponent, which affects learning quality. The amount of information needed by a learning technique typically depends on the model structure and the size of the parameter space that is to be learned. Therefore, a learning technique has to be assessed on negotiation domains of various sizes and of various complexity. Since in any negotiation the number of issues is one of the most important factors that determines the complexity of the preferences profile, a set of domains should be selected that range from a low number of issues to higher number of issues.

Predictability of the preferences. Most learning techniques for learning an opponent's preference profile use assumptions about the structure of the preference profile (e.g. see [2,8,22]). Among others such techniques may rely on the predictability of issue preferences [7]. Issues are called predictable when even though the actual evaluation function for the issue is unknown, it is possible to guess some of its global properties. For example, a price issue typically is rather predictable, where more is better for the seller, and less is better for the buyer, and the normal ordering of the real numbers is maintained; an issue concerning colour, however, is typically less predictable. Learning even ranking preferences related to issue values of unpredictable issues therefore is more difficult.

The set of selected negotiation domains for any experimental setup therefore ideally should consist of a balanced mix of predictable and unpredictable issues. In principle, the higher the number of unpredictable issues the more complicated the learning of a corresponding profile becomes.

Opposition of preferences. The results of analyzing negotiation dynamics presented in [7] revealed that some negotiation strategies are sensitive to preference profiles with compatible issues. Issues are compatible if the issue preferences of both negotiating parties are such that they both prefer the same alternatives for the given issue. Negotiation strategies may more or less depend on whether preferences of the negotiating parties are opposed or not on every issue. That is, using some strategies it is harder or even impossible to exploit such common ground and agree on the most preferred option by both parties for compatible issues (humans are reported to have difficulty with this as well; cf. [19]). A selection of preference profiles should therefore take into account that both preference profiles with and without compatible issues are included.

The notion of opposition can be made more precise. Conceptually, it represents a degree of conflict of interests between the parties. In other words, there is a conflict of interests if one party prefers outcome ω over outcome ω' and the other party prefers outcome ω' over outcome ω. In [10] a notion of local opposition based on the gradients of the utility functions of both parties is defined for each outcome in the negotiation domain. Intuitively, if the gradients point to opposite directions then the preferences of the negotiation parties are opposed. The more colinear the gradients are the closer (more compatible) the preferences of the parties. Although it is possible to generalize the notion of local opposition relative to an outcome to a more global notion of opposition of utility functions, we propose to reuse the distance measures for preference profiles to measure the level of opposition present.

As discussed, it is not clear how to randomly sample negotiation domains and we use the criteria discussed to select a number of negotiation domains to be used in our experimental setup. The selection we present is not intended to cover all variations in line with these criteria but rather is meant to illustrate these criteria. The following negotiation domains with predefined opponent profiles have been selected (also see Table 1 for details about profile distances):

- Second hand car selling, taken from [9]: a domain of 5 issues, of which only price is really predictable. That is, an agent can only reliably predict the other agent's preferences for this issue.
- Service-Oriented Negotiation, taken from [2], a domain with 4 issues for which domain knowledge is made available to the strategies.
- Employment contract negotiation domain, taken from [13] with 5 discrete issues. All issues have predictable values. The preference profiles have the strongest opposition in our setup.
- AMPO vs City, taken from [15], a domain with 10 issues, for which 7 are rather predictable, but 3 are not. This is the biggest domain in our experimental setup.
- Party domain is created for negotiation experiments with humans. It is a rather small domain with 5 discrete issues with 5 possible values each. All of the issues are unpredictable. The preference profiles have the lowest opposition in the experimental setup.

Table 1. Distance measures between utility space in the analyzed domains

| Domain | Utility spaces | | Weights | | Domain size | No. of Predictable |
	Ranking	Pearson	Ranking	Pearson		
AMPO vs. City	0.662	-0.482	0.422	-0.139	7,128,000	3 (10)
Party	0.540	-0.126	0.467	-0.276	3,125	0 (5)
SON	0.669	-0.453	0.833	-0.751	810,000	4 (4)
Employment contract	0.698	-0.584	0.600	-0.241	3,125	5 (5)
2nd hand car	0.635	-0.387	0.600	-0.147	18,750	1 (5)

3.3 Negotiation Strategies of the Opponent

The results of the analysis presented in [7] also have shown that the performance of a negotiation strategy can be significantly influenced by the negotiation strategy of the opponent. For example, the class of pure time-dependent tactics (TDT; see [3]) does not take into account the negotiation moves of opponents and selects the next offer to propose in a negotiation based on how close one is to the negotiation deadline. Whereas TDT tactics are insensitive to opponent moves, negotiation strategies in the class of behaviour-dependent tactics (BDT) do base their choice of offer on the offers received so far from the opponent. A variety of strategies therefore is needed to asses the quality of learning, which includes strategies that belong to the TDT class, the BDT class as well as mixes thereof.

The selection of strategies to be used in an experimental setup should be able to test the robustness of the learning technique with respect to various opponents that use different types of negotiation strategies. For example, to enable learning of opponent preferences from the observed negotiation moves (offers) typically a concession assumption is made (cf. [1,8,22]). Such rationality assumptions might however be exploited and it should be tested if a learning technique is robust against strategies like the Zero-Intelligence strategy that uses an irrational random tactic [5].

Again we do not claim to present an exhaustive coverage of the criteria discussed, but present a selection to illustrate. The following negotiation strategies have been used by the negotiating parties in our experimental setup:

- The ABMP strategy from [9], which is a concession oriented approach in the TDT class, and is taking no heed of knowledge about the domain or the opponent. The ABMP strategy uses a non-linear concession tactic. It conceeds more in the beginning of the negotiation when the gap between the opponents' negotiation positions is big and decreases the size of the concession when their negotiation positions approach each other. As such, it is an example of a so-called conceder tactic (cf. [3]).
- The Trade-off Strategy, taken from [4], uses so-called similarity criteria and exploits domain knowledge. The Trade-off strategy is an example of a Behaviour-dependent strategy. In our experiments we allowed three smart steps and a concession of 0.05 for the smart meta strategy.
- Zero-Intelligence, taken from [5], is a random strategy that makes random jumps through the outcome space. The ZI agent used a reservation point in our experiments to avoid making offers that have very low utility which was set to 0.6. The ZI strategy plays a role as a baseline strategy.

4   Application and Experimental Results

To show how the proposed method is used in practice we apply it to agents that make use of opponent's preferences learning techniques taken from [8]. This section presents the details of the experimental setup and presents some results obtained.

4.1   Experimental Setup

A learning technique based on Bayesian learning algorithm proposed in [8] is used as a subject of the analysis. The opponent model in [8] is based on learning probability over a set of hypothesis about evaluation functions and weights of the issues. The probability distribution is defined over the set of hypothesis that represent agent's belief about opponent's preferences. Structural assumptions about the evaluation functions and weights are made to decrease the number of parameters to be learned and simplify the learning task.

Authors propose two versions of the learning algorithm. In the first version of the algorithm each hypotheses represents a complete utility space as a combination of weights ranking and shapes of the issue evaluation functions. The size of the hypothesis space growth exponentially w.r.t. the number of issue and thus is intractable for negotiation domains with high number of issues.

The second version of the algorithm is a scalable variant for the first one. This version of the agent tries to learn probability distribution over the individual hypothesis about the value of the weight and shape of the issue evaluation function independently of other issues. The computational tractability of the learning is achieved by approximating the conditional distributions of the hypotheses using the expected values of the dependant hypotheses.

To test the proposed method for learning quality assessment an experimental setup is created. The method is applied in a tournament-like setup. In the tournament the Bayesian agent that uses a learning technique negotiates against the set of opponent strategies from the section 3.3. The tournament is repeated for all negotiation domains and preference profiles from the section 3.2.

The original code of the Bayesian agent was extended with a module that calculates the quality measures as explained in the section 3.1. This module is granted an access to the actual preference profile of the opponent that is needed to calculate the measures. The module calculates the distances between the current model of the opponent preference and the actual preferences profile of the opponent when the agent initializes the opponent model and after every update of the model. According to the algorithm of the Bayesian agent, the opponent model is updated when agent receives a bid from the opponent.

The authors realize that the learning power of such solution would degrade compared to the first version of the algorithm. However, the agent performs quite well on the negotiation domains of higher dimensionality (10 issues), see [8]. It is only reasonable to expect that the quality of learning degrades when the size of the negotiation domain is increased. In addition, the unscaleable version of the Bayesian learning agent is expected to perform less than the scalable version in terms of learning quality on the same negotiation domain.

The ZI agent is used to test the robustness of the Bayesian learning technique with respect to the opponent's negotiation strategy. Both versions of the Bayesian learning algorithm are expected to show worse performance when negotiating against the ZI agent because they rely on assumptions about the rationality of the opponent's negotiation strategy. Furthermore, the quality of learning of the Bayesian agent on the Party domain is expected to suffer from the upredictability of the preference of all the issues in this domain.

4.2   Evaluation

Due to space limitations, we only present the results of those experiments that give rise to some of the more significant conclusions. Figure 1 shows results that represent the quality of learning of the scalable version of the Bayesian agent on the Employment contract negotiation domain.

As explained in the previous section, the Bayesian agent updates the opponent model after receiving a bid from the opponent. Therefore, the horizontal axis of the charts represents the sequential number of the negotiation round. The first point of the curves corresponds to the distance between initial opponent model and the actual utility function of the opponent.

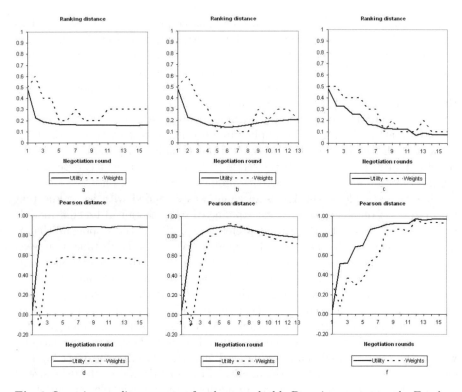

Fig. 1. Learning quality measures for the unscaleable Bayesian angent on the Employment contract negotiation domain against the Trade-off (a,d), ABMP (b,e), and ZI (c,f) strategies

The results show that the concession tactics of the opponent influences the quality of learning, as expected. The Bayesian agent learns the preferences of the opponent better when the opponent uses the Trade-off tactics rather than the ABMP strategy. The Trade-off tactics uses semi-linear concession tactics (see section 3.3), which is more consistent with the opponent tactics assumptions made in the Bayesian agent. As expected, the the Bayesian agent learns the opponent preference slower in case of the ZI negotiation strategy of the opponent. However, it is still capable of learning the opponent's preference quite well.

In general, the learning quality is better in smaller negotiation domains spaces. This follows from a comparison of the AMPO vs. City domain which is the largest domain with the SON contract negotiation domain in Figure 2. The Bayesian learning technique is able to perfectly learn a model of the ranking (ranking distance measure) in case of the SON domain and keeps improving the absolute values of the weights (cf. the results of the Pearson distance). In the AMPO vs. City domain the agent is able to learn the ranking of the weights to some extent. However, the results show that the learning of the outcome ranking is rather limited. This can be partly explained by the presence of a few issues with unpredictable preferences, which results in a lower learning quality of the

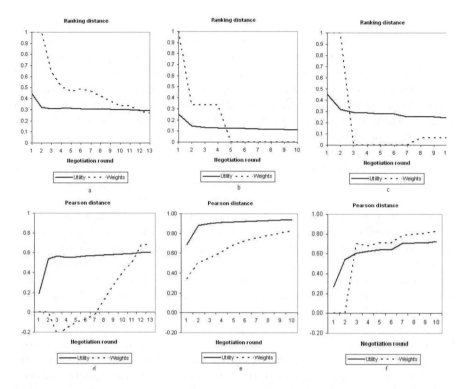

Fig. 2. Learning quality measures for the scaleable Bayesian agent against Trade-off strategy on the AMPO vs. City (a,d), SON (b,e), and Party (c,f) negotiation domains

evaluation functions and a lower learning quality of the utility function compared to the results for the SON domain.

Another interesting observation is that the learning algorithm approximates the absolute, cardinal values of the utility function and weights quite well, see Figure 2(b,e). This can be explained by the nature of the hypothesis space of the learning algorithm. The algorithm calculates opponent's utility values of a bid as an expected value of a random variable. The expected value is a sum of the utilities according to the hypothesis weighted with their probabilities. Thus, even if the more detailed structure of the opponent's preferences is not learned by the agent the information learned can still be used to approximate the utility function of the opponent as a linear combination of the set of all hypotheses.

5   Conclusion and Discussion

In this paper, a method for the analysis of the learning quality of learned opponent preference profiles in automated negotiation has been presented. The method consists of three components: (i) It uses distance measures between the actual preference profile of the opponent and the learned preference profile to assess the quality of the learned model; (ii) it propose criteria for the systematic classification of negotiation domains and preferences profiles to assess the impact of a variety of domains on the quality of the learned model; and (iii) it proposes some criteria to select a set of negotiation strategies. The method has been applied as an illustration to the agents introduced in [8], which use a Bayesian learning technique to learn preference profiles. The results confirmed the effectiveness of the learning technique, in particular that of the unscaleable version of the agent. The performance of the scalable agent is comparable to that of the unscaleable version on smaller negotiation domains. As is to be expected, the results showed that learning performance slowly degrades for the negotiation domains of higher dimensionality.

In addition, we believe that the results revealed interesting features of the learning algorithms that can be used to improve their performance. For instance, a more detailed analysis of the unscaleable version of the Bayesian agent proposed in [8] revealed that the learning algorithm typically approximates the opponent's preference profile with a weighted sum of the evaluation hypotheses instead of learning the evaluation function that best matches the actual function defined for a given issue. This indicates that it may be possible to reduce the hypothesis space of evaluation functions and use a smaller set of such functions which would still be sufficient to approximate a wide range of possible opponent preference profiles.

One issue that needs more research is the classification of both domains as well as strategies in order to systematically evaluate a learning technique used in negotiation. Though in principle, given that utility functions representing preference profiles are of a certain type, it is possible to generate random outcome and utility spaces to be used for evaluation. A method based on such random samples would potentially be more generic than the analysis of cases as used in this paper. It is not trivial to define such an approach, however, since the distribution used to generate samples should not favour particular situations (e.g. combinations of strictly opposed preference profiles over compatible preference profiles). Since it is also not completely clear how realistic certain preference profiles which lack sufficient structure are this poses another problem to be addressed before the use of random samples would make sense.

In this paper we have mainly focused on the learning of the opponent's preference profile. However, a negotiation strategy might also exploit other knowledge about the negotiating parties. Other parameters such as reservation value, or type of negotiation strategy however would require certain adaptations of the proposed method. We plan to extend our method with such tools along with a statistical toolbox useful in defining a testbed for automated negotiation agents.

References

1. Buffett, S., Spencer, B.: Learning opponents preferences in multi-object automated negotiation. In: Seventh International Conference on Electronic Commerce (ICEC 2005), pp. 300–305. ACM, New York (2005)
2. Coehoorn, R., Jennings, N.: Learning an opponents preferences to make effective multi-issue negotiation trade-offs. In: Proceedings of 6th International Conference on E-Commerce, pp. 59–68 (2004)

3. Faratin, P., Sierra, C., Jennings, N.R.: Negotiation decision functions for autonomous agents. Int. Journal of Robotics and Autonomous Systems 24(3-4), 159–182 (1998)
4. Faratin, P., Sierra, C., Jennings, N.R.: Using similarity criteria to make negotiation trade-offs. Journal of Artificial Intelligence 142(2), 205–237 (2003)
5. Gode, D.K., Sunder, S.: Allocative efficiency in markets with zero intelligence (zi) traders: Market as a partial substitute for individual rationality. Journal of Political Economy 101(1), 119–137 (1993)
6. Ha, V., Haddawy, P.: Similarity of personal preferences: Theoretical foundations and empirical analysis. Artificial Intelligence 146(2), 149–173 (2003)
7. Hindriks, K., Jonker, C., Tykhonov, D.: Negotiation dynamics: Analysis, concession tactics, and outcomes. In: Proceedings of the IEEE/WIC/ACM International Conference on Intelligent Agent Technology (IAT 2007), pp. 427–433 (2007)
8. Hindriks, K., Tykhonov, D.: Opponent modelling in automated multi-issue negotiation using bayesian learning. In: Proceedings of the AAMAS 2008 (2008)
9. Jonker, C.M., Robu, V., Treur, J.: An agent architecture for multi-attribute negotiation using incomplete preference information. Journal of Autonomous Agents and Multi-Agent Systems 15(2), 221–252 (2007)
10. Kersten, G.E., Noronha, S.J.: Rational agents, contract curves, and inefficient compromises report. Technical report, International Institute for Applied Systems Analysis (1997)
11. Lin, R., Kraus, S., Wilkenfeld, J., Barry, J.: An automated agent for bilateral negotiation with bounded rational agents with incomplete information. In: Proceedings of the International European Conference on AI (ECAI 2006), pp. 270–274 (2006)
12. Mok, W.W.H., Sundarraj, R.: Learning algorithms for single-instance electronic negotiations using the time-dependent behavioral tactic. ACM Transactions on Internet Technology 5(1), 195–230 (2005)
13. Nadler, J., Thompson, L., van Boven, L.: Learning negotiation skills: Four models of knowledge creation and transfer. Journal of Management Science 49(4), 529–540 (2003)
14. Narayanan, V., Jennings, N.: Learning to negotiate optimally in non-stationary environments. In: Klusch, M., Rovatsos, M., Payne, T.R. (eds.) CIA 2006. LNCS (LNAI), vol. 4149, pp. 288–300. Springer, Heidelberg (2006)
15. Raiffa, H.: The Art and Science of Negotiation. Harvard University Press, Cambridge (1982)
16. Raiffa, H., Richardson, J., Metcalfe, D.: Negotiation Analysis: The Science and Art of Collaborative Decision Making. Harvard University Press, Cambridge (2003)
17. Restificar, A., Haddawy, P.: Inferring implicit preferences from negotiation actions. In: Proceedings of the International Symposium on Artificial Intelligence and Mathematics (2004)
18. Robert, A.G.M., Guttman, H., Maes, P.: Agent-mediated electronic commerce: a survey. The Knowledge Engineering Review (1998)
19. Thompson, L.: The Mind and Heart of the Negotiator. Prentice-Hall, Englewood Cliffs (2004)
20. von Neumann, J., Morgenstern, O.: Theory of Games and Economic Behavior. Princeton University Press, Princeton (1944)
21. Zeng, D., Sycara, K.: Benefits of learning in negotiation. In: Proceedings of the Fourteenth National Conference on Artificial Intelligence, AAAI 1997 (1997)
22. Zeng, D., Sycara, K.: Bayesian learning in negotiation. International Journal of Human Computer Systems 48, 125–141 (1998)

Using a Memory Test to Limit a User to One Account

Vincent Conitzer

Department of Computer Science
Duke University
Durham, NC, USA
conitzer@cs.duke.edu

Abstract. In many Web-based applications, there are incentives for a user to sign up for more than one account, under false names. By doing so, the user can send spam e-mail from an account (which will eventually cause the account to be shut down); distort online ratings by rating multiple times (in particular, she can inflate her own reputation ratings); indefinitely continue using a product with a free trial period; place shill bids on items that she is selling on an auction site; engage in false-name bidding in combinatorial auctions; *etc.* All of these behaviors are highly undesirable from the perspective of system performance. While CAPTCHAs can prevent a bot from automatically signing up for many accounts, they do not prevent a human from signing up for multiple accounts. It may appear that the only way to prevent the latter is to require the user to provide information that identifies her in the real world (such as a credit card or telephone number), but users are reluctant to give out such information.

In this paper, we propose an alternative approach. We investigate whether it is possible to design an automated test that is easy to pass once, but difficult to pass a second time. Specifically, we design a memory test. In our test, items are randomly associated with colors (*"Cars are green."*). The user first observes all of these associations, and is then asked to recall the colors of the items (*"Cars are...?"*). The items are the same across iterations of the test, but the colors are randomly redrawn each time (*"Cars are blue."*). Therefore, a user who has taken the test before will occasionally accidentally respond with the association from the previous time that she took the test (*"Cars are...? Green!"*). If there is significant correlation between the user's answers and the correct answers from a previous iteration of the test, then the system can decide that the user is probably the same, and refuse to grant another account. We present and analyze the results of a small study with human subjects. We also give a game-theoretic analysis. In the appendix, we propose an alternative test and present the results of a small study with human subjects for that test (however, the results for that test are quite negative).

1 Introduction

Many Web-based applications require a user to sign up for an account first. Because of the anonymity that the Internet provides, it is typically not difficult

W. Ketter et al. (Eds.): AMEC/TADA 2008, LNBIP 44, pp. 60–72, 2010.
© Springer-Verlag Berlin Heidelberg 2010

for a single user to sign up for multiple accounts under fictional identities. Doing so can provide many benefits to the user, including at least the following:

1. The user can send spam e-mail from the fictional accounts. The service provider will typically realize that this is happening fairly quickly and shut down the account, but then the user can simply sign up for another account.
2. In online rating systems, the user can rate the same object many times and thereby distort the aggregate rating. This is especially valuable when the object being rated is a product that the user is selling, or when the object is the user's own reputation (on, say, an auction site).
3. When a product has a free trial period, the user can indefinitely continue using the product at no cost: once the trial period expires, she can simply start using the product under a different account.
4. In an online auction, the user can use another account to place shill bids on the items that she is selling, thereby driving up their selling prices.
5. In more complex economic mechanisms such as *combinatorial auctions*, in which multiple items are simultaneously for sale (for an overview, see [1]), it is often possible to obtain a bundle of items at a lower price by bidding under multiple identities [12,13]. It is possible to design mechanisms for which using multiple identities is not beneficial [12,10,13,11], but these are less efficient.
6. In online poker, the user can try to play on the same table under two or more distinct identities, allowing her to effectively collude with herself.

While all of the above behaviors are beneficial to the user who engages in them, they reduce the performance of the system as a whole. Users have to deal with potentially large volumes of unwanted e-mail, online ratings become meaningless, companies become reluctant to offer free trial periods, auction mechanisms become less efficient, people become reluctant to play poker online[1], *etc.* As a result, it may well be that *all* users, including those who choose to engage in the behavior, would prefer it if this behavior was impossible.[2]

In some cases, a user would benefit from owning a very large number of accounts. For example, if the accounts are used to send spam e-mail, then the service provider is likely to shut down the account as soon as it realizes that the account is being used to send spam; hence, many accounts are necessary to send out a significant amount of spam. In cases such as these, the user (spammer) may try to use a computer program, or *bot*, that repeatedly registers for an account. This (along with other applications) motivated the development of *CAPTCHAs* (*Completely Automated Public Turing Tests to Tell Computers and Humans Apart*) [8,9], which are automated tests that are easy to pass for humans, but difficult to pass for computers. A well-known CAPTCHA is *Gimpy*, where the

---

[1] Given online poker's murky legal status, one may debate whether this is a good or a bad thing.
[2] Game theory (for overviews, see [2,5,6]) provides many other examples where agents would prefer it if their most preferred actions were made unavailable, given that those actions are also made unavailable to the other agents: consider defection in the Prisoner's Dilemma, overgrazing in the Tragedy of the Commons, *etc.*

task is to read distorted text. Indeed, Gimpy is now widely used to screen out bots. It should be noted that several variants of Gimpy have been broken, that is, programs have been written that succeed on a large fraction of instances of the test [3,7,4]. This arguably represents a significant advance in computer vision. In fact, AI researchers should hope that *every* CAPTCHA that is designed will eventually be broken, since otherwise the CAPTCHA would represent a limit to artificial intelligence (more precisely, to the artificial intelligence that we as humans can create). But when a CAPTCHA is broken, we can in principle switch to using a different CAPTCHA, as long as artificial intelligence does not yet match human intelligence.

Unfortunately, CAPTCHAs are of little use in preventing a *human* from signing up for multiple accounts. Given how little revenue a spammer obtains from a single account, it is perhaps not economically feasible for a spammer to solve sufficiently many CAPTCHAs herself (or to hire people to do it for her). However, for all of the other uses for multiple accounts that we mentioned, only a few accounts are required. So, how can we prevent a human from signing up for multiple accounts? One possibility is to require her to provide information from which her identity in the real world can be established—for example, a credit card number or a phone number.[3] However, users tend to be very unwilling to provide such information, among other reasons because doing so entails giving up the privacy and anonymity that the Internet affords. Another possibility is to charge a price for each account (assuming that payments can be made anonymously), but again, Web users are notoriously unwilling to make payments. Also, if the payment is small enough, then the user may still want to sign up for multiple accounts.

It may seem that if account registrations are completely anonymous, and a user can sign up for one account, then she can always sign up for a second account in the same way. In this paper, we argue that this is not necessarily the case. We investigate whether it is possible to design an automated test that is easy to pass once, but difficult to pass a second time. The idea that we pursue is to have the user be affected by taking the test the first time, in a way that is detectable when she takes the test again. Specifically, we design a memory test. In this test, the user is asked to memorize and then recall a number of (item, color) associations. Across iterations of the test, the items are always the same, but the color associated with each item is randomly redrawn each iteration. Because of this, a user taking the test a second time is likely to get confused and occasionally respond with the association from the first time that she took the test. (This is related to the *proactive interference* phenomenon in psychology, where old memories interfere with the learning of new memories. However, this term typically refers to the decrease in performance on the later iteration of the test, rather than to the overlap in answers with the earlier iteration of the test.) Thus, if there is significant correlation between the user's answers and the correct

---

[3] One way to sign up for a Gmail™ account is to submit a mobile phone number, to which an invitation code is then sent. This is explicitly to prevent one person from signing up for many accounts.

answers from a previous iteration of the test, then the system can decide that the user is probably the same, and refuse to grant another account. The system must also refuse to grant the account if the user recalls too few associations correctly: otherwise, the user can just respond randomly, and thereby avoid confusion and overlap. Several other minor modifications are necessary to make the system work. For one, memory tests are easy to pass for computers; therefore, the test must be integrated with a CAPTCHA (in such a way that the CAPTCHA cannot simply be separated and given to a human). For example, the (item, color) pairs can be distorted as in Gimpy. Also, the test must be run at a speed that makes it infeasible for the user to write down and look up the associations.

In the remainder of this paper, we first present the specifics of the automated test that we designed. We then present the results of a small, formal study on human subjects. We also present a game-theoretic model of the test, and analyze the effects of different strategies for the user. Finally, we discuss future research. In the appendix, we discuss another (less effective) automated test that we designed, as well as the results of a small study on human subjects for that test.

2   Test Specifics

The specifics of the test that we designed are as follows. (The source code is available upon request.) There are 100 items in the test, which were chosen with a bias towards items that do not naturally have a color associated with them. (*E.g.*, "cars" was one of the items, "grass" was not. Of course, cars are still more associated with red than with pink; it seems impossible to avoid such association altogether.) There are 8 colors in the test: red, green, blue, yellow, white, black, orange, and pink. At the beginning of an iteration of the test, each item is randomly associated with one of the colors (*e.g.*, "Cars are green."). Each of these associations is then displayed to the user for 4 seconds (in random order). After all of the associations have been displayed, each of the items is displayed to the user for 3 seconds (in a different order[4]), during which the user has to recall the associated color. Thus, the total duration of the test is 700 seconds (11.7 minutes). Clearly, the length of the test makes it somewhat unattractive to take, but with fewer items we are unlikely to be able to recognize correlation with a previous iteration of the test (with statistical significance). In principle, a user would have to take the test only once, to obtain a master account which she can then use to sign up for other accounts. Besides the number of items, the other parameters are the number of colors, the amount of time each association is displayed, and the amount of time given to recall each item's color. Based on some informal experiments, these parameters were set to make the test difficult but not impossible, as well as to keep its length reasonable.

---

[4] Changing the order forces users to associate colors with items, rather than just remember a sequence of colors. It also makes it difficult to write down and look up the associations in time.

3   A Small Study with Human Subjects

We proceeded to conduct a small, formal study with human subjects, whose details and results we describe in this section. Each subject first did a practice run with a version of the system with only 10 items, which do not overlap with the "official" 100 items. Then, the subject did two full iterations of the main test (with the same 100 items, but re-randomized colors for each item). Each subject was compensated US \$7, plus US \$7 times the percentage of correct answers given in the two iterations of the main test. (Given that the test is somewhat exhausting, it was considered important to reward subjects for good performance, to keep them engaged.) Subjects were recruited by posting flyers. In the end, we obtained data from 7 subjects, all of whom are students at Duke University. The study was approved by the Institutional Review Board. It is very small, but it is enough to illustrate the key phenomena. Earlier, informal tests produced similar results.

Before presenting the results, it is useful to consider what results would indicate that our system is effective. Ideally, we would see: 1. high scores (percentage correct) for the first iteration (so that a user can obtain an account), and 2. either low scores for the second iteration, or significant overlap between the answers given by the user in the second iteration and the correct answers in the first iteration (so that a user will fail to obtain a second account, either because her performance is too poor or because the system can link her to her first attempt). We do *not* want to consider the overlap between given answers in the second iteration and *given* answers in the first iteration, because it is likely that there would be significant overlap between given answers even for two different users—for example, because people tend to answer "white" more often, or because they tend to answer "red" for cars, *etc.* However, the probability of giving the answer that was the *correct* answer for another iteration of the test, *given that the user never saw the correct answers for that iteration,*[5] is exactly $1/n_c$ (where n_c is the number of colors, 8 in our case), because the correct answers are randomly drawn. Thus, if the overlap between the given answers in one iteration of the test, and the correct answers in another iteration, is significantly greater than $1/n_c$, then we can be reasonably sure that the same user was involved in both iterations.

Unfortunately, it appears inevitable that some users will do poorly on their first iteration. If this happens, then we no longer have the same goal for the second iteration: if anything, we would like them to do *better* on their second iteration, since they would have failed to obtain an account the first time. Also, in this case, it is unreasonable to expect the correct answers from the first iteration to overlap much with the given answers in the second iteration, since these correct answers did not even overlap much with the given answers in the *first* iteration! So, to prevent users from signing up for multiple accounts, the key requirement is that people that perform well in the first iteration either perform poorly in the second iteration, or that their given answers in the second iteration have significant overlap with the correct answers from the first iteration. We are now ready to present the results of the study.

---

[5] ... or was otherwise (indirectly) influenced by the correct answers for that iteration.

Table 1. Experimental results for human subjects

subject	$c_1 = a_1$	$c_2 = a_2$	$c_1 = a_2$	$c_2 = a_1$
1	53	66	27	13
2	34	23	14	13
3	31	46	13	13
4	50	61	23	14
5	17	38	15	11
6	42	43	11	11
7	60	70	22	12

In the results, c_i stands for the correct answer in the ith iteration, and a_i for the given answer in the ith iteration ($i \in \{1,2\}$). Thus, the sequence $c_1 = a_1$ gives the score for the first iteration, $c_2 = a_2$ gives the score for the second iteration, $c_1 = a_2$ indicates how often the given answer in the second iteration is identical to the correct answer (for that item) in the first iteration (indicating the level of confusion that the subject experienced, and the extent to which the system can identify the subject as the same person that performed the first iteration), and $c_2 = a_1$ indicates how often the given answer in the first iteration is identical to the correct answer (for that item) in the second iteration. For the last sequence, the probability that these answers match is always 1/8 (because the second iteration's correct answer is drawn randomly after the user's answer has been given in the first iteration), so unsurprisingly, this sequence is closely clustered around $12.5 = 100/8$. (Had this not been the case, it could only have been due to a statistical fluke, a mistake in the experimental setup, or a failure of the random number generator.) So we focus on the three remaining sequences.

Unfortunately, not all the subjects do well on the first iteration. Thus, if we require a reasonably high score on the test, some users will be denied an account on their first attempt. However, in all but one case, performance improved on the second attempt. If we look at the three subjects who performed best (1, 4, and 7), we see, encouragingly, that their overlap ($c_1 = a_2$) is very high (27, 23, 22, respectively). The probability that an overlap of at least 22 would have occurred if the two iterations of the test were taken by different people (so that the probability of overlap on any individual answer would be 1/8) is only $\sum_{i=22}^{100} \binom{100}{i}(1/8)^i(7/8)^{100-i} = 0.0056$, so we can reject the second account application in these cases.[6] (Here, we are in some sense evaluating the cutoff of 22

---

[6] It should be noted that in a real system, we must compare the answers not just to *one* specific previous iteration of the test, but to *every* previous (successful) iteration of the test. If the number of users is large, then the probability of this much overlap occurring by chance in at least one of these comparisons is significant. For example, if nobody is trying to obtain multiple accounts and there have already been 100 iterations of the test with previous users, then the probability that the next user has an overlap of at least 22 with at least one previous iteration is $1-(1-0.0056)^{100} = .43$. That is, if we require that the overlap with *every* one of the previous 100 iterations is less than 22, then an honest agent has a chance of only 57% of getting an account on the first attempt (assuming that this agent is not rejected due to poor performance).

on the same data as the data on which we based this cutoff; for a more thorough evaluation, it would be desirable to have a separate training set, on which we base the cutoff, and test set, on which we evaluate the cutoff.) However, the fourth-best performer, subject 6, displayed no overlap at all in spite of performing reasonably well on both iterations. We conjecture that there are different memorization strategies that subjects used, and that while the most successful strategies tend to produce significant overlap, there are other strategies that are still somewhat successful and less prone to cause overlap. For example, a subject can split the colors into two sets of four each, restrict attention to colors in the first set in the first iteration, and to colors in the second set in the second iteration. Fortunately, such strategies will fail if the user is required to recall a large enough number of associations correctly.

4   A Game-Theoretic Analysis

Subjects were cautioned that the items in the second iteration would be the same as in the first iteration, with potentially different color associations, so that they should try to take care not to get confused. In reality, however, the reward structure of the study did not penalize subjects for giving an answer in the second iteration that was the correct answer in the first iteration (at least not more than it penalized them for giving any other wrong answer). Since the idea is to deny the request for an account if there is too much overlap with the correct answers from a previous iteration, an ideal study would have penalized subjects for such overlap; this perhaps would have made subjects more careful to avoid it. We chose not to pursue such a design for the study for the following reasons. First, it is *ex ante* not clear by how much to penalize subjects. Perhaps the most convincing design would have been to set strict criteria beforehand for when a subject "passed" the test (*i.e.*, would be awarded an account), and to pay subjects in proportion to the number of accounts that they obtained. However, this would have required us to set the requirements for passing the test before collecting any formal data. Moreover, the lack of any "partial credit" may have made it more difficult to attract subjects. A second reason for the design of our study is that by using a game-theoretic model that we present next, we can use the results of the study to infer what results a subject could have obtained by changing her strategy (assuming correctness of the model). The test designer and the user play a game where the designer sets criteria and the user subsequently tries to obtain multiple accounts.

We first introduce a (highly simplified) model of the limitations of human memory. Suppose that when the user is asked to recall the color of an item, one color (not necessarily the right one) pops up into her memory. In game-theoretic terms, this color can be referred to as a *signal* that she receives from her memory. Specifically, suppose that when a user takes the test a second time,

- with probability p_1 the signal is the correct answer (from the second iteration),

- with probability p_2 the signal is the correct answer from the first iteration, and
- with probability $p_3 = 1 - p_1 - p_2$ the signal is one of the colors drawn at random.

Presumably, $p_1 > p_2$. As for p_3, all of the following are reasonably possible: $p_3 \geq p_1$ (a forgetful user), $p_1 > p_3 \geq p_2$ (a user that is somewhat forgetful and does not get confused much), and $p_2 > p_3$ (a user that is not very forgetful but does get confused). Since the probability that the correct answer in the first iteration is the same as the correct answer in the second iteration is $1/n_c$, the (*ex ante*) probability that the correct answer pops up for a given item is $p_1 + p_2/n_c + p_3/n_c = p_1 + (1 - p_1)/n_c$. Similarly, the probability that the correct answer from the first round pops up is $p_1/n_c + p_2 + p_3/n_c = p_2 + (1 - p_2)/n_c$. The user does not receive any other signal from her memory (such as a confidence level that the answer is the correct one).

In this highly simplified model, for each item, the user must choose whether to respond with the color corresponding to her signal, or with some other color. (Since there is no way to distinguish the other colors, we may assume that she chooses one of the remaining colors at random in the latter case.) Thus, the only strategic decision that the user can make is the fraction q of items for which she responds with the signal. If she responds with the signal for an item, the probability that she is right is $p_1 + (1 - p_1)/n_c$. If she responds with a random other color, then the probability that she is right is $(1 - (p_1 + (1 - p_1)/n_c))/(n_c - 1) = (1 - p_1)/n_c$. Thus, the expected fraction of times that she is right is $p_1 q + (1 - p_1)/n_c = p_1(q - 1/n_c) + 1/n_c$. Similarly, it can be shown that the expected fraction of times that she responds with the correct answer from the first iteration is $p_2 q + (1 - p_2)/n_c = p_2(q - 1/n_c) + 1/n_c$. (If we, completely inaccurately, assume that in our experiment, all users had the same p_1 and the same p_2, and that they all set $q = 1$, then this produces estimates of $p_1 = .42$ and $p_2 = .06$.) If $q = 1/n_c$ (which corresponds to random guessing), both of these expressions are equal to $1/n_c$. Hence, intuitively, if a user wants to increase the first expression beyond $1/n_c$, the second expression must also increase beyond $1/n_c$, and the second increase must be p_2/p_1 times the first increase.

This suggests the following metric for evaluating whether a test taker is the same as the taker of a given previous iteration of the test.

- Take the percentage of answers that are correct (for the current iteration), minus $1/n_c$ (the percentage expected for random guessing). Call the resulting fraction f_1.
- Then, take the percentage of answers that coincide with the correct answers from the earlier iteration, minus $1/n_c$ (the percentage expected for random guessing). Call the resulting fraction f_2.
- Finally, take the ratio f_2/f_1.

Then, by the above, if the test taker is the same in both iterations, the resulting ratio must be somewhere close to $\frac{p_2(q - 1/n_c)}{p_1(q - 1/n_c)} = p_2/p_1$ (assuming that f_1 is significantly positive). (With our very rough experimental estimates from above, $p_2/p_1 = .06/.42 = .14$.) The following theorem makes this precise.

Theorem 1. *Suppose the following are true:*

- *the game-theoretic model proposed above is correct,*
- *the test taker is the same in both iterations,*
- *in the second iteration, the test taker sets q to a value above $1/n_c$ (i.e., she does not guess randomly).*

Then, for any $\epsilon > 0$, as the number of items n_i goes to infinity, the probability that $|f_2/f_1 - p_2/p_1| \geq \epsilon$ goes to zero.

Proof. For any $\epsilon_1 > 0$, as $n_i \to \infty$, the probability that $|f_1 - p_1(q - 1/n_c)| \geq \epsilon_1$ goes to zero (using the law of large numbers and the fact that $p_1(q - 1/n_c)$ is the expected value of f_1). Similarly, for any $\epsilon_2 > 0$, as $n_i \to \infty$, the probability that $|f_2 - p_2(q - 1/n_c)| \geq \epsilon_2$ goes to zero. Because $p_1 > 0$ and $q > 1/n_c$, it must be the case that $p_1(q - 1/n_c) > 0$, and hence, for any $\epsilon > 0$, as $n_i \to \infty$, the probability that $|f_2/f_1 - p_2/p_1| = |f_2/f_1 - \frac{p_2(q-1/n_c)}{p_1(q-1/n_c)}| \geq \epsilon$ goes to zero as well.

By contrast, if the iterations of the test had different test takers, then with high probability, the ratio f_2/f_1 is close to 0, because the expectation of f_2 must be 0. (This is assuming that performance on the current iteration is significantly better than random guessing, so that the expectation of f_1 is positive). Thus, if we require f_1 to be significantly above 0 to pass the test (that is, the user should be getting significantly more answers right than random guessing would give, and hence must set q to a value significantly greater than $1/n_c$ to have a good chance of passing), the number of items is sufficiently large, and $p_2 > 0$, then with sufficiently many items we can reliably detect when an applicant has taken the test before (because $p_2/p_1 > 0$).

5   Conclusions and Future Research

In many Web-based applications, there are incentives for a user to sign up for more than one account, under false names. By doing so, the user can send spam e-mail from an account (which will eventually cause the account to be shut down); distort online ratings by rating multiple times (in particular, she can inflate her own reputation ratings); indefinitely continue using a product with a free trial period; place shill bids on items that she is selling on an auction site; engage in false-name bidding in combinatorial auctions; participate in the same online poker game under multiple identities, allowing her to effectively collude with herself; *etc.* All of these behaviors can be beneficial to the individual user, but are highly undesirable from the perspective of system performance. Users end up receiving tons of unwanted e-mail; online ratings become meaningless; companies become unwilling to offer free trial periods; users become skeptical of online auctions and poker games; *etc.* CAPTCHAs offer a partial remedy in that they can prevent a bot from automatically signing up for many accounts.

However, they do not prevent a *human* from signing up for multiple accounts. It may appear that the only way to prevent the latter is to require the user to provide information that identifies her in the real world (such as a credit card or telephone number), but users are typically reluctant to give out such information. In this paper, we proposed an alternative approach. We investigated whether it is possible to design an automated memory test that is easy to pass once, but difficult to pass a second time. Specifically, we designed a memory test. In this test, items are randomly associated with colors (*"Cars are green."*). The user first observes all of these associations, and is then asked to recall the colors of the items (*"Cars are...?"*). The items are the same across iterations of the test, but the colors are randomly redrawn each time (*"Cars are blue."*). Therefore, a user who has taken the test before will occasionally accidentally respond with the association from the previous time that she took the test (*"Cars are...? Green!"*). If there is significant correlation between the user's answers and the correct answers from a previous iteration of the test, then the system can decide that the user is probably the same, and refuse to grant another account. We presented and analyzed the results of a small study with human subjects, in which each subject took the test twice. The results of this study were mixed. On the negative side, about half of the subjects did not perform very well on the tests. On the positive side, for subjects that performed well, there was significant overlap between their answers in the second iteration and the correct answers in the first iteration. Thus, the system may be effective at preventing multiple account registrations from the same person, but not at allowing everyone to obtain an account. To analyze whether there exists some strategy for users that is more successful at signing up for multiple accounts, we introduced a simple game-theoretic model. We showed that under this model, any strategy is likely to fail at signing up for multiple accounts, if the test is large enough.

There are several aspects of the proposed test design that limit its feasibility in practice. First, the test is long and exhausting, which would probably discourage users from signing up for accounts. Second, the study indicates that performance on the test is very variable (even when its takers are restricted to Duke University students). Because in addition, the study suggests that we must require a high percentage of correct answers for passing the test in order to see the desired confusion (that is, overlap) across iterations of the test, this means that some users would have serious difficulty passing the test. Third, while the study suggests that it is difficult to do well on the test twice without getting confused across iterations, the study took place under controlled conditions. In the real world, users may try to pass the test multiple times in different ways (by waiting a longer time between iterations,[7] getting other people to help them, trying to use tools to record the associations (though the speed at which the test is run makes this difficult), *etc.*), and we know little about the test's robustness to such behavior.

---

[7] This would still imply that the rate at which users can sign up for accounts has decreased.

While there are many obstacles that need to be overcome for this approach to be truly practical, we feel that the results are encouraging enough, and that the value of having a practical solution would be high enough, that it is very much worthwhile to pursue further research on this topic. Such research should probably investigate other variants of the basic test design. In the appendix, we present results for one alternative design that is based on face recognition by the subjects. Unfortunately, that design did not end up working very well, but the results are informative for future designs.

One can imagine numerous other designs. For example, a test based on procedural ("how-to") memory rather than declarative (fact-storing) memory may be more effective. To find the optimal design, it may be beneficial to reach out to researchers in cognitive psychology and cognitive neuroscience, to exploit known particularities of human memory. However, our approach can introduce incentives for test takers to behave in ways that are not beneficial in more typical memory tests. These incentives and the behavior that they are likely to cause must be rigorously studied, both in theory and through experimental evaluation. Creating a truly practical system is an ambitious goal, but one that, if reached, will make many existing Web-based applications much more efficient, and will probably make new ones feasible.

References

1. Cramton, P., Shoham, Y., Steinberg, R.: Combinatorial Auctions. MIT Press, Cambridge (2006)
2. Fudenberg, D., Tirole, J.: Game Theory. MIT Press, Cambridge (1991)
3. Mori, G., Malik, J.: Recognizing objects in adversarial clutter: Breaking a visual CAPTCHA. In: IEEE Conference on Computer Vision and Pattern Recognition (CVPR), vol. 1, pp. 134–141 (2003)
4. Moy, G., Jones, N., Harkless, C., Potter, R.: Distortion estimation techniques in solving visual CAPTCHAs. In: IEEE Conference on Computer Vision and Pattern Recognition (CVPR), vol. 2, pp. 23–28 (2004)
5. Myerson, R.: Game Theory: Analysis of Conflict. Harvard University Press, Cambridge (1991)
6. Osborne, M.J., Rubinstein, A.: A Course in Game Theory. MIT Press, Cambridge (1994)
7. Thayananthan, A., Stenger, B., Torr, P.H.S., Cipolla, R.: Shape context and chamfer matching in cluttered scenes. In: IEEE Conference on Computer Vision and Pattern Recognition (CVPR), vol. 1, pp. 127–133 (2003)
8. von Ahn, L., Blum, M., Hopper, N., Langford, J.: CAPTCHA: Using hard AI problems for security. In: Biham, E. (ed.) EUROCRYPT 2003. LNCS, vol. 2656, pp. 294–311. Springer, Heidelberg (2003)
9. von Ahn, L., Blum, M., Langford, J.: Telling humans and computers apart automatically: How lazy cryptographers do AI. Communications of the ACM 47(2), 56–60 (2004)
10. Yokoo, M.: The characterization of strategy/false-name proof combinatorial auction protocols: Price-oriented, rationing-free protocol. In: Proceedings of the Eighteenth International Joint Conference on Artificial Intelligence (IJCAI), Acapulco, Mexico, pp. 733–742 (2003)

11. Yokoo, M., Matsutani, T., Iwasaki, A.: False-name-proof combinatorial auction protocol: Groves mechanism with submodular approximation. In: International Conference on Autonomous Agents and Multi-Agent Systems (AAMAS), Hako-date, Japan, pp. 1135–1142 (2006)

12. Yokoo, M., Sakurai, Y., Matsubara, S.: Robust combinatorial auction protocol against false-name bids. Artificial Intelligence 130(2), 167–181 (2001)

13. Yokoo, M., Sakurai, Y., Matsubara, S.: The effect of false-name bids in combinato-rial auctions: New fraud in Internet auctions. Games and Economic Behavior 46(1), 174–188 (2004)

Appendix: Another Test Based on Recognizing Faces

In this appendix, we present the experimental results of another test, which turned out not to work as well as hoped. In this test, we used a database of 58 human faces (a subset of the Indian Face Database developed at IIT Kanpur). A subject was first shown 29 faces drawn at random from the 58, one face at a time, for 5 seconds per face. Subsequently, the subject was shown the full set of faces (one at a time, for 4 seconds per face); in this second phase, the subject was asked, for each face, whether she/he had seen the face in the first phase. Each subject took this test twice (using the same database of 58 faces each time, but with a new draw of 29 faces in the first phase of the second iteration). (Each subject also did a practice run beforehand on a few faces not in the 58.) Again, each subject received US $7, plus the percentage of correct answers times US $7.

The hope was that performance in the second iteration of the test would be worse than in the first iteration of the test, due to the fact that, in the second phase of the second iteration, if a face looks familiar to the subject it may be difficult for him/her to decide whether he/she had seen it in the first phase of the second iteration, or only at some point in the first iteration of the test (in the latter case, the correct answer would be "no"). If performance were consistent across subjects, and significantly worse in the second iteration, then perhaps we could set a threshold that everyone can pass the first time but not another time. Unfortunately, this turned out not to be the case, as the results below show.

While for some subjects, there was a drop in performance in the second it-eration, these drops were generally not significant, and some subjects' scores actually increased in the second iteration. It appears that subjects did experi-ence some confusion in the second iteration, but at the same time, there was a learning effect: subjects became generally better at remembering the faces, and this canceled out the confusion effect. Perhaps this learning effect can be removed by making subjects practice beforehand, but this would make the duration of the test unreasonable.

One may also wonder if it is possible to observe correlations across iterations of this test, as we did for the test in the main part of this paper. In the experiment, it was the case that most of the subjects' wrong answers in the second iteration occurred when the correct answer for a face in the second iteration was not the same as the correct answer for that face in the first iteration; however, this effect

Table 2. Experimental results for human subjects in the face-based test

subject	# correct in iteration 1	# correct in iteration 2
1	53	45
2	47	49
3	48	44
4	43	42
5	45	45
6	41	51
7	46	47
8	36	34

does not appear strong enough to confidently conclude that two iterations of the test correspond to one person (especially because subjects generally did not have that many wrong answers in this test).

Multi-attribute Regret-Based Dynamic Pricing

Janyl Jumadinova* and Prithviraj Dasgupta

Computer Science Department
University of Nebraska, Omaha, NE 68182, USA
{jjumadinova,pdasgupta}@mail.unomaha.edu

Abstract. In this paper, we consider the problem of dynamic pricing by a set of competing sellers in an information economy where buyers differentiate products along multiple attributes, and buyer preferences can change temporally. Previous research in this area has either focused on dynamic pricing along a limited number of (e.g. binary) attributes, or, assumes that each seller has access to private information such as preference distribution of buyers, and profit/price information of other sellers. However, in real information markets, private information about buyers and sellers cannot be assumed to be available *a priori*. Moreover, due to the competition between sellers, each seller faces a tradeoff between accuracy and rapidity of the pricing mechanism. In this paper, we describe a multi-attribute dynamic pricing algorithm based on minimax regret that can be used by a seller's agent called a *pricebot*, to maximize the seller's utility. Our simulation results show that the minimax regret based dynamic pricing algorithm performs significantly better than other algorithms for rapidly and dynamically tracking consumer attributes without using any private information from either buyers or sellers.

Keywords: Dynamic pricing, pricebots, minimax regret.

1 Introduction

With the increasing automation of e-commerce applications, intelligent agents are becoming an essential part of various business transactions. Over the past decade, several services such as automated comparison shopping tools including MySimon[2] and PriceGrabber[3], and seller ratings Websites such as Bizrate [1] have enabled online buyers make rapid and informed decisions before purchasing products over the Internet. As the number of buyers who rely on these services increases, it is becoming advantageous for online sellers to use automated pricing-setting techniques in an attempt to maximize profits. Intelligent agents called *pricebots* [14] provide a suitable paradigm for online sellers to rapidly update the price of a product in response to changes in market parameters such as buyer preferences in an online economy.

Consumers who purchase products online are frequently willing to pay an elevated price for enhanced values on particular product attributes such as delivery time, seller reputation, and after-sales service[1]. Different consumers have

---

* Primary author, student.

W. Ketter et al. (Eds.): AMEC/TADA 2008, LNBIP 44, pp. 73–87, 2010.
© Springer-Verlag Berlin Heidelberg 2010

also been reported to prefer different product attributes and these preferences vary over time depending on exogenous factors such as sales promotion, aggressive advertising and even time of the year [16]. Therefore, it is important for an online seller to differentiate a product it sells along multiple attributes, and, determine a potential buyer's purchase preferences over the different product attributes, so that it can tailor its offer to meet the buyer's requirements, and, improve its profits. Online markets are also characterized by multiple sellers for the same product. To remain competitive in such a market, a seller has to offer a price that is more attractive than its competitors prices to potential buyers. To achieve this, each seller has to use a dynamic pricing algorithm that calculates a profit maximizing price for the seller. Previous research on dynamic pricing algorithms requires each seller to possess *a priori* information about the market parameters such as buyers' reservation prices, the number of buyers, preferences of buyers over different product attributes and prices and profits of other competing sellers in the market. However, in real-life economies accurate knowledge of such market parameters cannot be assumed to be available with sellers. In this paper, we make two contributions to the problem of dynamic pricing in a market where buyers differentiate products along multiple attributes. First, we describe a preference elicitation algorithm based on minimax regret that can be used by a seller's pricebot to determine the distribution of buyer preferences along different product attributes. Then, we describe a minimax regret based algorithm that enables a seller to dynamically update the posted price of a product to improve its profit. Both these algorithms do not require any *a priori* knowledge about market parameters such as buyer's preferences over product attributes, buyers' reservation prices and other competing sellers' prices and profits. These algorithms only require a seller's private history including its posted prices, profits and purchase decisions from different buyers for their calculations. Our simulation results show that the minimax regret-based attribute prediction algorithm is able to predict the preferred attributes of different buyers with more than 90% accuracy in most cases, even when the buyers' preferences over different attributes change dynamically over time. When used with the attribute prediction algorithm in a competitive market, a seller using the minimax regret based dynamic pricing algorithm is able to obtain $9-13\%$ more profits than competing sellers using other dynamic pricing strategies.

2   Dynamic Pricing over Multiple Product Attributes

Current real-life internet economies involve complex interactions between several buyers, sellers and possibly brokers that facilitate trading. We have made certain simplifying assumptions of an online economy to simplify analysis while retaining the essential features of the market. Our online market model is based on the shopbot economy model of Kephart and Greenwald [14]. We consider an economy that consists of a set of S sellers who compete to provide a set of B buyers with a single homogeneous product, where $\mid B \mid \gg \mid S \mid$. Each seller behaves as a profit maximizer and has a sufficient supply of the product to last the lifetime

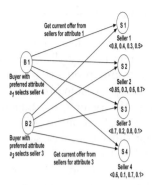

Fig. 1. A hypothetical market showing two buyers with preferred attributes as a_1 and a_3 respectively making a quote request to four sellers and selecting the seller that offers the best price for the product on their respective attributes. The tuple $< p_{a_1}, p_{a_2}, p_{a_3}, p_{a_4} >$ below each seller denotes the normalized price offered by each seller on the different product attributes.

of the buyers. Buyers come back to the market repeatedly to re-purchase the product. A product is differentiated by buyers and sellers on multiple attributes such as offered price, delivery time, product quality, seller reputation, previous experience with seller, etc. Here, we assume that each product has a set of A different attributes, and, the buyers and sellers in the market are aware of this set of product attributes.

Every buyer in the market selects one of the product's attribute as its preferred attribute and is willing to pay a slightly elevated price to purchase the product along its preferred attribute. In online markets, buyers also change their preferred attribute for a product dynamically [16]. For example, when buyers purchase products under time constraints, they prefer the 'delivery- time' attribute of the product. On the other hand, when buyers do not consider time as a critical factor, product quality or seller reputation are possible attributes that determine their purchase decision. The choice of the preferred product attribute of a buyer can also be affected by exogenous factors such as time of the year, previous purchase experiences, etc.[18]. To model this, we assume that every buyer in our market has one of the product's attributes as its preferred attribute and the preferred attribute of a buyer can vary with time. Sellers are unaware of buyers' preferred attributes and the temporal variation of the preferred attributes for each buyer. A seller offers a slightly different price for the product along each product attribute $a_i \in A$. To improve its profits in a market with multiple sellers offering the same product, each seller has to dynamically adjust its posted prices along the different product attributes so that it can continue to offer a competitive price and attract buyers. When a buyer requests a price quote, the buyer's preferred attribute is not known to a seller. Therefore, the objective of a profit maximizing seller is to determine a buyer's preferred attribute in response to the buyer's quote request. The seller can then calculate a competitive price of the product along the buyer's preferred attribute and make an attractive offer to the buyer.

An illustration of the operation of our market is shown in Figure 1. A seller j enters the market with an initial price $p^0_{a_i,j}$ for a unit of the product under attribute a_i. Each seller has a unit production cost p_{co} below which it is not willing to sell the product. A buyer wishing to purchase a product first requests a price quote from the sellers. We assume that buyers use comparison shopping services [3] to discover sellers and are aware of all the sellers in the market. Since we analyze pricing algorithms for sellers, seller discovery is not treated as a major issue in the model. Each seller j receiving a buyer's quote request responds with a price vector $\bar{P}^t_j = < p^t_{a_i,j} >$, where $p^t_{a_i,j}$ represents the price charged by seller j during interval t along product attribute a_i. This price is updated by the seller's pricebot at intervals τ_j using a dynamic pricing algorithm. Different sellers update their product prices asynchronously and each seller uses its own pricing strategy. When a buyer that had made quote requests receives the offers from different sellers, it compares the offers made by the different sellers. Each buyer b has a reservation price for the product p_{r,b,a_i} along attribute a_i, above which it is not willing to buy the product. The utility of the product to a buyer b from seller j along attribute a_i is given by $U_{b,a_i,j} = p_{r,b,a_i} - p^t_{a_i,j}$, where $p^t_{a_i,j}$ is the posted price of the product offered by seller j along attribute a_i during interval t. The purchase decision is made by buyer b by comparing the utilities from the different sellers along the preferred attribute a_i of the product, and, selecting seller S_k given by $S_k = \arg_S \max U_{b,a_i,S}$. In case, more than one seller offers the same lowest price along the buyer's preferred attribute, one of the sellers offering the highest utility is chosen randomly by the buyer. Buyer b then pays seller S_k the posted price of the product and the seller delivers the product. Payment and product delivery are not discussed any further here as we concentrate on seller's preferred attribute prediction and pricing strategies. In the next two sections, we present the minimax regret-based dynamic pricing algorithm that is used by sellers to estimate buyers' preferences and dynamically update the posted prices over the different product attributes.

3   Minimax Regret-Based Algorithms

The parameters used in our market model are given below:

A Set of product attributes.

B Set of buyers.

S Set of sellers.

p_{r,b,a_i} Buyer b's reservation price along attribute a_i.

p_{co} Unit production cost for a seller(assumed to be uniform over all attributes)

τ_j Price update interval for seller j.

$p^t_{a_i,j}$ Posted price of the product by seller j along attribute a_i during interval t.

$\pi^t_{a_i,j}$ Profit obtained by seller j along attribute a_i during interval t.

u^t_{b,a_i} Upper bound on the buyer's purchase value for attribute a_i.

l^t_{b,a_i} Lower bound on the buyer's purchase value for attribute a_i.

3.1   Minimax Regret-Based Attribute Prediction

To remain competitive in a market where buyers can change their preferred attribute, each seller should attempt to accurately determine the current preferred attribute of the buyers that request price quotes from it, so that the seller can charge a profit maximizing price along the buyers' preferred attribute. However, dynamically determining the buyers' preferred attribute without any knowledge of the buyers' demand and attribute variance function is a challenging task facing the seller. In this paper, we describe a preference elicitation based technique that can be used by sellers to predict the buyers' preferred attribute.

Most of the previous literature on user preference elicitation uses considerable information extracted from users to determine the user's preferences over different choices. However, in our model there are three challenges in collating consumer data for analysis by sellers for preference elicitation: (1) A buyer's preferred product attribute changes over time and a seller needs to continuously update the buyer's preferences over the different product attributes to be able to determine the current preferred attribute of the buyer. (2) A seller and a buyer interact for a limited duration and the only information that the seller is able to get from a buyer is the purchase decision (yes or no) of the buyer from that seller. (3) Because a seller is not aware of the prices offered by other sellers in the market, when a buyer does not purchase a product from the seller after receiving the seller's offer, the seller does not have any mechanism for inferring whether the negative purchase decision resulted from incorrect calculation of buyer's preferred product attribute, or, whether another seller offered a more attractive price to the buyer along the buyer's preferred attribute.

To address these issues, we first make the observation that elicitation of the full buyer preferences captured by the utility function of the buyer might be unnecessary in determining the buyer preferred product attribute. A reasonable estimate of the buyer preferences can be obtained by a seller from the purchase decision made by a buyer after the buyer requests a quote from the seller. To elicit the buyer preferences from the purchase decision information of a seller, each seller in our model uses the minimax regret technique of preference elicitation described by Boutilier et $al.$ in [6]. To enable the preference elicitation mechanism, each seller assumes that there is a set of bounds on every buyer's expected purchase value of the product. These bounds keep track of the price levels at which a buyer will purchase the product and can be used as an indicator for both the buyer's valuation(reservation price) of the product as well as the prices charged by the competing sellers at which the buyer has recently purchased the product. The minimax decision criterion suggests that the seller makes a decision that gives the minimum max-regret, where max-regret is the largest value by which the seller could regret making that decision. It is therefore a decision the seller would regret the least and minimizes the worst-case loss the seller would encounter after making that decision.

In our model, sellers have to make a decision at the end of each interval about which attribute to predict for each buyer. To realize this, each seller keeps an upper bound u_{b,a_i} and a lower bound l_{b,a_i} for every buyer on their expected purchase values for each attribute of the product. To enable the elicitation of buyers' preferences, we consider the buyer-seller interaction as a querying process. Essentially sellers are sending a query to a buyer every time they respond to that buyer's quote request with the product's posted prices.

We can consider this query as a bound query of type: "Is your valuation of the product greater than or equal to my offered price?" Given a "yes" response,

```
function minimax_attrib_predict returns
     input: int τ_j;          // time interval length (in quotes)
     variables: int qr;        // number of quote requests received by seller
                int t;          // time interval
                double p^t_{a_i,j};    // seller j's price along attribute a_i
                set B^t_j;       // set of buyers that have accessed j during interval t
                set B[a_i];      // index set of buyers under attribute a_i
                t ← 0; B^t_j ← ∅;
     while(seller remains in market)
1.       for every a_i ∈ A
2.           p^t_{a_i,j} ← p | p ∈ U[p_{co}, 1]
3.           while (qr < τ_j)
4.               if some buyer b ∈ B requests quote from seller
5.                   qr ← qr + 1;
6.                   B^t_j ← B^t_j ⋃ b;
7.               if some buyer b' ∈ B^t_j purchases product with preferred attribute a_i
8.                   B^t_{j,a_i,pos} ← B^t_{j,a_i,pos} ⋃ b'
9.
10.      for every buyer b ∈ B^t_j
11.          for every a_i ∈ A
12.              if(b ∈ B^t_{j,a_i,pos})
13.                  l^t_{b,a_i} ← l^t_{b,a_i} + ε;
14.              else
15.                  u^t_{b,a_i} ← u^t_{b,a_i} − ε;
16.                  B^t_{j,a_i,neg} ← B^t_{j,a_i,neg} ⋃ b;
17.      // condition u_{b,a_i} and l_{b,a_i} values
18.      for every a_i ∈ A
19.          u^t_{b,a_i} ← Σ^h_{k=0} λ_k u^{t−k}_{b,a_i} | Σ λ_k = 1, λ_{k−1} > λ_k;
20.          l^t_{b,a_i} ← Σ^h_{k=0} λ_k l^{t−k}_{b,a_i} | Σ λ_k = 1, λ_{k−1} > λ_k;
21.      for every buyer b ∈ B^t_j
22.          for every a_i ∈ A
23.              R(a_i, a_{−i}) ← u^t_{b,a_{−i}} − l^t_{b,a_i};
24.              R(a_i, a_i) ← 0;
25.              for every a_i ∈ A
26.                  MR_{a_i} ← max_{a_{−i}∈A} R(a_i, a_{−i});
27.              a_l ← arg_{a_i} min MR_{a_i};
28.          Place buyer b in B[a_l];
29.          Remove buyer b from any other B[a_{−l}];
30.      t ← t + 1;
```

Fig. 2. Algorithm used by the sellers to predict buyers preferred attributes at the end of each time interval

the seller modifies that buyer's lower bound and given a "no" response, the seller adjusts buyer's upper bound, thus tightening the bounds of the buyer's purchase valuation. The algorithm describing the attribute prediction process is presented in Figure 2. Initially, seller j sets its price along each attribute randomly (lines 1-2). Seller j keeps track of the number of quotes it receives and records whether a purchase was made or not by the buyers (lines 3-9). When the number of quote requests received by seller j reaches τ_j (time interval for price update measured in number of buyer quote requests), seller j updates its bounds on the purchase valuation of every buyer that has purchased from it over the current time interval. A positive purchase decision by a buyer raises the lower bound of the purchase valuation while a negative purchase decision lowers the upper bound of the purchase valuation (lines 10-16). Seller j then weighs both of these bounds over the historical values of the previous h bounds used by it, with higher weights given to more recent bounds, to prevent wide fluctuations in these values(lines 17-19). To calculate the minimax regret, seller j first calculates the pairwise regret $R(a_i, a_{-i})$ of attribute $a_i \in A$ with respect to other attributes $a_{-i} \in A$. This value corresponds to the regret the seller feels for predicting attribute a_i instead of any other attribute a_{-i}. Seller j then selects the attribute a_l corresponding to the minimum of the maximum regrets from these pairwise regret values as the preferred attribute for buyer b. This calculation is repeated for every buyer b that purchases from the seller in the current time interval (line 22-26).

3.2   Regret-Based Dynamic Pricing

At the end of each time interval, seller j predicts the buyer's preferred attribute and then updates its price along each attribute a_i. A seller's objective is to calculate a profit maximizing price along each product attribute while considering the number of buyers that were determined to have that attribute as its preferred attribute during that time interval using the attribute prediction technique in Section 3.1. The algorithm for achieving this dynamic pricing is described in Figure 3. Seller j first calculates the average bounds on the purchase valuations across all buyers for each product attribute (lines 1-2). It then calculates a historical weighted average price $\overline{p}^t_{a_i, j}$ using prices in h previous intervals (line 3). The seller then calculates the normalized number of buyers, n_{a_i}, with preferred attribute a_i, using the number of buyers under each product attribute determined by the $minimax\_attrib\_predict$ function (line 27, Figure 2). This value is then used to determine the regret-based price $p'^t_{a_i, j}$ by seller j (lines 4-5).

Since the goal of the seller is to maximize its profit, the seller keeps track of its profit direction changes and adjusts its prices so that the profits are increasing. The seller observes the direction of price movement predicted by the average regret-based price and the historical average of prices. If the direction of this price movement is the same as the direction of the profit change in the last interval, the seller sets the new posted price during interval $(t + 1)$ along attribute a_i as the weighted average of regret-based price and historical average price with the larger weight given to regret-based price. Regret-based price

---

function minimax_regret_pricing return double[ ] $< p_{a_i,j}^t >$
  for every $a_i \in A$

1. $\overline{u}_{b,a_i}^t \leftarrow \sum_{b \in B[a_i]} u_{b,a_i}^t / |B[a_i]|;$

2. $\overline{l}_{b,a_i}^t \leftarrow \sum_{b \in B[a_i]} l_{b,a_i}^t / |B[a_i]|;$

3. $\overline{p}_{a_i,j}^t \leftarrow \sum_{k=0}^h \lambda_k p_{a_i,j}^{t-k} \mid \sum \lambda_k = 1, \lambda_{k-1} > \lambda_k;$ // historical average

4. $n_{a_i} \leftarrow \frac{|B[a_i]|}{|B|};$

5. $p'_{a_i,j}^t \leftarrow n_{a_i} \overline{u}_{b,a_i}^t + (1 - n_{a_i}) \overline{l}_{b,a_i}^t;$ // average regret-based price

6.   if $\left(sign(p'_{a_i,j}^t - \overline{p}_{a_i,j}^t) * sign(\pi_{a_i,j}^t - \pi_{a_i,j}^{t-1}) = 1 \right)$

7. $p_{a_i,j}^{t+1} \leftarrow \lambda_1 p'_{a_i,j}^t + (1 - \lambda_1) \overline{p}_{a_i,j}^t;$

8.   else

9. $p_{a_i,j}^{t+1} \leftarrow p_{a_i,j}^t + sign(\pi_{a_i,j}^t - \pi_{a_i,j}^{t-1}) * \epsilon;$

  return $< p_{a_i,j}^{t+1} >$

Fig. 3. Minimax regret-based dynamic pricing algorithm used by sellers to update prices at the end of each interval

accounts for the buyers' predicted preference distribution, whereas historical average price is used to account for some "noise" in the market, which can make the buyers' predicted preference distribution less accurate. Using past price trends, sellers can eliminate sudden changes in the prices that are caused by the inaccurate prediction of the buyers' preference distribution. On the other hand, if the direction of predicted price movement and the direction of profit change are opposite to each other, the seller will still want to update its prices based on the profit changes, since that will yield it more profit. The opposite direction of the predicted price movement to the profit change can happen as a result of some error in the attribute prediction algorithm or some noise in the market. In this case, the seller sets the posted price during interval $(t + 1)$ as the price during the last interval t plus a small amount ϵ in the direction of the profit change (lines 6-9).

4   Simulation Results

We have tested our minimax regret based attribute prediction and dynamic pricing algorithm within a simulated market economy. All simulation results have been averaged over 10 simulation runs. Following is a list of parameters and their values we have used in our simulations:

4.1   Comparison Strategies

To quantify the performance of our minimax regret based algorithm with other algorithms for dynamic pricing, we have compared the minimax regret based algorithm with the following strategies: **(1) Fixed Pricing.** In fixed pricing, a seller does not change the posted price of a product. **(2) Derivative Follower Pricing Strategy.** In the derivative follower (DF) strategy, a seller determines the price for the next interval based on the profits obtained from the pricing in

Table 1. Parameters used for the simulation experiments

Parameter	Value
Number of buyers	500 or 1000
Number of sellers	3 or 5
Number of product attributes	5
Rate at which buyers send quote requests to sellers	5000 ms
Unit production cost for seller	0.1
Entry price of sellers in market	$U[p_{co}, 1.0]$
Number of past intervals, h	10
Interval for price updates for seller	40 quote requests from buyers[1]
Weight of average regret based price (λ_1 in line 7, Figure 3)	0.8

the current interval. The price update equation along attribute a_i used by a seller j using the derivative follower strategy is given by: $p_{a_{i,j}}^{t+1} = p_{a_{i,j}}^t + sign(\pi_{a_{i,j}}^t - \pi_{a_{i,j}}^{t-1}) * \epsilon$, where $\epsilon \in U[0.1, 0.2]$. **(3) Goal Directed Strategy.** In the goal-directed pricing strategy described by DiMicco *et al.*[10], a seller calculates the average number of a units of the product it should sell per interval that enables it to clear the inventory by its last interval in the market. It then observes the number of units it is able to sell during the current interval. If the actual number of units sold is above(below) the expected clearance value, the seller responds by raising(lowering) the price of the product for the next interval.

Variation of Buyer Attribute Preferences. Buyers have a set of discrete probability distributions P_n according to which they vary their preferred attributes. When a buyer enters the market, it randomly selects one of the probability distributions, $p_n \in P_n$. Each probability distribution consists of $| A |$ probabilities, $p_n = < p_{a_i} > | i = 1, ..., | A |$. Each p_{a_i} corresponds to a buyer's probability of selecting that attribute as its preferred attribute. To model the temporal variation in preferred attributes, each buyer changes its selected probability distribution from p_n to $p_{n'} \in p_{-n}$ at random times.

Attribute Prediction Algorithms. For comparing the minimax regret based attribute prediction algorithm, we have used a collaborative filtering based attributed prediction technique used in dynamic pricing. Collaborative filtering algorithms [17] are used extensively in recommender systems for recommending products to a user by matching the user's preferences along different product attributes with the preferences of other users collected over time. [5,9] have employed collaborative filtering techniques to determine consumer attributes for the dynamic pricing problem. In these collaborative filtering mechanisms, each seller predicts the buyers' preferred attributes based on the purchase history of buyers with that seller. To achieve this, each seller associates each product attribute with a cluster of buyers. For every buyer that has purchased from the seller, the seller calculates a set of probabilities $W_t = w_i^t$ for placing the buyer under cluster(attribute) $a_i \in A$ during interval t. Each seller updates these probabilities at the end of every interval based on the purchase decision of the buyer during the interval and the historical values of the probabilities, as outlined below: (1) Update w values: $w_i^{t+1} = (w_i^t)^{\frac{p_i^t}{p} - \frac{n_i^t}{n}}$, where p_i^t is number of purchases during interval t along cluster i and n_i^t is the number of no-purchases, p is the total number of purchases along attribute i and n is the total number of no-purchases.

Find w_i^{t+1} values for each attribute, $i = 1.. \mid A \mid$ and put them into the W_{t+1} vector (2) Find the cosine similarities of W_{t+1} with all previous cluster probability vectors that are in the history table according to the following equation: $sim = \frac{W_{t+1} . W_j}{||W_{t+1}|| * ||W_j||}$, where j represents elements in the history table. (3) Select the probability vector W_{t-j} that is most similar to W_{t+1} and calculate of weighted sum of W_{t-j} and its h successive probability vectors: $W_{t+1}' = \Sigma_{k=0}^h \lambda_k W_{t-j+k}$ (4) The probability values in W_{t+1}' are then used to assign buyers into clusters during next interval $t + 1$.

4.2   Experimental Results

Attribute Prediction. In our first set of simulations, we compare the attribute prediction accuracy, independent of price setting, using the collaborative filtering and the minimax regret-based techniques. Figure 4(a) shows the attribute prediction comparison along attribute $a_2 \in A$ in a market with 3 sellers and 500 buyers, where two of the sellers use the minimax regret based attribute prediction while the remaining seller uses the collaborative filtering technique for attribute prediction. We observe that sellers using the minimax regret-based attribute prediction technique are able to predict the number of buyers with preferred attribute a_2 within $0 - 15\%$ accuracy of the actual number of buyers under the attribute. Although the collaborative filtering based technique performs comparably, it shows intermittent excursions in the attribute prediction resulting in the preferred attribute being incorrectly predicted for as many as 80% of the buyers in the market. The relative inaccurate predictions of the collaborative filtering algorithm can be attributed to the fact that collaborative filtering performance is highly dependent on other buyers purchase decisions and might introduce biased effects. This causes the overall most preferred attributes to be recommended more often and prevents the seller from adjusting to changes in buyer preferences. In Figure 4(b), we show the comparison results for the two attribute prediction techniques in a market with 5 sellers and 1000 buyers, where three of the sellers use the minimax regret based attribute prediction while the remaining two sellers use the collaborative filtering technique for attribute prediction. Once again, we observe that the minimax regret based technique is able to predict the attribute of the buyers accurately most of the time and has a maximum error of only 10% during the entire simulation. On the other hand, the collaborative filtering based technique performs considerably poorly with errors ranging from $20 - 30\%$ through most of the simulation. The reason for the poor performance of the collaborative filtering algorithm can be attributed to the probability values varying significantly with a big change in the number of purchases which results in most buyers being classified under one attribute. This contributes to sellers

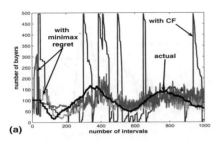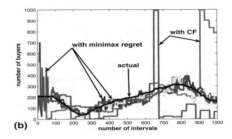

Fig. 4. Attribute prediction using minimax regret based attribute prediction and collaborative filtering techniques. (a) In a market with 3 sellers and 500 buyers and (b) in a market with 5 sellers and 1000 buyers.

using collaborative filtering predicting one attribute for most of the buyers during some intervals and resulting in large inaccurate oscillations in the number of predicted buyers The average prediction accuracy for our simulations in Figure 4 was 89% for minimax regret-based attribute prediction and 69% for attribute prediction using the collaborative filtering approach.

Dynamic Pricing. In our next set of simulations we compared the performance of different pricing strategies used by different sellers in our simulated market economy. For the first set of experiments, we used a market with 500 buyers and 3 sellers. Two of the sellers used the minimax regret based dynamic pricing strategy while the remaining seller used the strategy being compared. Figure 5(top) shows the profit comparisons and price competition of two sellers using the minimax regret-based dynamic pricing and one seller who sets a fixed price. In our simulations, fixed-price sellers set the price for each attribute randomly when they enter the market. Figure 5(top) illustrates that even when the fixed price is initially below the prices set randomly by the minimax regret-based dynamic pricing sellers, sellers using minimax regret-based pricing strategies adjust their prices as they compete with each other and end up with the majority of the market profit share (49.2 % and 50.3%). Figure 5(middle) presents the profits and the price variations of three sellers over time, two of the sellers use minimax regret-based dynamic pricing and the other seller uses goal-directed pricing technique. For goal-directed strategy price computation, the parameter *daysInMarket* is set to 1,000 intervals and *initialInventory* is set to 20,000 units. The sellers using the minimax regret-based pricing technique are able to get higher shares of the profits, 35% and 42%, in Figure 5(middle), while the seller using goal-directed strategy gets about 23% of the total market profit share. Our simulations show that even in the market in which a seller has a limited supply of products, minimax regret-based pricing can outperform the goal-directed strategy. Finally, Figure 5(bottom) illustrates the profit and price profiles of three sellers that use either the derivative-follower or the minimax regret-based dynamic pricing strategies. The market prices fluctuate consistently due to the competition between sellers. The seller using the derivative-follower

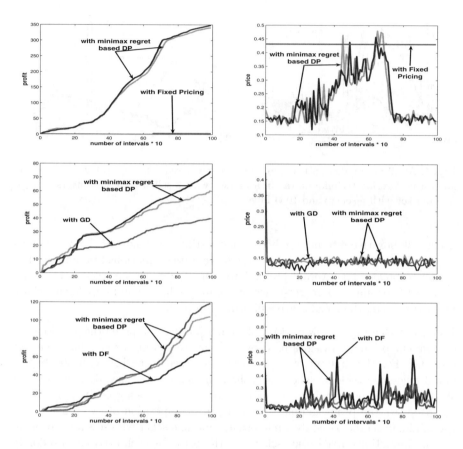

Fig. 5. Profit profile and the price competition between 3 sellers in the market with 500 buyers using Fixed Pricing or Minimax Regret (top), Goal-Directed (GD) or Minimax Regret (middle) and Derivative Follower (DF) or Minimax Regret (bottom) techniques

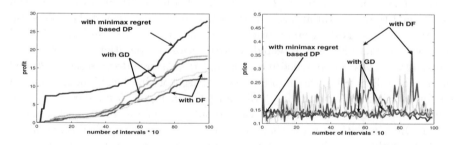

Fig. 6. Profit and price profiles of 5 sellers in the market with 1000 buyers using Goal-Directed (GD), Derivative Follower (DF) or Minimax Regret-based Dynamic Pricing techniques

pricing strategy ends up with the smallest market profit share (about 23% of the total profit in the market). The sellers that use the minimax regret-based dynamic pricing get the larger share of the market profit share (about 38% and 39%). The sellers that use the minimax regret for attribute prediction adjust to the buyers preferences and other market changes to obtain more profits.

Figure 6 illustrates the profit and price competition in a market with 1000 buyers and 5 sellers where 1 of the sellers use the minimax regret-based strategy and each of the remaining sellers use the goal-directed or derivative-following strategy. The two goal-directed sellers end up receiving 20% and 19% of the market's profits respectively. This is because the goal directed strategy is unable to reduce the posted price in response to price cuts by the other sellers because the strategy is dependent on the surplus inventory at the end of each interval. The derivative-follower seller raises prices until its profit goes down and then significantly lowers the price. The price adjustments by the derivative-follower are not very effective when the sellers using goal-directed and minimax regret-based pricing are simultaneously in the market with it. Consequently, the two sellers using derivative follower strategy for dynamic pricing receive 13% and 16% of the profits in the market. As sellers compete for profit shares, the sellers using minimax regret-based pricing adjust their prices more accurately and capture 32% of the market profit.

5   Related Work

Over the past few years, several researchers have considered the problem of automated dynamic pricing by sellers using software agents called pricebots. Kephart and Greenwald [14] analyze various dynamic price strategies such as game-theoretic, myopically optimal, derivative-following strategy, and Q-learning price setting strategy. An extension of this work [11] describes a no-regret learning based technique for automated dynamic pricing by sellers. In these algorithms sellers are assumed to have prior knowledge of some market parameters such as reservation prices of buyers, the distribution of buyers under each attribute of the product, and prices or profits of competing sellers. However, in most real-life economies, knowledge of such market parameters is either unavailable or has to be learned by the seller in real time. In contrast, in this paper, we do not assume prior knowledge of the reservation prices of buyers, the distribution of buyers under different product attributes and competitors' price information. Moreover, the minimax regret based attribute prediction and dynamic pricing techniques presented in this paper can determine product prices for sellers when the preferences of buyers over different product attributes change dynamically with time. In [12,4], the authors have also considered the problem of dynamic pricing products. However, their settings contain only one seller and the main problem considered is to determine the optimal bundle of products and the price of the bundle that maximizes the seller's profit. Preference elicitation of consumers in a market has also been an active research topic in the area of decision support systems[13]. Recently, Lahaie and Parkes [15] have developed techniques based on machine learning for preference elicitation from consumers. Bayesian methods for preference elicitation have been researched in [7] where preference uncertainty is probabilistically quantified. In contrast, in our work, sellers don't use a density over possible utility functions and dynamically calculate the distribution of buyers over different product attributes. In [6,19], Boutilier *et al.* use minimax regret as a decision criterion in constraint-based decision making. We have used a similar minimax regret-based technique to enable a seller's price-bot learn the consumer's preferences over different attributes and dynamically update the product's posted price. In contrast to the work in [6], sellers in our model cannot explicitly send queries to consumers to elicit their preferences. We have therefore considered the price quote sent by a seller to the buyer as a bound query and used the purchase decision made by the buyer after receiving the seller's price quote as a response to the bound query. Conitzer [8] showed that single-peaked preferences can be elicited using comparison queries if prior knowledge of some preference order structure or the preferences of one agent exists. However, in our model sellers interact with buyers only while offering price quotes or receiving an affirmative purchase decision. Therefore, our model is not amenable to comparison queries.

6   Conclusion

In this paper, we have described an algorithm that can be used by sellers to determine temporally changing buyer preferences across multiple product attributes, and, to dynamically update the posted product prices in a competitive market without explicit knowledge of various market parameters. There are several directions we plan to expand this work in the future. First, we are interested in investigating dynamic pricing algorithms in markets where sellers have information, possibly partially, about competitors' prices. With partial information about competitors' prices a seller could possibly infer the reason for a negative purchase decision by a buyer more efficiently and improve its buyer attribute prediction as well as its dynamic pricing performance, resulting in improved profits. Secondly, we plan to investigate a scenario where buyers are able to exchange information about sellers with each other. This results in more informed purchase decisions between buyers and could even lead to collisions between buyers to affect the prices being charged by sellers. Dynamic pricing over multiple attributes by competing sellers in a market with limited information about market parameters is a relevant yet challenging problem and we envisage that appropriate solution techniques in this direction will result in improved success of e-commerce technologies.

References

1. Bizrate Inc., http://www.bizrate.com
2. MySimon, http://www.mysimon.com
3. PriceGrabber, http://www.pricegrabber.com

4. Balcan, M.-F., Blum, A.: Approximation algorithms and online mechanisms for item pricing. In: Proc. ACM-EC, pp. 29–35 (2006)
5. Bergemann, D., Ozmen, D.: Optimal pricing with recommender systems. In: Proc. ACM-EC, pp. 43–51 (2006)
6. Boutilier, C., Patrascu, R., Poupart, P., Schuurmans, D.: Constraint-based optimization and utility elicitation using the minimax decision criterion. Artificial Intelligence 170(8), 686–713 (2006)
7. Chajewska, U., Koller, D., Parr, R.: Making rational decisions using adaptive utility elicitation. In: Proc. of the 17th National Conference on AI, pp. 363–369 (2006)
8. Conitzer, V.: Eliciting single-peaked preferences using comparison queries. In: Proc. AAMAS, pp. 408–415 (2007)
9. Dasgupta, P., Hashimoto, Y.: Multi-attribute Dynamic Pricing for Online Markets using Intelligent Agents. In: Proc. AAMAS, pp. 277–284 (2004)
10. DiMicco, J.M., Greenwald, A., Maes, P.: Dynamic Pricing Strategies under a Finite Time Horizon. In: Proc. ACM-EC, pp. 95–104 (2001)
11. Greenwald, A., Kephart, J.: Probabilistic Pricebots. In: Proc. of the 5th International Conference on Autonomous Agents, pp. 560–567 (2001)
12. Guruswami, V., Hartline, J., Karlin, A., Kempe, D., Kenyon, C.: On profit-maximizing envy-free pricing. In: Proc. 16th annual ACM-SIAM Symposium on Discrete Algorithms, pp. 1164–1173 (2005)
13. Keeney, R., Raiffa, H.: Decisions with Multiple Objectives. Cambridge University Press, Cambridge (1993)
14. Kephart, J., Hanson, J., Greenwald, A.: Dynamic pricing by software agents. Computer Networks 32(6), 731–752 (2000)
15. Lahaie, S., Parkes, D.: Applying learning algorithms to preference elicitation. In: Proc. of the ACM Conference on Electronic Commerce, pp. 180–188 (2004)
16. Li, N., Zhang, P.: Consumer Online Shopping Attitudes and Behavior: An Assessment of Research. In: 8th Americas Conference on Information Systems (2002)
17. Shardanand, U., Maes, P.: Social Information Filtering: Algorithms for Automating "Word of Mouth". In: Proc. ACM Conference on Human Factors in Computing Systems, pp. 210–217 (1995)
18. Wei, Y.: Future Orientation, Chronological Age and Product Attributes Preference. PhD Thesis, Georgia State University (2007)
19. Wang, T., Boutilier, C.: Incremental utility elicitation with the minimax regret decision criterion. In: Proc. IJCAI 2003, pp. 309–316 (2003)

On the Economic Effects of Competition between Double Auction Markets

Kai Cai[1], Jinzhong Niu[1], and Simon Parsons[1,2]

[1] Department of Computer Science, Graduate Center
City University of New York, 365, 5th Avenue
New York, NY 10016, USA
{kcai,jniu}@gc.cuny.edu
[2] Department of Computer and Information Science
Brooklyn College, City University of New York
2900 Bedford Avenue, Brooklyn, NY 11210, USA
parsons@sci.brooklyn.cuny.edu

Abstract. Real market institutions, stock and commodity exchanges for example, do not occur in isolation. The same stocks and commodities may be listed on multiple exchanges, and traders who want to deal in those goods have a choice of markets in which to trade. While there has been extensive research into agent-based trading in individual markets, there is little work on this kind of multiple market scenario. Our work seeks to address this imbalance. In particular, this paper examines how allocative efficiency, the standard measure of a market's ability to extract surplus, is affected by the presence of multiple markets for the same good. We find that while dividing traders between several small markets typically leads to lower efficiency than grouping them into one large market, the movement of traders between markets, and price incentives for changing markets, can reduce this loss of efficiency.

1 Introduction

An *auction*, according to [7], is a market mechanism in which messages from traders include some price information — this information may be an offer to buy at a given price, in the case of a *bid*, or an offer to sell at a given price, in the case of an *ask* — and which gives priority to higher bids and lower asks. The rules of an auction determine, on the basis of the offers that have been made, the allocation of goods and money between traders. When well designed [11], auctions achieve desired economic outcomes like high *allocative efficiency* whilst being easy to implement. Auctions have been widely used in solving real-world resource allocation problems [12], and in structuring stock or futures exchanges [7].

There are many different kinds of auction. One of the most widely used kinds is the *double auction* (DA), in which both buyers and sellers are allowed to exchange offers simultaneously. Since double auctions allow dynamic pricing on both the supply side and the demand side of the marketplace, their study is of great importance, both to theoretical economists, and those seeking to implement real-world market places. The *continuous double auction* (CDA) is a DA in which traders make deals continuously

W. Ketter et al. (Eds.): AMEC/TADA 2008, LNBIP 44, pp. 88–102, 2010.
© Springer-Verlag Berlin Heidelberg 2010

throughout the auction. The CDA is one of the most common exchange institutions, and is in fact the primary institution for trading of equities, commodities and derivatives in markets such as the New York Stock Exchange (NYSE) and Chicago Mercantile Exchange (CME). Another common kind of double auction market is the *clearing-house* (CH) in which the market clears at a pre-specified time, allowing all traders to place offers before any matches are found. The CH is used, for example, to set stock prices at the beginning of trading on some exchange markets.

Our focus in this paper is on the behavior of multiple auctions for the same good. This interest is motivated by the fact that such situations occur in the real world. For example, company stock is frequently listed on several stock exchanges. Indian companies can be listed on both the National Stock Exchange (NSE) and the Bombay Stock Exchange (BSE) [21]. US companies may be listed on both the NYSE, NASDAQ and, in the case of larger firms, non-US markets like the London Stock Exchange (LSE). Other examples of multiple markets for the same good are the various commodity exchanges, prediction markets such as [1,6], and internet auctions, though the latter are not typically structured as double auctions.

The interactions between related markets can be complex, as when the NSE opened and proceeded to claim much of the trade volume from the established BSE [21], or when unfulfilled orders on the CME overflowed onto the NYSE during the global stock market crash of 1987 [13]. This kind of interaction between markets has not been widely studied, especially in the context of automated traders. Our work addresses exactly this issue.

2 Background

Double auctions have been extensively studied using both human traders and computerized agents. Starting in 1955, Smith carried out numerous experiments investigating the behavior of such markets, documented in papers such as [22,23]. The experiments in [22], for example, involved human traders and showed that even with limited information available, and only a few participants, the CDA can achieve very high efficiency, comes close to the theoretical equilibrium, and responds rapidly to changing market conditions. This result was in contrast to classical theory, which suggested that high efficiency would require a very large number of traders, and led some to suggest that the form of the market itself was sufficient to ensure efficiency. In other words, Smith's results led to the suggestion that double auction markets are bound to lead to efficiency irrespective of the way that traders behave. Gode and Sunder [9] tested this hypothesis, introducing two automated trading strategies which they dubbed *zero intelligence without constraint* (ZI-U) and *zero intelligence with constraint* (ZI-C). ZI-U traders make offers at random, while ZI-C traders make offers at random, but are constrained so as to ensure that traders do not make a loss (it is easy to see that ZI-U traders can make a loss, and so can lead to low efficiency markets). In the experiments reported in [9], the ZI-C traders gained high efficiency and came close enough to the performance of human traders for Gode and Sunder to claim that trader intelligence is not necessary for the market to achieve high efficiency and that only the constraint on not making a loss is important.

This position was attacked by Cliff [4], who showed that if supply and demand are asymmetric, the average transaction prices of ZI-C traders can vary significantly from the theoretical equilibrium. Cliff then introduced the *zero intelligence plus* (ZIP) trader, which uses a simple machine learning technique to decide what offers to make based on previous offers and the trades that have taken place. ZIP traders outperform ZI-C traders, achieving both higher efficiency and approaching equilibrium more closely across a wider range of market conditions (though [4][page 60] suggests conditions under which ZIP will fail to attain equilibrium), prompting Cliff to suggest that ZIP traders embodied the minimal intelligence required. A range of other trading algorithms have been proposed — including those that took part in the Santa Fe double auction tournament [19], the reinforcement learning *Roth-Erev* approach (RE) [18] and the expected-profit maximizing *Gjerstad-Dickhaut* approach (GD) [8] — and the performance of these algorithms evaluated under various market conditions.

This work on trading strategies is only one facet of the research on auctions. Gode and Sunder's results suggest that the structure of the auction mechanisms plays an important role in determining the outcome of an auction, and this is further borne out by the work of [26] (which also points out that results hinge on both auction design and the mix of trading strategies used). For example, if an auction is *strategy-proof*, traders need not bother to conceal their private values and in such auctions complex trading agents are not required.

As mentioned above, there has been little work on multiple market scenarios. We have presented some initial results on the dynamics of auctions that compete for traders [15] and the design of such auctions is the focus of the TAC Market Design competitions. This paper is a further contribution in the same direction, considering the impact of multiple markets on the efficiency of trading.

3   Experimental Setup

3.1   Software

To experiment with multiple markets, we used the Java-based server platform JCAT [10]. JCAT provides the ability to run multiple double auction markets populated by traders that use a variety of trading strategies, and was used to support the 2007 and 2008 TAC Market Design competition [3,16]. Auctions in JCAT follow the usual pattern for work on automated trading agents, running for a number of trading *days*, with each day being broken up into a series of *rounds*. A round is an opportunity for agents to make offers (shouts) to buy or sell, and we distinguish different days because at the beginning of a day, agents have their inventories replenished. As a result, every buyer can buy goods every day, and every seller can sell every day. Days are not identical because agents are aware of what happened on the previous day. Thus it is possible for traders to learn, over the course of several days, the optimal way to trade.

We run a number of JCAT markets simultaneously, allowing traders to move between markets at the start of a day. In practice this means that traders need a decision mechanism that picks which market to trade in. Using this approach, agents are not only learning how best to make offers, which they will have to do anew for each market, but they are also learning which market is best for them. Of course, which market is best will depend partly on the properties of different markets, but also on which other agents are in those markets.

3.2 Traders

Traders in our experiments have two tasks. One is to decide how to make offers. The mechanism they use to do this is their *trading strategy*. The other task is to choose market to make offers in. The mechanism for doing this is their *market selection strategy*. We studied markets in which all the traders used the same trading strategy, and considered three such strategies:

- Gode and Sunder's zero intelligence with constraint (ZI-C) strategy [9];
- A variant of Cliff's zero intelligence plus strategy [4] which we call ZIQ; and
- Roth and Erev's reinforcement learning strategy (RE) [18].

The reason for picking the first of these is that given by [14,25], that since ZI-C is not making bids with any intelligence, any effects we see have to be a result of market structure, rather than a consequence of the trading strategy, and hence will be robust across markets inhabited by different kinds of trader. The reason for picking the ZIP variant and RE is that given by [17]. The first of these strategies is typical of the behavior of automated traders, while the second can be a good model of human bidding behavior (though it does not match human performance in a CDA). Using both will give us results indicative of markets with both human and software traders.

The market selection strategy is based on a simple model for reinforcement learning. Traders treat the choice of market as an n-armed bandit problem that they solve using an ϵ-greedy exploration policy [24]. Using this approach the behavior of the agents is controlled by two parameters ϵ and α. A trader chooses what it estimates to be the best market, in terms of daily trading profit, with probability $1 - \epsilon$, and randomly chooses one of the remaining markets otherwise. ϵ may remain constant or be variable over time, depending upon the value of the parameter α [24]. If α is 1, ϵ remains constant, while if α takes any value in $(0, 1)$, ϵ will reduce over time. For these experiments, we set α to 1, and ϵ to 0.1. The results from or previous work on the interactions between multiple markets [15] suggest that market selection behavior is rather insensitive to the parameters we choose here.

JCAT is typically set up to use the market selection strategy to decide which market each trader should participate in at the start of each day. Since this facility can be disabled, however, we can experiment with two different kinds of trader movement:

- Mobile: traders choose a market at the start of each day (this may be the same market in which the traders participated the previous day).
- Stationary: traders always remain in the same market.

Each trader is permitted to buy or sell at most five units of goods per day, and each trader has a private value for these goods, a value which is drawn from a uniform distribution between \$50 and \$150. A given trader is assumed to have the same private value for all goods that it trades throughout the entire experiment.

3.3 Markets

All of our experiments consider five markets which we refer to as $M0$, $M1$, $M2$, $M3$ and $M4$. While JCAT allows markets to charge traders in a variety of ways, we used just four kinds of charge in the work reported here:

- Shout fees, charges made by the market for each shout made by a trader.
- Information fees, charges made by the market for information about shouts made by other traders in the market.
- Transaction fees, charges made by the market for each transaction executed by a trader.
- Profit fees, charges made by the market on the bid/ask spread of any transactions they execute.[1].

We set shout, information and transaction fees to constant, low, figures — $0.1, $2 and $0.1 respectively. These are values typical of those adopted by entrants in the 2007 TAC Market Design Competition, and, as [16] discusses, are sufficient to provide a small negative reinforcement that encourages traders to leave markets in which they are not managing to make trades.

We used three different mechanisms for setting the profit fees:

- Fixed: a constant proportion, in this case 10% ($M0$), 20% ($M1$), 30% ($M2$), 40% ($M3$) and 50% ($M4$) of the surplus on a transaction, is taken as a fee.
- Lure-or-learn fast (LL): a version of the ZIP strategy for traders [5] adapted for markets and introduced by [15] under the name "zero intelligence"[2]. A LL market adjusts its charges to be just lower than that of the market that is the most profitable. If it is the most profitable market, it raises its charges slightly. In these experiments, initial charges are the same as for the fixed markets.
- Free: no profit fees are charged.

In all of our experiments the markets are populated by 100 traders, evenly split between buyers and sellers.

3.4 Experiments

Our main aim in this work was to answer the questions "what is the economic effect of running a number of parallel markets?", and "what is the effect of different charging regimes?", so our basic comparisons are between the situation in which all traders transact in a single market, and the situation in which traders are split across a number of markets for different charging mechanisms. We were also interested in the effect of traders moving between markets — the results we published in [15] tell us that traders

---

[1] The name arose since the bid/ask spread is the transaction surplus, and with the $k = 0.5$ rule we usually use for allocating the surplus is thus directly related to the profit realized by both agents.

[2] We found that calling it "zero-intelligence" caused confusion with the trading strategies, and the current name is inspired by WOLF [2].

move between markets due to the charges imposed by markets, but it does not say anything about the effect of that movement on the overall performance of the markets in economic terms.

These considerations led us to compare the performance of the single market, and the multiple markets in different scenarios. We considered six different scenarios — one scenario for each combination of charging mechanism (fixed, LL and free) and traders that are either mobile or stationary. For a given trading strategy, we considered all six of these scenarios for both CH and CDA exchanges.

Thus we ran a total of 36 experiments, six scenarios for the two different kinds of market and the three different kind of trading strategy. For each experiment we obtained results for both traders split across five markets and all the traders concentrated in one market. Each of these 36 experiments was run for 400 trading days, with each day being split into 50 0.5-second-long rounds. We repeated each experiment 50 times.

3.5   Measurements

The effectiveness of a market can be measured in a number of different ways. *Allocative efficiency*, E_a, is used to measure how good a market is at extracting possible profits. The *actual overall profit*, P_a, of an auction is:

$$P_a = \sum_i |v_i - p_i| \tag{1}$$

for all agents who trade, where p_i is the price of a trade made by agent i and v_i is the private value of agent i. The *equilibrium profit*, P_e, is:

$$P_e = \sum_i |v_i - p_0| \tag{2}$$

for all buyers whose private value is no less than the equilibrium price, p_0, and all sellers whose private value is no greater than p_0. The equilibrium price is the price at which supply and demand curves cross, and can be computed from the private values of the traders assuming that no trader makes a loss. E_a, is then P_a/P_e expressed as a percentage. This tells us how close a market is to theoretical equilibrium in terms of profits made. However, it says nothing about how close a market is to trading at the equilibrium price. For the latter we use the *coefficient of convergence* α, introduced by Smith [22]. α actually measures the deviation of transaction prices from the equilibrium price:

$$\alpha = \frac{\sqrt{\frac{1}{n} \sum_i (p_i - p_0)^2}}{p_0} \times 100 \tag{3}$$

For the multiple market experiments, we measure the efficiencies and convergence of each individual market, but also what we call the *global* values which assess the measurements across all the parallel markets. Global efficiency E_a^g is computed as:

$$E_a^g = \frac{\sum_j \sum_i |v_i^j - p_i^j|}{\sum_j \sum_i |v_i^j - p_0|} \tag{4}$$

where v_i^j is the private value of agent i in market j, p_i^j is the price paid by agent i in market j, and p_0 is the equilibrium price that would hold were all the traders in a single market. Thus the equilibrium profit term is the equilibrium profit for all the traders together in the same market, while the actual profit is the sum of the actual profits made in each individual market. The global value of α is computed similarly, using the transaction prices that are obtained in each of the individual markets and the equilibrium price from one large market that contains all the traders. These global values give us some idea how closely the set of markets approaches the performance of one large market containing all the traders.

4   Results

Figure 1, which summarizes the results of the experiment that places mobile ZIQ traders in CH markets that adjust their profit charges using the LL mechanism, show the typical way that markets change over time. All the other experiments have very similar results, and the results parallel those we reported in [15].

Figure 1 (a) shows the number of traders leaving each of the five markets at the end of each day. The lines plotting these numbers for each of the markets are superimposed over each other since the performances of the markets in this regard are indistinguishable. Over the first 50 days, the amount of "churn" falls steadily and eventually the movement between markets stabilizes and settles to a constant value. However, because the market selection strategy always keeps exploring, on average each market still has two traders leave each day. (On average, the same number of traders also enter).

This movement of traders necessarily has a effect on the trading that takes place in each of the markets. Whereas we would expect a single market to rapidly approach equilibrium after just a few days at most, in the multiple market case, this does not happen. Figure 1(b), which plots the *change* in equilibrium price in each market (to be

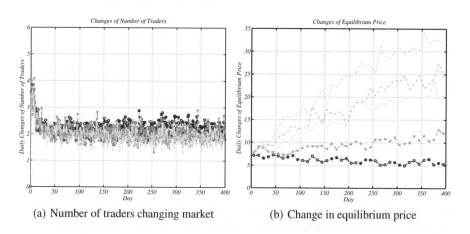

(a) Number of traders changing market   (b) Change in equilibrium price

Fig. 1. How individual markets change over time. Mobile ZIP traders in CH markets that use LL to set charges on trader profits. The values for change in equilibrium price are 10-day averages.

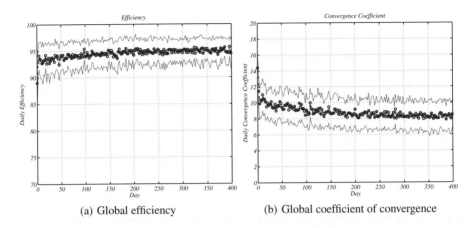

(a) Global efficiency   (b) Global coefficient of convergence

Fig. 2. How individual markets change over time. Mobile ZIP traders in CH markets that use LL to set charges on trader profits. The plots show average value and standard deviation.

precise, it plots the ten-day moving average — there is a lot of variation from day to day and the trends are much clearer in these smoothed plots), is testimony to the way that that the markets don't have a settled equilibrium. Every market has a non-zero daily change, even at the end of the 400 days of the experiment. However, we do see a certain level of stability emerge — by the end of 400 days, there is a clear separation between the change seen in the different markets, and for several of the markets this has settled towards a relatively stable value over the last 100 days.

In case these results suggest that there is no overall pattern, consider Figure 2. This plots the global values of efficiency and the coefficient of convergence for the same experiment as in Figure 1. As described above, global efficiency is computed by summing actual trader profits and then dividing by the theoretical profit that would be made *if all the traders were in the same market*. It thus gives us a picture of our set of markets taken as a whole, and shows that, despite the churn, the overall picture has settled down after around 200 days.

Having sketched the overall behavior of the markets in our experiments, the main results of this paper are given in Tables 1–3. These give, for each of the experiments outlined above, the efficiencies of markets M0 to M4, the global efficiency, and the efficiency of a single market containing all the traders. This latter differs from the global measure in that the actual trader profits are obtained in the single market rather than in the individual markets (while the theoretical profit is the same in both cases). The values of the efficiency given is averaged over the last 100 days of each experiment as well as across the 50 runs of each experiment.

The first point to make is that, just as one would expect from usual theoretical analysis, say [20], the efficiency of the single market of 100 traders is greater than the global efficiency (though there is an exception). Not only is this in agreement with the theory, but it is not surprising. The theoretical profit is the same in both cases, so for the global efficiency to be higher, the individual markets would have to do a better job of matching

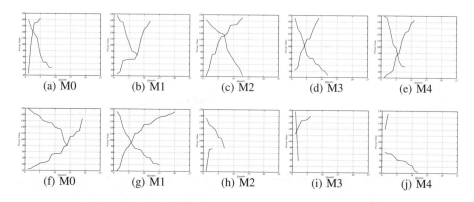

Fig. 3. Typical final day supply and demand curves for the fixed charging CDA markets (a)–(e) with stationary traders and (f)–(j) with mobile traders

traders than the single market. Clearly the churn will make any optimal matching hard to sustain even if it occurs in the first place.

Some other interesting points emerge. First, looking just at the global values, we see that across all three trading strategies, markets with mobile traders are more efficient than markets with stationary traders. It therefore seems to be the case that trader mobility leads to higher efficiency. Traders that move to maximize their own expected profit, which is the effect of the market selection strategy we use, end up improving the performance of the markets as a whole. Second, again across all three trading strategies, the best performing (in terms of efficiency) individual markets with mobile traders that make charges on profits, outperform any of the corresponding individual markets that do not charge[3]. Thus, not only does it seem that mobility leads to higher efficiency, but it also seems that charging does.

Third, the effect of charging is strong enough that with ZIQ and RE traders (the ones that might be considered more rational because they pick offers that aim to maximize their profits) these best performing individual markets do so well that they lift the global performance of the charging markets with mobile traders above that of the markets that don't charge. (This despite the fact that the higher charging individual markets have considerably lower efficiencies than the markets that do not charge). Thus, not only do individual markets benefit from the charges, but it seems that *overall* the markets benefit — they certainly manage to extract more total profits that way.

5   Discussion

An explanation for the effects that we see is provided by Figure 3. This compares one typical set of supply and demand curves for the final trading day of five parallel CDA markets, all of which charge. The difference between the two sets is that in

---

[3] In other words, M0 under fixed and LL charging has greater efficiency than any of the markets which are free.

Table 1. Market allocative efficiency for ZIC traders in single-market and multiple-market scenarios

			multiple markets					single market
			M0	M1	M2	M3	M4	global	
CDA	Mobile	Fixed	87.14	80.67	71.47	65.90	64.99	85.45	⋆**88.86**
			11.96	*20.07*	*27.04*	*29.85*	*30.99*	*3.49*	*2.05*
		LL	87.15	80.88	78.36	66.25	60.49	85.54	⋆**87.58**
			12.17	*20.65*	*22.89*	*30.09*	*32.26*	*3.31*	*2.35*
		Free	78.80	76.37	78.27	79.36	78.24	85.66	⋆**88.92**
			22.46	*25.48*	*22.41*	*22.22*	*23.31*	*3.03*	*2.01*
	Stationary	Fixed	83.10	82.71	83.59	82.91	83.86	77.02	⋆**88.86**
			11.11	*9.19*	*9.19*	*8.25*	*8.40*	*5.80*	*2.05*
		LL	82.38	84.70	81.65	80.51	81.51	77.18	⋆**87.58**
			10.63	*10.42*	*12.08*	*13.49*	*14.91*	*6.05*	*2.35*
		Free	81.20	81.83	81.65	80.58	81.20	77.25	⋆**88.92**
			11.05	*10.86*	*12.48*	*11.29*	*12.55*	*5.37*	*2.01*
CH	Mobile	Fixed	***84.99***	75.05	69.12	57.41	55.83	81.16	⋆**81.99**
			20.01	*24.85*	*30.87*	*30.87*	*31.30*	*3.20*	*2.99*
		LL	***87.41***	79.55	69.29	60.43	57.81	⋆**83.52**	81.30
			7.17	*16.02*	*25.13*	*29.86*	*30.89*	*2.94*	*2.63*
		Free	74.58	76.38	71.83	72.94	77.90	83.72	⋆**83.89**
			24.73	*22.10*	*24.96*	*25.31*	*21.37*	*3.14*	*2.76*
	Stationary	Fixed	86.40	86.26	85.56	86.74	***87.67***	77.80	⋆**81.99**
			8.47	*8.85*	*7.63*	*8.72*	*8.72*	*5.11*	*2.99*
		LL	79.78	81.08	***81.72***	78.62	77.69	76.09	⋆**81.30**
			9.50	*9.95*	*7.99*	*12.24*	*13.73*	*5.13*	*2.63*
		Free	79.35	80.77	82.46	80.32	81.29	76.86	⋆**83.89**
			11.82	*10.48*	*9.11*	*10.12*	*11.86*	*4.66*	*2.76*

Italic numbers are standard deviations, **bold** numbers indicate the better of the global and single market values, ***bold italic*** identifies the largest value on each line, and ⋆ denotes that where these comparisons are significant at the 95% level. The charges on profit rise linearly from M0 (10%) to M4 (50%). In the case of the LL markets, these are the figures from which charges start.

Note that in a single market it makes no sense for traders to move since there is no market to move to or from. As a result, figures for mobile and stationary traders are the same.

one the traders are allowed to move while in the other the are stationary. Whereas in the markets with stationary traders the numbers of intra-marginal traders (to the left of the intersection between supply and demand curves) and extra-marginal traders (to the right of the intersection) are fairly well balanced, as one would expect of a random allocation of private values, this is not the case in the markets with the mobile traders. In these latter markets the traders have sorted themselves so that market M0 has no extra-marginal buyers, market M2 has no extra-marginal traders at all, M4 has

Table 2. Market allocative efficiency for ZIQ traders in single-market and multiple-market scenarios

			multiple markets						single market
			M0	M1	M2	M3	M4	global	
CDA	Mobile	Fixed	97.06	96.24	96.11	94.60	93.24	94.53	*__97.93__
			5.59	*7.54*	*7.76*	*11.84*	*14.38*	*2.59*	*1.27*
		LL	96.79	96.91	96.63	94.43	93.49	94.51	*__98.55__
			7.15	*5.34*	*5.74*	*12.68*	*14.30*	*2.62*	*1.04*
		Free	96.04	96.39	96.17	95.88	95.63	94.22	*__99.49__
			8.19	*6.80*	*7.34*	*8.26*	*9.18*	*2.63*	*0.47*
	Stationary	Fixed	97.47	97.86	97.46	***98.05***	96.98	91.14	*__97.93__
			3.03	*3.23*	*3.34*	*4.96*	*4.16*	*4.16*	*1.27*
		LL	97.66	97.85	97.80	97.97	97.87	90.37	*__98.55__
			2.96	*2.72*	*2.76*	*3.25*	*2.65*	*4.15*	*1.04*
		Free	97.27	97.59	97.60	97.55	97.54	89.62	*__99.49__
			4.11	*3.75*	*3.49*	*4.57*	*4.16*	*5.10*	*0.47*
CH	Mobile	Fixed	98.85	98.53	97.52	96.38	95.09	96.62	*__99.74__
			4.74	*8.25*	*11.25*	*13.75*	*13.75*	*2.10*	*0.52*
		LL	98.56	97.89	96.88	96.65	94.17	96.74	*__99.68__
			4.71	*7.50*	*10.07*	*10.86*	*16.45*	*2.34*	*0.49*
		Free	97.96	97.79	98.41	98.24	98.17	96.91	*__99.75__
			6.77	*7.62*	*4.60*	*5.02*	*5.98*	*2.06*	*0.49*
	Stationary	Fixed	99.04	99.01	99.36	99.22	99.01	90.54	*__99.74__
			3.45	*2.06*	*3.40*	*3.96*	*4.98*	*4.98*	*0.52*
		LL	99.35	99.16	99.21	99.32	99.03	92.50	*__99.68__
			1.79	*2.82*	*2.67*	*2.04*	*4.11*	*4.19*	*0.49*
		Free	99.29	98.56	99.06	99.06	99.19	91.34	*__99.75__
			2.55	*5.66*	*3.35*	*2.97*	*2.91*	*4.76*	*0.49*

Italic numbers are standard deviations, **bold** numbers indicate the better of the global and single market values, ***bold italic*** identifies the largest value on each line, and ⋆ denotes that where these comparisons are significant at the 95% level. The charges on profit rise linearly from M0 (10%) to M4 (50%). In the case of the LL markets, these are the figures from which charges start.

Note that in a single market it makes no sense for traders to move since there is no market to move to or from. As a result, figures for mobile and stationary traders are the same.

no intra-marginal traders, and M3 has virtually no intra-marginal traders. Since, as [27] points out, the reason that CDA markets lose efficiency is because of extra-marginal traders "stealing" transactions from intra-marginal traders (who for a given transaction will, by definition, generate a larger profit), the segregation that we observe will lead to increased efficiency. In addition, as we observed in [16], charges have the effect of prodding traders that aren't making profits — and so are not adding to the efficiency

Table 3. Market allocative efficiency for RE traders in single-market and multiple-market scenarios

			multiple markets						single market
			M0	M1	M2	M3	M4	global	
CDA	Mobile	Fixed	*89.89*	88.62	79.54	68.81	68.57	85.79	★**89.14**
			9.29	*29.06*	*39.19*	*40.06*	*3.07*	*3.07*	*1.68*
		LL	*89.94*	89.20	79.69	70.43	66.90	86.55	★**87.39**
			2.93	*8.41*	*29.40*	*38.49*	*41.10*	*3.21*	*2.46*
		Free	86.97	87.29	85.85	85.37	84.93	85.59	★**89.37**
			14.74	*12.08*	*17.89*	*18.11*	*18.58*	*3.00*	*1.69*
	Stationary	Fixed	88.47	*89.79*	88.17	88.26	89.40	82.07	★**89.14**
			4.85	*4.80*	*5.33*	*4.70*	*4.92*	*4.92*	*1.68*
		LL	87.75	87.62	87.12	86.97	*88.09*	81.42	★**87.39**
			5.53	*7.25*	*6.74*	*5.66*	*5.49*	*5.49*	*2.46*
		Free	88.64	*89.53*	87.93	88.74	87.72	81.15	★**89.37**
			5.94	*5.18*	*5.65*	*4.98*	*5.59*	*5.26*	*1.69*
CH	Mobile	Fixed	99.01	97.73	94.52	89.83	87.90	95.90	★***99.33***
			5.30	*15.90*	*24.81*	*27.67*	*27.67*	*2.94*	*0.86*
		LL	98.86	97.71	95.74	92.48	87.57	95.83	★***99.42***
			2.30	*6.76*	*12.84*	*20.95*	*28.84*	*3.28*	*0.78*
		Free	97.18	97.87	97.41	97.23	97.27	95.51	★***99.20***
			6.28	*8.34*	*8.84*	*8.54*	*8.54*	*2.90*	*0.92*
	Stationary	Fixed	98.46	98.51	98.50	98.56	98.89	91.99	★***99.33***
			2.79	*2.73*	*2.62*	*2.41*	*4.60*	*4.60*	*0.86*
		LL	98.65	98.66	98.58	98.81	98.84	88.13	★***99.42***
			2.49	*2.36*	*2.57*	*2.48*	*2.13*	*6.42*	*0.78*
		Free	98.44	98.66	98.73	98.65	98.59	89.48	★***99.20***
			2.58	*2.30*	*2.52*	*2.86*	*5.59*	*5.59*	*0.92*

Italic numbers are standard deviations, **bold** numbers indicate the better of the global and single market values, ***bold italic*** identifies the largest value on each line, and ★ denotes that where these comparisons are significant at the 95% level. The charges on profit rise linearly from M0 (10%) to M4 (50%). In the case of the LL markets, these are the figures from which charges start.

Note that in a single market it makes no sense for traders to move since there is no market to move to or from. As a result, figures for mobile and stationary traders are the same.

of a given market — to try different markets, allowing markets to rid themselves of unproductive traders.

Figure 3 also shows us that the increased efficiency in mobile markets is not purely the result of all traders collecting in the lowest charging market — there are still significant numbers of traders in the higher charging markets. (Subsequent work, which we do not have room to discuss here, provides further evidence that this is the case.)

In CH markets, of course, extra-marginal traders cannot "steal" trades away from intra-marginal traders (at least not if they make rational offers). However, the movement of traders can still increase profits by allowing a trader that is extra-marginal in one market to become intra-marginal in another. Again, this behavior is encouraged by the combination of the market selection strategy and the charges imposed by the markets.

Finally, we should note that the efficiencies of the individual markets and the global efficiencies are rather low compared with those often reported for the trading strategies we use (in contrast the single market values are much the same as one would expect given the random allocation of private values to traders). We attribute this, at least in part, to churn. When a trader moves from one market to another, any learning it underwent in the old market is no use any more, and may even be detrimental. Similarly, the influx of new traders into a market can invalidate the learning previously undertaken by traders that have not moved.

6   Conclusions

The main conclusion of this paper is that while dividing traders into multiple markets leads to a loss of efficiency, this loss is reduced when traders are allowed to move between markets in search of greater profits, and this movement is encouraged by the imposition of fees on the traders. This result holds because the movement of traders between markets serves to segment those markets. Since the movement is profit-driven — traders choose markets with a probability that is proportional to the average profit that they make in those markets — traders migrate towards markets that allow them to make good trades. Overall this increases the total surplus generated by the set of markets, and this in turn increases the global efficiency. The effect is sharpened by the application of fees since fees tend to reduce the profits recorded by traders (the fees charged by a market are counted by the trader as negative profits from trading in the market while not affecting the values used in computing efficiency) and so further discourage agents from remaining in markets that are unprofitable for them.

Our current work extends the investigation reported here. We are examining: the robustness of our results against traders who use different algorithms to do market selection[4]; the effect of different levels of charging on the changes in efficiency that we observe; and the influence of network effects, such as restrictions on the mobility of traders, on the effects that we observe here.

Acknowledgments. This work was partially funded by the National Science Foundation under grant NSF IIS-0329037 *Tools and Techniques for Automated Mechanism Design*, and from the UK EPSRC under grant GR/T10657/01 *Market Based Control of Complex Computational Systems*. The authors are grateful for support from the computational facility at the CUNY Graduate Center.

---

[4] Especially since the n-armed bandit algorithm we use is not particularly effective when payoffs change, as they do here.

References

1. Berg, J., Forsythe, R., Nelson, F., Rietz, T.: Results from a dozen years of election futures markets research. In: Plott, C., Smith, V. (eds.) Handbook of Experimental Economic Results. Elsevier, Amsterdam (2001)
2. Bowling, M., Veloso, M.: Multiagent learning using a variable learning rate. Artificial Intelligence 136, 215–250 (2002)
3. http://www.marketbasedcontrol.com/
4. Cliff, D.: Minimal-intelligence agents for bargaining behaviours in market-based environments. Technical Report HPL-97-91, Hewlett-Packard Research Laboratories (1997)
5. Cliff, D., Bruten, J.: Less than human: Simple adaptive trading agents for CDA markets. Technical Report HP-97-155, Hewlett-Packard Research Laboratories (1997)
6. http://www.ideafutures.com/ and http://www.ideosphere.com/
7. Friedman, D.: The double auction institution: A survey. In: Friedman, D., Rust, J. (eds.) The Double Auction Market: Institutions, Theories and Evidence, pp. 3–25. Perseus Publishing, Cambridge (1993)
8. Gjerstad, S., Dickhaut, J.: Price formation in double auctions. Games and Economic Behavior 22, 1–29 (1998)
9. Gode, D.K., Sunder, S.: Allocative efficiency of markets with zero-intelligence traders: Market as a partial substitute for individual rationality. Journal of Political Economy 101(1), 119–137 (1993)
10. http://jcat.sourceforge.net/
11. Klemperer, P.: How (not) to run auctions: The European 3G telecom auctions. European Economic Review 46, 829–845 (2002)
12. McMillan, J.: Reinventing the Bazaar: A Natural History of Markets. W. W. Norton & Company (2003)
13. Miller, M.H., Hawke, J.D., Malkiel, B., Scholes, M.: Findings of the Committee of Inquiry Examining the Events Surrounding (October 19, 1987); Technical report, Chicago Mercantile Exchange (Spring 1988)
14. Niu, J., Cai, K., Parsons, S., Sklar, E.: Reducing price fluctuation in continuous double auctions through pricing policy and shout improvement. In: Proceedings of the 5th International Conference on Autonomous Agents and Multi-Agent Systems, Hakodate, Japan (2006)
15. Niu, J., Cai, K., Parsons, S., Sklar, E.: Some preliminary results on competition between markets for automated traders. In: Proceedings of the Workshop on Trading Agent Design and Analysis, Vancouver, BC (2007)
16. Niu, J., McBurney, P., Gerding, E., Parsons, S.: Characterizing effective auction mechanisms: Insights from the 2007 tac market design competition. In: Proceedings of the 7th International Conference on Autonomous Agents and Multi-Agent Systems, Estoril, Portugal (2008)
17. Phelps, S., Parsons, S., McBurney, P.: An evolutionary game-theoretic comparison of two double auction markets. In: Faratin, P., Rodríguez-Aguilar, J.A. (eds.) Agent Mediated Electronic Commerce VI: Theories for and Engineering of Distributed Mechanisms and Systems, pp. 101–114. Springer, Heidelberg (2004)
18. Roth, A.E., Erev, I.: Learning in extensive-form games: Experimental data and simple dynamic models in the intermediate term. Games and Economic Behavior 8, 164–212 (1995)
19. Rust, J., Miller, J.H., Palmer, R.: Characterizing effective trading strategies. Journal of Economic Dynamics and Control 18, 61–96 (1994)
20. Rustichini, A., Satterthwaite, M.A., Williams, S.R.: Convergence to efficiency in a simple market with incomplete information. Econometrica 62(5), 1041–1063 (1994)
21. Shah, A., Thomas, S.: David and Goliath: Displacing a primary market. Global Financial Markets 1(1), 14–21 (2000)

22. Smith, V.L.: An experimental study of competitive market behaviour. Journal of Political Economy 70(2), 111–137 (1962)
23. Smith, V.L.: Experimental auction markets and the Walrasian hypothesis. The Journal of Political Economy 73(4), 387–393 (1965)
24. Sutton, R.S., Barto, A.G.: Reinforcement learning: An introduction. MIT Press, Cambridge (1998)
25. Walia, V., Byde, A., Cliff, D.: Evolving market design in zero-intelligence trader markets. Technical Report HPL-2002-290, Hewlett-Packard Research Laboratories, Bristol, England (2003)
26. Walsh, W., Das, R., Tesauro, G., Kephart, J.O.: Analyzing complex strategic interactions in multi-agent systems. In: Proceedings of Workshop on Game-Theoretic and Decision-Theoretic Agents (2002)
27. Zhan, W., Friedman, D.: Markups in double auction markets. Technical report, LEEPS, Department of Economics, University of Santa Cruz (2005)

A Multiagent Recommender System with Task-Based Agent Specialization

Fabiana Lorenzi[1,2], Fabio Arreguy Camargo Correa[1], Ana L.C. Bazzan[1],
Mara Abel[1], and Francesco Ricci[3]

[1] Instituto de Informatica, UFRGS
Caixa Postal 15064, 91.501-970 Porto Alegre, RS, Brazil
faccorrea,bazzan,abel@inf.ufrgs.br
[2] Universidade Luterana do Brasil
Av. Farroupilha, 8001 Canoas, RS, Brazil
lorenzi@ulbra.br
[3] Free University of Bozen-Bolzano
Bolzano, Italy
fricci@unibz.it

Abstract. This paper describes a multiagent recommender system where agents maintain local knowledge bases and, when requested to support a travel planning task, they collaborate exchanging information stored in their local bases. A request for a travel recommendation is decomposed by the system into sub tasks, corresponding to travel services. Agents select tasks autonomously, and accomplish them with the help of the knowledge derived from previous solutions. In the proposed architecture, agents become experts in some task types, and this makes the recommendation generation more efficient. In this paper, we validate the model via simulations where agents collaborate to recommend a travel package to the user. The experiments show that specialization is useful hence providing a validation of the proposed model.

1 Introduction

Internet is a rich source of information where users search information about products and services related to their interests and preferences. However, this has generated new information problems. In fact, the overabundance of information may *overload* the users and ultimately can make very hard to locate the *right* information [9]. Moreover, the information required for a topic or a service (e.g., rent a car) is usually distributed in several repositories.

In order to cope with these issues, Recommender Systems have been proposed [11]. They are based on data mining algorithms, are capable to learn about user preferences over time, and can automatically identify relevant products or information that fit the user needs [1]. Different approaches are used in their core recommendation algorithms, such as collaborative filtering, content-based filtering or knowledge-based approaches [1]. Recommender systems have been applied in several domains [5] such as book recommendation (amazon.com) or

W. Ketter et al. (Eds.): AMEC/TADA 2008, LNBIP 44, pp. 103–116, 2010.
© Springer-Verlag Berlin Heidelberg 2010

movie recommendation (netflix.com). It is worth noting that these web sites can fully support the purchase (or rent) process, they manage huge catalogues of products and they can rely on the user information acquired by direct contact with their customers (logs).

However in some application domains it may be possible that a single information source (web site) does not manage all the information needed to run the full recommendation process. The data available may be fragmented, overspecialized or overgeneralized, or even irrelevant to the recommendation at hand. There are several data sources and services distributed in Internet, which are not always available, and sometimes can they offer information that can be ambiguous or erroneous.

To cope with these problems, we propose the application and integration of two technologies: distributed recommender systems and multiagent technologies. We claim that a multiagent recommender system can be applied for retrieving, filtering and using information that is relevant to the recommendation task, and can better deal with the dynamic changes in the information source compared with more traditional non-distributed recommender systems [2,10].

In the tourism domain, for instance, a travel package recommendation is typically supported by several service providers for flights, hotels and attractions. Moreover, specific knowledge is required to assemble all the components [12]. Usually this information cannot be found in a single repository. The tourism market is by its nature distributed, and several service providers and intermediaries manage and store in their databases (or in informal repositories) service information and users data [17]. In order to recommend a travel package, an intermediary (travel agent) must construct a model representing all the elements (information) required for generating this recommendation. This model can be implicitly defined in her mind, or explicitly documented in a formal plan in the travel agency. These elements would include resources (information, products or services), customers and their requirements, factors influencing the recommendation (such as the season), immediate strategies for finding the best options for the user, and so on. However, planning a travel and building a package is not performed by an intermediary alone. Collaboration among travel agents is required to integrate individual experiences into a coherent plan that satisfies user's preferences.

The main goal of a Multiagent Recommender System is therefore to implement this cooperation among the agents. Each agent should work as an expert and participate to the composition of the final recommendation. This work presents a distributed, and knowledge-based, recommender system implemented in a multiagent environment. The recommendation computation (travel package) is based on the collaboration of multiple agents exchanging information stored in their local knowledge bases. A recommendation request is decomposed into sub-tasks handled by different agents, each one maintaining its own knowledge base and working as an expert helping to compose the final recommendation. The proposed model supports agent specialization, i.e., the agents become experts in specific tasks. This agent specialization mimics what happens in the real world, where it is common for travel agents to specialize in a particular kind of service (hotel, flights, interchanges, conferences, etc) in order to provide better and better advises to the customers. Specialization increases agent's confidence and improves quality of service. We want to replicate this in our multiagent scenario, and generate expert agents by letting them to specialize.

This paper is structured as follow: the next section discusses some related work on Multiagent Recommender Systems and Recommender Systems. Section 3 describes the multiagent recommender model and Section 4 presents the experiments we conducted. Finally section 5 summarizes the paper's contributions.

2   Related Work

Our approach explores the ability of multiagent systems to decompose a complex recommendation problem into smaller ones. This allows specific knowledge to be applied in solving each subproblem and updated when changes occur in the domain. The baseline technologies applied in our research are introduced in this section.

2.1   Recommender Systems

As mentioned above the three major recommendation techniques are: collaborative filtering, content-based filtering and knowledge-based systems. The most popular technique is collaborative filtering that aggregates customer's preferences, expressed as product ratings, to recommend new products [11]. In collaborative filtering the system predicts the target user ratings and select the products with highest rating. However, a large number of ratings from similar users are required to build reliable recommendations for a target user. This is hard to achieve and "data sparsity" is the primary source of erroneous recommendations.

Amazon.com is a very popular e-Commerce site that exploits collaborative-filtering. In its book section for instance, the system encourages direct feedback from customers about books that they have already read [13]. After this, the customer may request recommendation for books that he/she might like.

In content-based filtering the preferences of a specific customer are exploited to build new recommendations to her. NewsDude [4], for instance, observes what online news stories the user has read and not read and learns which articles the user may be interested in reading. In content-based systems only data related to the current user are exploited in building a recommendation. It requires a description of user interests that either matches the items' catalog or provides an input for the user model that was learned in order to output a recommendation.

Collaborative and content-based filtering can deliver poor recommendations if not trained with an adequate number of examples (product ratings or pattern of user preferences). This limitation mostly motivates the knowledge-based approach. A knowledge-based system learns about user preferences over time and automatically suggests products that fit the user model. This technique tries to better use preexisting knowledge, which is specific to the application domain, in order to build a more accurate prediction model still based on a limited number of training instances.

Usually knowledge-based approaches, such as case-based reasoning [14,6], are combined with collaborative or content-based filtering to provide better recommendations. Knowledge about customers and the application domain are used to reason about the products that fit the customer's preferences. The most important advantage of the combined approach is that it does not depend (exclusively) on customer's rates, hence avoiding the mentioned difficulty to bootstrapping the system. The knowledge that improves the recommendation can be expressed as a detailed user model; a model of the selection process or a description of the items that will be suggested.

Travel recommendation is a complex task and there are still many open issues. In this paper we are mostly focussed on the integration of different information sources distributed over the Internet, and to exploit experts' specific knowledge in the recommendation. In order to deal with these issues, we propose a multi-agent recommender system.

2.2   Multiagent Recommender Systems

Multiagent systems (MAS) can be applied to retrieve, filter and use information relevant to recommendations [16] [8]. MAS can deal with distributed information sources and there are several advantages in developing these systems [15], such as: 1) the information sources may be already distributed, and it would be wasteful to replicate agent information gathering and problem solving capabilities for each user and each application; 2) agents can interact flexibly in new configurations on demand; and 3) the system performance can degrade gracefully when some agents are out of service temporarily.

Classical recommendation technologies can be described as *single agent*, as one single intelligent system provides the recommendation function [10]. In a multiagent recommender system a collection of interacting agents manage the recommendation generation process, trying to improve the recommendation quality obtained by a single agent. The agents cooperate and negotiate in order to satisfy the users, interacting among themselves to complement their partial solutions or even to solve conflicts that may arise.

CASIS [7] is an example of multiagent case-based recommender system [14,6], where the authors proposed a metaphor from swarm intelligence to help the negotiation process among agents. The honey bees' dancing metaphor is applied with case-based reasoning approach to recommend the best travel to the user. The recommendation process works as follows: the user elicits her preferences; the bees visit all cases in the case base and when they find the best case (according to the user's preferences) they dance to that case, recruiting other bees to that case; and the case with the most number of bees dancing for it is the one recommended to the user.

The advantage of this application is that the bees always return some recommendation to the user. Normally, case-based recommender systems use similarity-based retrieval to identify the best cases. The recommendation results depend on the retrieval algorithm (similarity function, similarity threshold, feature weights, etc.) and sometimes the system does not find cases that sufficiently match the probe (problem definition). In a real travel package recommendation, the travel agent always recommend something to the user, even if there is not a travel package that matches the customer's preferences. The travel agent always provides to the customer an answer, as the customer could always switch to another travel agency. Because of this, CASIS always returns some recommendation. However, the main disadvantage of this system is that the case-base is unique and centralized. It is not possible to search information located in other sources.

Another example of multiagent recommender system is presented in [8]. This system arranges meetings for several participants taking into account constraints for personal agendas. In this system, three different agents were proposed: the *personal assistant agent* is the interface between the user and the MAS; the *flight travel agent* is connected to a database of flights; and the *accommodation hotel agent* is responsible to find an accommodation on the cities involved in the meeting. A disadvantage found in this approach is that the problem is not solved dynamically because the recommender system has to collect information from different information gathering agents to model the problem-solving.

3   MAS Recommendation Model

This section describes the proposed Multiagent System (MAS) approach and uses the tourism domain as motivating scenario. Planning a travel is a difficult task even for an expert travel agent. She needs to know many details about the destination chosen by the passenger and many features of the whole trip such as the attractions' details, hotels or flights times and costs. In several cases, this knowledge is distributed among different travel agents, and they must communicate and exchange information to compose the final recommendation.

3.1   The Agents

Using the travel recommendation example, we have created a multiagent system where a community of agents share a common goal (the travel package recommendation) as well as individual goals (the travel components that each one must identify). A community C of agents consists of n Searcher (Src) agents $a_1, a_2, ..., a_n$.

When the user asks for a recommendation, a list of tasks, here restricted to flights, hotels or attractions, is created and communicated to the Src agents. The agents choose a task from the received list and perform it. When a task is performed by an agent, it is marked as *not available*, which means that another agent can perform that task at the same time.

The Src agent is represented by $a = (P, LocalKB)$ where P is the agent's profile and $LocalKB$ is the agent knowledge base.

The agent's profile is defined as $P = (id, status, tcurrent, confind)$; id is the identification id of the agent, $status$ indicates if the agent is *online, offline* or *not available* to perform a task. The agent can be offline if, for example, the computer is switched off or the network is down. In this case, it will not be able to perform a task. When the agent is performing a task its status becomes *not available*. $tcurrent$ is the current chosen task and *confind* are the confidence indexes of the agent to each type of task.

Each confidence index is calculated through the number of tasks performed of the respective type and the evaluation of each task done by the user. Each task solved by an agent receives an evaluation from the user, with a rating ranging from 0 to 10, where 0 is the worst and 10 is the best rating. The task evaluation is then used in the agent confidence index computation so that the agent increases more the confidence when it solved better the task.

Two features are desired when addressing the set of evaluations: quality and uniformity. The first one is quite obvious, the goal is to give the best recommendation to obtain a high evaluation. The second one relates to the evaluations homogeneity. Here, the lower the variability of evaluations the more reliable will be the results. Thus, we search for a set of evaluations with a high average evaluation and low standard deviation.

$$confind^{(n)}(t) = \frac{confind^{(n-1)}(t) + F^{(n-1)}(t)}{\sum_{i \in T} F^{(n-1)}(i)} \times evaluation \qquad (1)$$

Equation 1 shows the *confind* (confidence indexes) update function of an agent, where t is the task type, T is the set of task types, $confind^{(n)}(t)$ is the new confidence index of task type t, $F^{(n)}(t)$ is the number of tasks of type t performed by the agent in the instant n. Finally, the *evaluation* is defined as follow:

$$evaluation = \begin{cases} \alpha \left(\frac{\mu(t)}{\sum_{j \in T} \mu(j)} \right) & \text{if } \sum_{k \in T} \sigma(k) = 0 \\ \alpha \left(\frac{\mu(t)}{\sum_{j \in T} \mu(j)} \right) + (1 - \alpha) \left(\frac{\frac{1}{\sigma(t)}}{\sum_{k \in T} \frac{1}{\sigma(k)}} \right) & \text{otherwise} \end{cases} \qquad (2)$$

where: $\mu(t)$ is the evaluation average of type task t performed by the agent; $\sigma(t)$ is the evaluation standard deviation of type task t performed by the agent.

In order to get the normalized evaluations average value of the type task t, the value is divided by the sum over all task types evaluations. The standard deviation value is calculated in the same way. Since the formula is a recurrence equation, it was necessary to set initial conditions, such as:

- Each agent has performed one task of each type;
- Each performed task got an evaluation equal to 5 (a neutral rate);
- There is no standard deviation in instant 0, which means that the standard deviation was not considered in instant 0.

The α coefficient determines the relevance of the average and the standard deviation over the confidence indexes. In the experiments, described later, α was set to 0.5. That means that the average and the standard deviation have the same importance in the calculation of the confidence index.

Thus, the confidence index must be proportional to the average and inversely proportional to the standard deviation, which means that we will get best results with a high average evaluation and a low standard deviation. Equation 2 expresses the influence that the tasks evaluations have over the confidence index.

The agent updates the confidence indexes every time it must choose a task to execute. Based on those indexes, it can check which task type, among those available, is better considering. However, sometimes the agent can be forced to choose a task that is not its specialty (for example, a flight recommendation is required but the flight expert is missing and only the (agent) expert in hotels is available).

This behavior helps the agent to become an expert in a task type. The agent specialization improves the system performance. If the agent has enough information about a task type in its knowledge base, it can provide a faster recommendation for that kind of service. But more importantly, it gives, in the long run, high quality recommendations because the agent becomes an expert in that type of recommendations.

LocalKB stores the knowledge the agent has already used to solve previous recommendations. Figure 1 shows the agent's model. The user's preferences and the list of tasks (appearing inside the box) do not belong to the agent, but they are needed to understand the agent's LocalKB. *Id* is the task's identification. *type* is the task's type (flight, hotel or attractions) and *timespent* represents the time spent by the agent to perform the task. *requirements* represent the user's preferences, i.e., the user's query. *Solution* represents the task already performed by the agent. The combination of the *requirements* and the *solution* attributes represents a case, i.e., the description of the problem and the description of the solution, respectively.

The agent's knowledge base is increased with the number of tasks it decides to save. The bigger the knowledge base becomes, the worse becomes the search performance. On the other hand, a small knowledge base forces the agent to search in the community or in the Web, which results in a waste of time and slower performance. For this reason, it is important for the agent to control

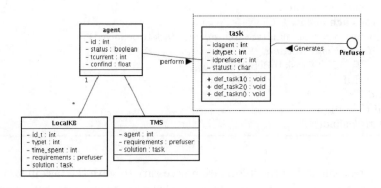

Fig. 1. Agent's model

the size of its knowledge base. It must have enough knowledge to give good recommendations. The confidence indexes help to control the knowledge base size according to the tasks the agent has performed. After performing the task, the agent checks if that task has increased or not its confidence index and it decides to keep or not the task in its knowledge base.

3.2   The Recommendation Algorithm

As shown in the previous subsections, each agent performs a task (of type flight, hotel or attraction) to contribute to the final complete recommendation, i.e., a travel package.

When the user explicit her preferences, the recommendation process starts and the list of tasks is created. Let us now consider a hypothetical scenario where the user has chosen Paris as destination to her vacation; she would like to travel on March 10th, to stay in a three-stars hotel and would like to know the possible attractions in Paris. Three new tasks are created with these preferences.

After that, each agent picks a task (considering its confidence indexes) and turns its status to *not available*. This choice is made in a decentralized manner, where the agent chooses the task it has the highest confidence index. A task can be performed only by one agent which means that two different agents cannot pick the same task. When an agent chooses a task, it chance its status and this task is not available anymore.

Algorithm 1. Multiagent Recommendation

$\{C$ is the agent community$\}$
$\{\mathcal{T}$ is the set of tasks to be solved$\}$
Procedure Recommendation $(agent_x, t, C)$
repeat
   taskToBeSolved = PickTask$(agent_x, t)$
   $\mathcal{T} = \mathcal{T} \setminus \{taskToBeSolved\}$
   Solution = SearchLocalKB(taskToBeSolved)
   if $Solution = \emptyset$ **then**
     for each $agent_x \in C$
     Solution = CommunitySearch$(agent_y$, taskToBeSolved$)$
     if $Solution = \emptyset$ **then**
       $\mathcal{T} = \mathcal{T} \cup \{$ taskToBeSolved $\}$
     end if
   end if
until $(\mathcal{T} \neq \emptyset)$
UpdateConfind()

The agent might find the information necessary to solve the task in two ways: searching in its own knowledge base or exchanging information with agents in the community. As shown in algorithm 1, two levels of information search are proposed.

Through the *SearchLocalKB* procedure, agents search for the information necessary to complete their selected tasks in their own knowledge bases. Each agent has a knowledge base that stores the task episodes already performed by the agent. These episodes are stored as cases with attributes describing the user's preferences (the description of the problem) and attributes describing the task itself (the solution of that recommendation episode).

If the agent does not find the information required to complete the selected task in its knowledge base, then it proceeds with the second type of search, here called *CommunitySearch*. In this stage, the agent communicates with the available agents to exchange information. This communication is important because the agent can find another agent that is expert in the selected task and exchanging information with this expert agent, it will better solve the task. It is important to note that the *CommunitySearch* is not exploited in this paper and it will be detailed in a future work.

4   Experimental Results

In order to validate the multiagent recommender approach in the tourism domain, a preliminary experiment was done, where we have simulated different users asking for different recommendations and 35 users queries were generated. From these queries, 100 new tasks to be performed were created (i.e, the list of tasks was created from these new queries).

The agents were developed in the JADE (Java Agent Development Framework) framework [3]. An acquisition knowledge step was done in a travel agency and the *Src* agents' knowledge bases were populated randomly with real cases of clients of this agency.

Here we assume that, at instant 0, each agent has performed one task for each type and these tasks got an evaluation equal to 5 (a neutral rate). That means that the agent has all confidence indexes with the same value and therefore at the beginning it will choose the task randomly.

Another goal of the experiments was to validate the scalability of the system. For this reason, the experiments were done with different number of available agents. We have calculated the average evaluation of agents in each solved task and we shall show how this value changes during the whole tasks performed by the agents.

We have run the same experiment under two conditions, to show that specializing the agents can be useful. In the first one, the agents confidence indexes were calculated and the agents used these values to select the task to execute. In the second one, the agents did not considered the indexes and they chose the tasks randomly.

Figure 2 shows the average evaluation values for the 54 tasks performed, where 3 agents were available to perform tasks. The average evaluation value of expert agents was high (almost 7) which means a better result comparing to the non-expert agents that reached only 5.

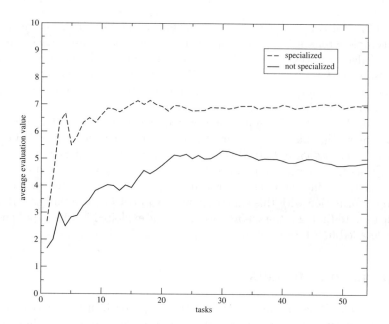

Fig. 2. Average evaluation value - 3 agents (54 tasks)

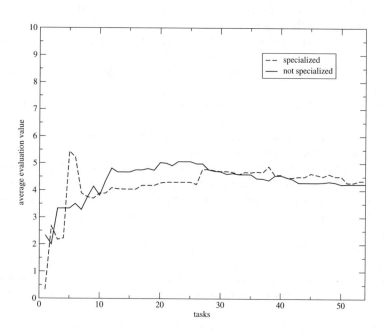

Fig. 3. Average evaluation value - 10 agents (54 tasks)

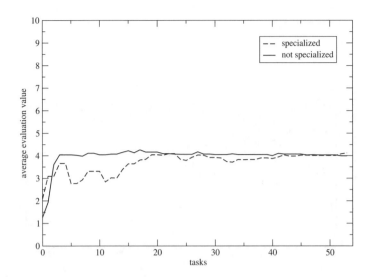

Fig. 4. Average evaluation value - 15 agents (54 tasks)

In the second run, 10 agents were available to perform tasks. Since we have more agents for the same number of tasks, and the same number of task types, the individual performance decreases. The objective was understand how the agents behave if we increase the number of available agents to perform the tasks. Figure 3 shows that, as expected, that increasing the number of agents and keeping the same number of tasks, the average evaluation value is lower for the specialized agents, than the previous scenario (with 3 agents).

Figure 4 confirms the behavior shown in the previous figure. Here we have 15 agents and 54 tasks and the average evaluation value was around 4 for both agents: expert and non-expert. Similarly the results from the previous experiment, as larger the number of agents performing tasks, lower is the average evaluation value.

We also have run a second experiment, where we increased the number of tasks to perform (and kept the same number of types). In this experiment we had 100 tasks to be performed. The same number of agents were used in the experiments: 3, 10, and 15.

Figure 5 shows the average evaluation value of specialized and non-specialized agents, through the 100 tasks performed, with only 3 agents available. Both non-expert and expert agents had unstable average evaluation values in the beginning. However, the expert agents had better results in the end.

In figure 6 we can see the average evaluation value of expert and non-expert agents with 10 agents working. Expert agents got better results than non-expert agents. They reached 4.5 of evaluation average value and the result was stable starting from the thirties task. Considering that we have 10 agents and 100 tasks to be performed, the results of expert agents were good. It was almost the same results got in the experiment with less tasks.

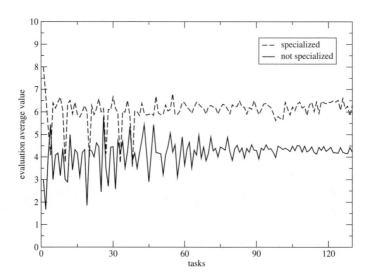

Fig. 5. Average evaluation value - 3 agents (100 tasks)

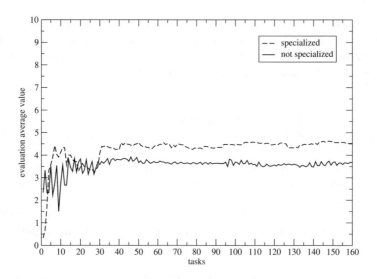

Fig. 6. Average evaluation value - 10 agents (100 tasks)

Figure 7 shows the average evaluation value when we used 15 agents working to solve the tasks. Despite the expert agents started with unstable values, the evaluation average became stable soon and kept the same performance until all the tasks were completed.

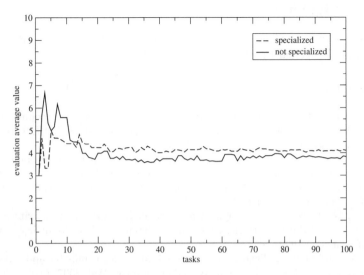

Fig. 7. Average evaluation value - 15 agents (100 tasks)

5   Conclusions

This paper presented a distributed knowledge-based multiagent model applied to the tourism domain. The agents are cooperative and recommend travel packages to the user.

A recommendation is divided in small pieces called tasks and each agent is responsible to perform some tasks not necessarily for the same travel-package request. As long as the agents will perform different tasks, they become experts in a specific task type. The agents become travel agents, where each one have specific knowledge and the cooperation among them can bring good recommendations.

It is important to mention that the tourism domain was chosen to validate the architecture but we believe that the approach can answer the requests of other applications that deal with problems that require the application of a dynamic and distributed knowledge to solve that application tasks. Testing the reusability of the proposal is going to be done in a next phase of this work.

Decomposing the problem and distribute it to several different agents that are becoming more and more specialized can yield good recommendations, even when applied to tourism that is a complex domain that needs specific knowledge distributed over different sources. The agents can be considered experts, i.e., thanks to the confidence indexes that were added in the agent's model in order to help the agent to select the tasks that it is more prepared to attend.

Another interesting point is that the ideas presented here are being validated in a real scenario. A knowledge acquisition phase was conducted and the agents' knowledge bases were created with knowledge from a real travel agency. The queries used in the experiments were obtained from the travel agency as well, which provide a real scene for collecting and understand the requirements of the application.

Acknowledgments

This work is supported by the Brazilian Council of Research - CNPq through the founding Universal Program, Process 475597/2006-0.

References

1. Adomavicius, G., Tuzhilin, A.: Toward the next generation of recommender systems: A survey of the state-of-the-art and possible extensions. IEEE Transactions on Knowledge and Data Engineering 17(6), 734–749 (2005)
2. Balabanovic, M., Shoham, Y.: Fab: Content-based, collaborative recommendation. Communications of the Association for Computing Machinery 40(3), 66–72 (1997)
3. Bellifemine, F., Caire, G., Greenwood, D.: Developing Multi-Agent Systems with JADE. Wiley, Chichester (2007)
4. Billsus, D., Pazzani, M.: A hybrid user model for news story classification. In: Proceedings of the Seventh International Conference on User Modeling, UM 1999, Banff, Canada (1999)
5. Goy, A., Ardissono, L., Petrone, G.: Personalization in e-commerce applications. In: Brusilovsky, P., Kobsa, A., Nejdl, W. (eds.) Adaptive Web 2007. LNCS, vol. 4321, pp. 485–520. Springer, Heidelberg (2007)
6. Lorenzi, F., Ricci, F.: Case-based recommender systems: a unifying view. In: Mobasher, B., Anand, S. (eds.) Intelligent Techniques for Web Personalization, pp. 89–113. Springer, Heidelberg (2005)
7. Lorenzi, F., Santos, D.S., de Oliveira, D., Bazzan, A.L.C.: Task allocation in case-based recommender systems: a swarm intelligence approach. In: Lin, H. (ed.) Architectural Design of Multi-Agent Systems. Information Science Reference, pp. 268–279 (2007)
8. Macho, S., Torrens, M., Faltings, B.: A multi-agent recommender system for planning meetings. In: Workshop on Agent-based recommender systems (2000)
9. Maes, P.: Agents that reduce work and information overload. Commun. ACM 37(7), 30–40 (1994)
10. Montaner, M., López, B., de la Rosa, J.L.: A taxonomy of recommender agents on the internet. Artificial Intelligence Review 19(4), 285–330 (2003)
11. Resnick, P., Iacovou, N., Suchak, M., Bergstrom, P., Riedl, J.: Grouplens: An open architecture for collaborative filtering of netnews. In: Proceedings ACM Conference on Computer-Supported Cooperative Work, pp. 175–186 (1994)
12. Ricci, F.: Travel recommender systems. IEEE Intelligent Systems 17(6), 55–57 (2002)
13. Schafer, J., Konstan, J., Riedl, J.: E-commerce recommendation applications. Data Mining and Knowledge Discovery 5(1/2), 115–153 (2001)
14. Smyth, B.: Case-based recommendation. In: Brusilovsky, P., Kobsa, A., Nejdl, W. (eds.) Adaptive Web 2007. LNCS, vol. 4321, pp. 342–376. Springer, Heidelberg (2007)
15. Sycara, K.: Multiagents systems. AI Magazine 19(2), 79–82 (1998)
16. Wei, Y., Moreau, L., Jennings, N.: Recommender systems: A market-based design. In: Proceedings Second International Joint Conference on Autonomous Agents and Multi Agent Systems (AAMAS 2003), Melbourne, Australia, July 2003, pp. 600–607 (2003)
17. Werthner, H., Ricci, F.: E-commerce and tourism. Commun. ACM 47(12), 101–105 (2004)

Towards Automated Bargaining in Electronic Markets: A Partially Two-Sided Competition Model

Nicola Gatti, Alessandro Lazaric, and Marcello Restelli

Dipartimento di Elettronica e Informazione
Politecnico di Milano
Piazza Leonardo da Vinci 32, I-20133 Milano, Italy
{ngatti,lazaric,restelli}@elet.polimi.it

Abstract. This paper focuses on the prominent issue of automating bargaining agents within electronic markets. Models of bargaining in literature deal with settings wherein there are only two agents and no model satisfactorily captures settings in which there is competition among buyers, being they more than one, and analogously among sellers. In this paper, we extend the principal bargaining protocol, i.e. the alternating-offers protocol, to capture bargaining in markets. The model we propose is such that, in presence of a unique buyer and a unique seller, agents' equilibrium strategies are those in the original protocol. Moreover, we game theoretically study the considered game providing the following results: in presence of one-sided competition (more buyers and one seller or *vice versa*) we provide agents' equilibrium strategies for all the values of the parameters, in presence of two-sided competition (more buyers and more sellers) we provide an algorithm that produce agents' equilibrium strategies for a large set of the parameters and we experimentally evaluate its effectiveness.

1 Introduction

A bargaining situation involves two parties, which can cooperate towards the creation of a commonly desirable surplus, over whose distribution both parties are in conflict [1]. The alternating-offers [2] is considered the main protocol for bilateral negotiations and it has received a lot of attention both in economics to analyze human transactions [3] and in computer science both to automate electronic transactions [4] and to solve dynamic distributed optimizations [5]. The study of bargaining is commonly carried out by employing tools provided by game theory in which one distinguishes the *protocol* from the *strategies*. The protocol sets the negotiation mechanism, whereas the strategies define agents' behavior. Rational agents employ strategies that are in equilibrium.

The alternating-offers protocol is simple: an agent makes an offer; the opponent can accept it or exit or make a counteroffer; if a counteroffer is made, the process is repeated. The utility function of each agent depends on her reservation price, her time discount factor, and her temporal deadline.

W. Ketter et al. (Eds.): AMEC/TADA 2008, LNBIP 44, pp. 117–130, 2010.
© Springer-Verlag Berlin Heidelberg 2010

Although the analysis of bargaining in presence of real-world settings is currently far from being addressed, some recent results are promising for its future employment: multiple issue bargaining can be reduced in polynomial time (in the number of issues) to single issue bargaining [6], the situation wherein agents have uncertain weights over the issues can be solved in polynomial time (in the number of agents' types), and the situation with one-sided uncertain over deadlines can be solved in time asymptotically independent of the number of agent's types [7].

A crucial setting that is not satisfactory studied in literature is the setting where the two bargaining agents act in a market. This setting will be common in real-world electronic markets. Within a market of bargaining agents two aspects coexist: the matching of two opponents (a buyer and a seller) and the negotiation between two matched opponents. Classic models from literature does not effectively capture the matching between two agents, usually assuming that the matching is random [1,3,8]. Moreover, these models make assumptions too restrictive to be employed in real-world applications: all the buyers (sellers) are the same and agents do not have deadlines. The lack of a satisfactory model for bargaining in markets pushes researchers to develop more effective models.

In this paper, we consider a complete information setting where there are more buyers and more sellers with deadlines and agents can be different, i.e. agents' parameters can be different. The original contributions we present in this paper are the followings. (*i*) We provide an extension of the alternating-offers protocol to capture bargaining in markets where agents can choose the opponent with whom negotiating and, once matched, they negotiate as in the original protocol. The proposed model satisfactorily extends the alternating-offers protocol since, in presence of a unique buyer and a unique seller, agents' equilibrium strategies are those in the original protocol. (*ii*) In presence of one-sided competition (when there are one buyer and more sellers or more buyers and one seller) we provide agents' equilibrium strategies for all the values of the parameters. In presence of two-sided competition (more buyers and more sellers) we provide an algorithm that efficiently produces agents' equilibrium strategies for a large set of the parameters and we experimentally evaluate the effectiveness of the proposed algorithm.

The paper is organized as follows. In Section 2 we review the classic alternating-offers protocol presenting the mechanism and agents' equilibrium strategies. In Section 3 we describe our protocol that extends the classic alternating-offers. In Section 4 we study agents' equilibrium strategies. Section 5 concludes the paper.

2   Alternating-Offers Bargaining with Agents' Deadlines

Alternating-offers bargaining is an extensive-form game where a buyer agent **b** and a seller agent **s** try to agree on the value of one or more issues. (In this paper, we consider only single-issue bargaining, since, as showed in [6], with complete information multi-issue bargaining can be casted into single-issue bargaining in polynomial time with respect to the number of issues.) A *player* *function* $\iota : \mathbb{N} \to \{\mathbf{b}, \mathbf{s}\}$ returns the agent that acts at time t and is such that $\iota(t) \neq \iota(t+1)$. At time $t > 0$ the action $\sigma_{\iota(t)}(t)$ of agent $\iota(t)$ can be: (i) *offer*(x), where $x \in \mathbb{R}$; (ii) *exit*; (iii) *accept*. At $t = 0$ agent $\iota(0)$ can make only (i) or (ii). If $\sigma_{\iota(t)}(t) = accept$ the game stops and the *outcome* is the agreement (x, t), where x is the value such that $\sigma_{\iota(t-1)}(t-1) = offer(x)$. If $\sigma_{\iota(t)}(t) = exit$ the game stops and the outcome is *NoAgreement*. Otherwise the bargaining continues to the next time point.

The utility of an agreement (x, t) for agent i is given by a utility function $U_i : (\mathbb{R} \times \mathbb{N}) \cup \{NoAgreement\} \to \mathbb{R}$ that depends on three parameters of agent i: the *reservation price* $RP_i \in \mathbb{R}^+$, the *temporal discount factor* $\delta_i \in (0, 1]$, and the *deadline* $T_i \in \mathbb{N}$, $T_i > 0$. If the outcome of the bargaining is (x, t), then the utility functions $U_{\mathbf{b}}$ and $U_{\mathbf{s}}$ are:

$$U_{\mathbf{b}}(x, t) = \begin{cases} (RP_{\mathbf{b}} - x) \cdot \delta_{\mathbf{b}}^t & \text{if } t \leq T_{\mathbf{b}} \\ -1 & \text{otherwise} \end{cases},$$

$$U_{\mathbf{s}}(x, t) = \begin{cases} (x - RP_{\mathbf{s}}) \cdot \delta_{\mathbf{s}}^t & \text{if } t \leq T_{\mathbf{s}} \\ -1 & \text{otherwise} \end{cases}.$$

If the outcome is *NoAgreement*, then $U_{\mathbf{b}}(NoAgreement) = U_{\mathbf{s}}(NoAgreement) = 0$. Notice that the assignment of a strictly negative value (we have chosen by convention the value -1) to U_i after agent i's deadline allows one to capture the essence of the deadline: an agent, after her deadline, strictly prefers to exit the negotiation rather than to reach any agreement. Finally, we standardly assume the *feasibility* of the problem, i.e. $RP_{\mathbf{b}} \geq RP_{\mathbf{s}}$, and the *rationality* of the agents, i.e. each agent will act to maximize her utility.

With complete information the appropriate solution concept for the game we are dealing with is the *subgame perfect equilibrium* [9]. In subgame perfect equilibrium strategies, agents' strategies are of equilibrium in every possible subgame. Such a solution can be found by *backward induction*. We briefly revise the use of backward induction in this setting; details can be found in [10].

Initially, it is determined the time point $\overline{T}$ where the game rationally stops: it is $\overline{T} = \min\{T_{\mathbf{b}}, T_{\mathbf{s}}\}$. The equilibrium outcome of every subgame starting from $t \geq \overline{T}$ is *NoAgreement*, since at least one agent will make *exit*. Therefore, at $t = \overline{T}$ agent $\iota(\overline{T})$ would accept any offer x which gives her a utility not worse than *NoAgreement*, namely, any offer x such that $U_{\iota(\overline{T})}(x, \overline{T}) \geq 0$. From $t = \overline{T} - 1$ back to $t = 0$ it is possible to find the optimal offer agent $\iota(t)$ can make at t, if she makes an offer, and the offers that she would accept. We denote by $x^*(t)$ the optimal offer of agent $\iota(t)$ at t. Easily, $x^*(t)$ is the offer such that, if $t < \overline{T} - 1$, agent $\iota(t + 1)$ is indifferent at $t + 1$ between accepting it and rejecting it to make her optimal offer $x^*(t + 1)$ and, if $t = \overline{T} - 1$, agent $\iota(t + 1)$ is indifferent at $t + 1$ between accepting it and making *exit*. Formally, $x^*(t)$ is such that $U_{\iota(t+1)}(x^*(t), t) = U_{\iota(t+1)}(x^*(t + 1), t + 1)$ if $t < \overline{T} - 1$ and $U_{\iota(t+1)}(x^*(t), t) = 0$ if $t = \overline{T} - 1$. The offers agent $\iota(t)$ would accept at t are all those offers that gives her a utility no worse than the utility given by offering $x^*(t)$. The equilibrium strategies of any subgame starting from $0 \leq t < \overline{T}$ prescribe that agent $\iota(t)$ offers $x^*(t)$ at t and agent $\iota(t + 1)$ accepts it at $t + 1$.

In order to provide a recursive formula for $x^*(t)$, we introduce the notion of backward propagation: given value x and agent i, we call *backward propagation* [6] of value x for agent i the value y such that $U_i(y, t-1) = U_i(x, t)$; we employ the arrow notation $x_{\leftarrow i}$ for backward propagations. Formally, $x_{\leftarrow \mathbf{b}} = RP_{\mathbf{b}} - (RP_{\mathbf{b}} - x) \cdot \delta_{\mathbf{b}}$ and $x_{\leftarrow \mathbf{s}} = RP_{\mathbf{s}} + (x - RP_{\mathbf{s}}) \cdot \delta_{\mathbf{s}}$. If a value x is backward propagated n times for agent i, we write $x_{\leftarrow n[i]}$, e.g. $x_{\leftarrow 2[i]} = (x_{\leftarrow i})_{\leftarrow i}$. If a value is backward propagated for more than one agent, we list them left to right in the subscript, e.g. $x_{\leftarrow i2[j]} = ((x_{\leftarrow i})_{\leftarrow j})_{\leftarrow j}$. The values of $x^*(t)$ can be calculated recursively from $t = \overline{T} - 1$ back to $t = 0$ as follows:

$$x^*(t) = \begin{cases} RP_{\iota(t+1)} & \text{if } t = \overline{T} - 1 \\ (x^*(t+1))_{\leftarrow \iota(t+1)} & \text{if } t < \overline{T} - 1 \end{cases}.$$

Finally, agents' equilibrium strategies can be defined on the basis of $x^*(t)$ as follows:

$$\sigma_{\mathbf{b}}^*(t) = \begin{cases} t = 0 & offer(x^*(0)) \\ 0 < t < \overline{T} & \begin{cases} \text{if } \sigma_{\mathbf{s}}(t-1) = offer(x) & accept \\ \quad \text{with } x \leq (x^*(t))_{\leftarrow \mathbf{b}} \\ \text{otherwise} & offer(x^*(t)) \end{cases} \\ \overline{T} \leq t \leq T_{\mathbf{b}} & \begin{cases} \text{if } \sigma_{\mathbf{s}}(t-1) = offer(x) & accept \\ \quad \text{with } x \leq RP_{\mathbf{b}} \\ \text{otherwise} & exit \end{cases} \\ T_{\mathbf{b}} < t & exit \end{cases}$$

$$\sigma_{\mathbf{s}}^*(t) = \begin{cases} t = 0 & offer(x^*(0)) \\ 0 < t < \overline{T} & \begin{cases} \text{if } \sigma_{\mathbf{b}}(t-1) = offer(x) & accept \\ \quad \text{with } x \geq (x^*(t))_{\leftarrow \mathbf{s}} \\ \text{otherwise} & offer(x^*(t)) \end{cases} \\ \overline{T} \leq t \leq T_{\mathbf{s}} & \begin{cases} \text{if } \sigma_{\mathbf{b}}(t-1) = offer(x) & accept \\ \quad \text{with } x \geq RP_{\mathbf{s}} \\ exit & \text{otherwise} \end{cases} \\ T_{\mathbf{s}} < t & exit \end{cases}$$

In Fig. 1 and in Fig. 2 we report agents' optimal offers in two different games. The parameters in both games are $RP_{\mathbf{b}} = 1$, $\delta_{\mathbf{b}} = 0.95$, $T_{\mathbf{b}} = 11$, $RP_{\mathbf{s}} = 0$, $\delta_{\mathbf{s}} = 0.95$, and $T_{\mathbf{s}} = 12$. We denote by $\Gamma(0, \mathbf{s}, \mathbf{b})$ the bargaining starting from $t = 0$ between $\mathbf{s}$ and $\mathbf{b}$ where $\iota(0) = \mathbf{s}$; agents' optimal offers in $\Gamma(0, \mathbf{s}, \mathbf{b})$ are reported in Fig. 1. Analogously, $\Gamma(0, \mathbf{b}, \mathbf{s})$ denotes the bargaining starting from $t = 0$ between $\mathbf{s}$ and $\mathbf{b}$ where $\iota(0) = \mathbf{b}$; agents' optimal offers in $\Gamma(0, \mathbf{b}, \mathbf{s})$ are reported in Fig. 2. The lines connecting two consecutive offers are isoutility curves. In both examples $\overline{T} = \min\{T_{\mathbf{b}}, T_{\mathbf{s}}\} = 11$. Consider $\Gamma(0, \mathbf{s}, \mathbf{b})$: $\iota(11) = \mathbf{b}$. Therefore, $x^*(10) = RP_{\mathbf{b}} = 1$, $x^*(9) = (x^*(10))_{\leftarrow \mathbf{s}} = .95$, $x^*(8) = (x^*(9))_{\leftarrow \mathbf{b}} = .9525$, and so on. Consider $\Gamma(0, \mathbf{b}, \mathbf{s})$: $\iota(11) = \mathbf{s}$. Therefore, $x^*(10) = RP_{\mathbf{s}} = 0$, $x^*(9) = (x^*(10))_{\leftarrow \mathbf{b}} = .05$, and so on.

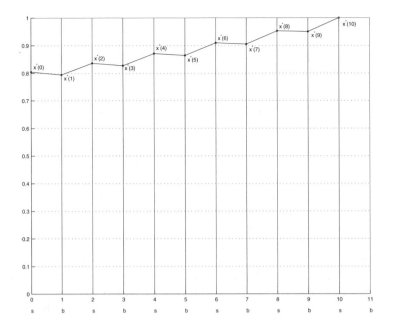

Fig. 1. Optimal offers in $\Gamma(0, \mathbf{s}, \mathbf{b})$: $RP_{\mathbf{b}} = 1$, $RP_{\mathbf{s}} = 0$, $\delta_{\mathbf{b}} = \delta_{\mathbf{s}} = 0.95$, $T_{\mathbf{b}} = 11$, $T_{\mathbf{s}} = 12$, $\iota(0) = \mathbf{s}$

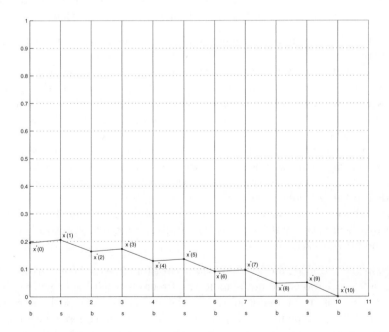

Fig. 2. Optimal offers in $\Gamma(0, \mathbf{s}, \mathbf{b})$: $RP_{\mathbf{b}} = 1$, $RP_{\mathbf{s}} = 0$, $\delta_{\mathbf{b}} = \delta_{\mathbf{s}} = 0.95$, $T_{\mathbf{b}} = 11$, $T_{\mathbf{s}} = 12$, $\iota(0) = \mathbf{b}$

3   The Proposed Model

In this section, we propose a bargaining model, as extension of the model discussed in the previous section, to capture the situation where there are m buyer agents and n seller agents such that:

- the items sold by the sellers are equal;
- all the sellers have exactly one item to sell;
- all the buyers are interested in buying exactly one item.

We denote by $\mathbf{b}_i$ the i-th buyer agent – her parameters will be $RP_{\mathbf{b}_i}$, $T_{\mathbf{b}_i}$, and $\delta_{\mathbf{b}_i}$ – and by $\mathbf{s}_j$ the j-th seller agent – her parameters will be $RP_{\mathbf{s}_j}$, $T_{\mathbf{s}_j}$, and $\delta_{\mathbf{s}_j}$. Furthermore, each agent, both $\mathbf{b}_i$ and $\mathbf{s}_j$, will be characterized by a time point denoted by $A_{\mathbf{b}_i}$ and $A_{\mathbf{s}_j}$, respectively, where she enters the market. Easily, an agent i can act in a market from $t = A_i$.

Within a market two different aspects coexist: (1) the matching of two opponents (a buyer $\mathbf{b}_i$ and a seller $\mathbf{s}_j$) and (2) the negotiation between two matched opponents. According to classical literature these two aspects can overlap. Indeed, several models allow agents that are negotiating to leave the negotiation they are currently carrying on and match other opponents with whom starting a new negotiation. This is usually captured by introducing an action, named *outside option* [8,11], available to the agents. For the sake of simplicity, in this paper we provide a market model for bargaining agents where agents cannot match other opponents during the negotiation. We will consider this option in future works. Precisely, we design our bargaining model such that:

- (exclusively) non-matched agents can match (exclusively) non-matched opponents;
- two agents that match at t will start to negotiate at $t+d$ where $d \in \mathbb{N}, d > 0$ (the value of d captures a possible delay due to the negotiation platform or set by the electronic institution; we assume that the platform grants the negotiation to begin exactly at $t+d$ and then the value of d is known *a priori* by the agents);
- given two agents matched at t, the agent that opens the negotiation at $t+d$ is chosen randomly with a probability .5 by the negotiation platform;
- two matched agents negotiate as prescribed by the bargaining model provided in the previous section;
- in presence of one buyer agent and one seller agent, agents' equilibrium strategies are exactly those in the classic alternating-offers protocol described in the previous section.

Finally, in the proposed model we partially capture two-sided competition, since agents' allowed actions are not symmetric. Precisely, each buyer will announce whether she wants to be matched and, in the affirmative case, will announce by which seller wants to be matched, whereas each seller will choose which buyer to match (we report details below). Fully two-sided competition will be studied in future works. Our extension of the original bargaining model develops in three points. We discuss them one by one.

(1) We introduce three actions to rule the matching between two opponents, i.e. $matchable(\mathbf{s}_j)$, $nonmatchable$, and $match(\mathbf{b}_i)$, and one action to allow agents to wait for the next time point, i.e. $wait$. The actions $matchable(\mathbf{s}_j)$ and $nonmatchable$ are available at t to the buyers that are not matched at such time point and the effect of the first one is to signal that the buyer is ready at t to be matched by the specific seller $\mathbf{s}_j$, whereas the effect of the second one is that the buyer does not want to be matched. In order for $matchable(\mathbf{s}_j)$ to be valid at t, $\mathbf{s}_j$ must be present in the market and must be non-matched at such time point. The action $match(\mathbf{b}_i)$ is available to the non-matched sellers and the effect is that $\mathbf{s}_j$ matches the buyer $\mathbf{b}_i$. Obviously, to be $match(\mathbf{b}_i)$ a valid action for $\mathbf{s}_j$ at t, $\mathbf{b}_i$ must have made $matchable(\mathbf{s}_j)$ at such time point. The action $wait$ is available to both buyers and sellers, and allow them to wait for the next time point. We discuss below, at point (3), when and how agents can employ these actions.

(2) We redefine the action $exit$: if an agent made $exit$, then she leaves the market and her outcome is $NoAgreement$. Our choice is directed to exclude agents' non-feasible behaviors: it can be easily observed that if action $exit$ does not impose agents to leave the market, then in presence of a unique buyer and a unique seller the equilibrium strategies are different from those prescribed by Rubinstein's equilibrium. We will show that in the next section.

(3) We modify the mechanism of the game dividing each time point in two sequential stages, denoted by 1 and 2, and inhibiting and allowing actions according to the actual state in which an agent is. Precisely, in a market an agent $\mathbf{b}_i$ (or $\mathbf{s}_j$) can be in three different states: (i) $\mathbf{b}_i$ (or $\mathbf{s}_j$) is non-matched, (ii) $\mathbf{b}_i$ (or $\mathbf{s}_j$) have been matched with $\mathbf{s}_j$ (or $\mathbf{b}_i$) and is waiting for starting to negotiate, or (iii) $\mathbf{b}_i$ (or $\mathbf{s}_j$) is negotiating with $\mathbf{s}_j$ (or $\mathbf{b}_i$). Consider state (i). If $\mathbf{b}_i$ is not matched, then her allowed actions are the following. In the first stage of every time point t she can make $nonmatchable$ or $matchable(\mathbf{s}_k)$ where $\mathbf{s}_k$ must not be matched at t. In the second stage of every time t point she can make $wait$ or $exit$; this second action is allowed only if in the first stage of t $\mathbf{b}_i$ has made $nonmatchable$: we exclude non-reasonable situations wherein at the same time point a buyer announces to be ready to be matched with a specific seller and subsequently leaves the market. If $\mathbf{s}_j$ is not matched, then her allowed actions are the following. In the first stage of every time point t, no action is allowed. In the second stage of every time point t, she can make $wait$ or $match(\mathbf{b}_k)$ where $\mathbf{b}_k$ must not be matched or $exit$. Consider state (ii). If $\mathbf{b}_i$ (or $\mathbf{s}_j$) is matched and is waiting for starting to negotiate, no action is allowed. Consider state (iii). If $\mathbf{b}_i$ (or $\mathbf{s}_j$) is negotiating, then she acts alternately and her allowed actions are exactly those in the alternating-offers protocol discussed in the previous section: $offer(x)$, $accept$, and $exit$. For the sake of clarity, the actions available to agents are summarized in Tab. 1.

Agents' utility functions are exactly those defined in the previous section. Since every agent negotiate exclusively on one item, once a negotiation has been concluded with an acceptance, the two negotiators leave the market. When $m >$

Table 1. Actions available to the agents

state	stage	agent	time points	available actions
$\mathbf{b}_i$ ($\mathbf{s}_j$) is not matched	1	$\mathbf{b}_i$	any	$nonmatchable, matchable(\mathbf{s}_k)$ if $\mathbf{s}_k$ is not matched
	2	$\mathbf{b}_i$	any	$wait, exit$ if $\mathbf{b}_i$ has made $nonmatchable$
		$\mathbf{s}_j$	any	$wait, match(\mathbf{b}_i)$ if $\mathbf{b}_i$ has made $matchable(\mathbf{s}_j)$, $exit$
$\mathbf{b}_i$ and $\mathbf{s}_j$ are negotiating	2	$\mathbf{b}_i$	alternately	$offer(x), accept, exit$
		$\mathbf{s}_j$	alternately	$offer(x), accept, exit$

n (or $m < n$) $m - n$ buyer agents (or $n - m$ seller agents) will never take part in any negotiation and therefore their outcome will be *NoAgreement*.

4   Equilibrium Strategies

In this section we provide agents' equilibrium strategies when $A_i = A_j = 0$ for all i, j. The analysis of the general case will be produced in future works.

4.1   Base Case: One Buyer and One Seller

We consider the setting wherein there are a unique buyer $\mathbf{b}_1$ and a unique seller $\mathbf{s}_1$. We can state the following lemma.

Lemma 41 *Once two opponents have started to negotiate, they employ the equilibrium strategies prescribed in Section 2.*

The proof is omitted, being trivial. It is based on the fact that, if $RP_{\mathbf{b}_1} > RP_{\mathbf{s}_1}$, agents strictly prefer to negotiate rather than to make *exit*. We state now the following lemma.

Lemma 42 *If $\mathbf{b}_1$ and $\mathbf{s}_1$ are both present in the market at $t < \overline{T} - d$ and they are not matched, then they prefer to match immediately rather than to match subsequently or not to match.*

Proof. Call $x_{\mathbf{b}_1}^*(t)$ and $x_{\mathbf{s}_1}^*(t)$ the optimal offers of $\mathbf{b}_1$ and $\mathbf{s}_1$, respectively, at t. Notice that $x_{\mathbf{b}_1}^*(t)$ is defined in $\Gamma(t, \mathbf{b}_1, \mathbf{s}_1)$, whereas $x_{\mathbf{s}_1}^*(t)$ is defined in $\Gamma(t, \mathbf{s}_1, \mathbf{b}_1)$. We study $\mathbf{b}_1$'s optimal actions ($\mathbf{s}_1$'s ones can be similarly studied). We consider the case with $d = 1$; when $d > 1$ the proof is analogous.

We need to prove that $\mathbf{b}_1$'s expected utility of starting a negotiation at t is greater than her expected utility of starting a negotiation at $t + 1$. Formally, we need to prove that:

$$\left(\frac{1}{2}x_{\mathbf{s}_1}^*(t+1) + \frac{1}{2}x_{\mathbf{b}_1}^*(t+1)\right)_{\leftarrow \mathbf{b}_1} > \frac{1}{2}x_{\mathbf{s}_1}^*(t) + \frac{1}{2}x_{\mathbf{b}_1}^*(t).$$

We consider the worst case, i.e. when $\delta_{\mathbf{s}_1} = 1$, and we show that in the worst case the above inequality holds. Precisely, we can make the following substitutions: $x^*_{\mathbf{b}_1}(t) = x^*_{\mathbf{s}_1}(t+1)$ and $x^*_{\mathbf{s}_1}(t) = RP_{\mathbf{b}_1} - (RP_{\mathbf{b}_1} - x^*_{\mathbf{b}_1}(t+1))\delta_{\mathbf{b}_1}$. We obtain:

$$\frac{1}{2} \cdot (1 - \delta_{\mathbf{b}_1}) \cdot (RP_{\mathbf{b}_1} - x^*_{\mathbf{s}_1}(t+1)) > 0.$$

Since $RP_{\mathbf{b}_1} - x^*_{\mathbf{s}_1}(t+1) > 0$ by construction and $1 - \delta_{\mathbf{b}_1} > 0$ by definition, the above inequality holds.   □

From Lemmas 41 and 42, it trivially follows the following theorem.

Theorem 43 *In presence of one buyer and one seller, agents equilibrium strategies are:*

$$\sigma_{\mathbf{b}_1}(t) = \begin{cases} \text{if matched} & \text{strategies prescribed in Section 2} \\ \text{if non-matched} & \begin{cases} t < \overline{T} - d & \begin{cases} \text{stage 1} & matchable(\mathbf{s}_1) \\ \text{stage 2} & wait \end{cases} \\ \overline{T} - d \leq t & \begin{cases} \text{stage 1} & nonmatchable \\ \text{stage 2} & exit \end{cases} \end{cases} \end{cases}$$

$$\sigma_{\mathbf{s}_1}(t) = \begin{cases} \text{if matched} & \text{strategies prescribed in Section 2} \\ \text{if non-matched} & \begin{cases} t < \overline{T} - d & \{\text{stage 2} \quad match(\mathbf{b}_2) \\ \overline{T} - d \leq t & \{\text{stage 2} \quad exit \end{cases} \end{cases}$$

We show now that, if action *exit* does not impose agents to leave the platform, then Lemma 41 does not hold and therefore, in presence of a unique buyer and a unique seller, agents' equilibrium strategies are different from those in the original protocol presented in Section 2.

Consider the bargaining setting with one buyer $\mathbf{b}_1$ and one seller $\mathbf{s}_1$, with $d = 1$, and where both agents enter the market at $t = 0$: agents' optimal offers are reported in Fig. 3. It can be easily observed that agents will immediately match themselves and then they will start to negotiate at $t = 1$. If agents can make *exit* without leaving the market, then they will make it at $t = 1$. Consider $\Gamma(1, \mathbf{s}_1, \mathbf{b}_1)$: $\mathbf{s}_1$ opens the negotiation (the analysis of $\Gamma(1, \mathbf{b}_1, \mathbf{s}_1)$ is analogous). If $\mathbf{s}$ employs the strategies provided in Section 2, i.e. $offer(x^*(1))$ with $x^*(1) \simeq 0.1$, then she gains $U_{\mathbf{s}_1}(x^*(1), 0) \simeq 0.1$. If $\mathbf{s}$ makes *exit* and subsequently $match(\mathbf{b}_1)$ at $t = 2$, then she gains $\simeq 0.45$. Exactly, the computation of the expected utility of making *exit* at $t = 1$ and subsequently $match(\mathbf{b}_1)$ at $t = 2$ is: with probability $.5$ $\mathbf{s}_1$ acts at $t = 3$ offering $x^*(3) = 0.05$ and with probability $.5$ $\mathbf{b}_1$ acts at $t = 3$ offering $x^*(3) = 0.95$; since these agreements are reached at $t = 4$, their utility must be discounted by $\delta^2_{\mathbf{s}_1}$. Notice that agents prefer to offer rather than to exit at $t = 3$ (otherwise agents would not reach any agreement).

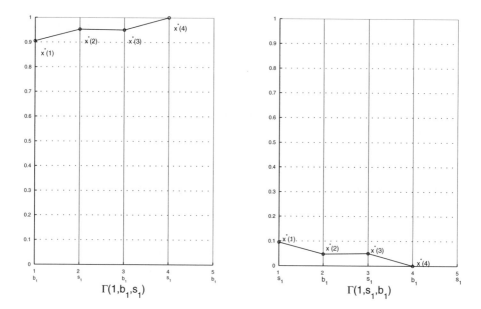

Fig. 3. Subgames $\Gamma(1, \mathbf{b}_1, \mathbf{s}_1)$ and $\Gamma(1, \mathbf{s}_1, \mathbf{b}_1)$ where $RP_{\mathbf{b}_1} = 1$, $\delta_{\mathbf{b}_1} = 0.95$, $T_{\mathbf{b}_1} = 5$, $RP_{\mathbf{s}_1} = 0$, $\delta_{\mathbf{s}_1} = 0.95$, $T_{\mathbf{s}_1} = 12$, and $d = 1$

4.2   One-Sided Competition I: One Buyer and More Sellers

We consider the setting wherein there are one buyer $\mathbf{b}_i$ and more sellers $\mathbf{s}_j$ with $j \in \{1, \ldots, n\}$. We denote by $x^*_{\mathbf{b}_i}(t, \mathbf{s}_j)$ the optimal offer of $\mathbf{b}_i$ at t in the negotiation with $\mathbf{s}_j$ and, analogously, by $x^*_{\mathbf{s}_j}(t, \mathbf{b}_i)$ the optimal offer of $\mathbf{s}_j$ at t in the negotiation with $\mathbf{b}_i$.

The analysis of the considered setting is straightforward. Indeed, all the sellers $\mathbf{s}_j$ (with $RP_{\mathbf{s}_j} < RP_{\mathbf{b}_1}$) prefer to negotiate and reach an agreement rather than not to negotiate and reach thus *NoAgreement*. The buyer $\mathbf{b}_1$ will choose the seller to match in order to maximize her profit. Exactly, the utility expected by $\mathbf{b}_1$ from being matched by a seller $\mathbf{s}_j$ at t is: $\frac{1}{2}U_{\mathbf{b}_1}(x^*_{\mathbf{s}_j}(t, \mathbf{b}_1), t + d) + \frac{1}{2}U_{\mathbf{b}_1}(x^*_{\mathbf{b}_1}(t, \mathbf{s}_j), t + d + 1)$. Indeed, with probability .5 $\mathbf{s}_j$ will open the negotiation at $t + d$ and with probability .5 $\mathbf{b}_1$ will open the negotiation. Among all the possible $\mathbf{s}_j$s, $\mathbf{b}_1$ will choose the one that maximize her expected utility. By trivial mathematics we can write:

$$\mathbf{s}^*(\mathbf{b}_1, t) = \arg \min_{\mathbf{s}_j \in \{\mathbf{s}_1, \ldots, \mathbf{s}_n\}} \left\{ x^*_{\mathbf{s}_j}(t + d, \mathbf{b}_1) + x^*_{\mathbf{b}_1}(t + d, \mathbf{s}_j) \right\},$$

where $\mathbf{s}^*(\mathbf{b}_1, t)$ is the seller that $\mathbf{b}_1$ will match at t on the equilibrium path. We state the following theorem, whose proof trivially follows from the above considerations.

Theorem 44 *In presence of one buyer and more sellers, $\mathbf{b}_1$ and $\mathbf{s}^*(\mathbf{b}_1, t)$'s equilibrium strategies are exactly the ones reported in Theorem 43 where $\mathbf{s}_1$ is substituted by $\mathbf{s}^*(\mathbf{b}_1, t)$ and equilibrium strategies of all the other $\mathbf{s}_j s$ are to make exit.*

4.3 One-Sided Competition II: More Buyers and One Seller

We consider the setting wherein there are more buyers $\mathbf{b}_i$ with $i \in \{1, \ldots, m\}$ and one seller $\mathbf{s}_1$. The analysis of the considered setting is analogous to the previous one. All the buyers $\mathbf{b}_i$ (with $RP_{\mathbf{b}_i} > RP_{\mathbf{s}_1}$) prefer to negotiate and reach an agreement rather than not to negotiate and reach thus *NoAgreement*. The seller $\mathbf{s}_1$ will choice the buyer to match in order to maximize her profit. Exactly, the utility expected by $\mathbf{s}_1$ from being matched by a buyer $\mathbf{b}_i$ at t is: $\frac{1}{2}U_{\mathbf{s}_1}(x^*_{\mathbf{s}_1}(t, \mathbf{b}_i), t + d) + \frac{1}{2}U_{\mathbf{s}_1}(x^*_{\mathbf{b}_i}(t, \mathbf{s}_1), t + d + 1)$. Among all the possible $\mathbf{b}_i s$, $\mathbf{s}_1$ will choose the one that maximize her expected utility. By trivial mathematics we can write:

$$\mathbf{b}^*(\mathbf{s}_1, t) = \arg\max_{\mathbf{b}_i \in \{\mathbf{b}_1, \ldots, \mathbf{b}_m\}} \left\{ x^*_{\mathbf{s}_1}(t + d, \mathbf{b}_i) + x^*_{\mathbf{b}_i}(t + d, \mathbf{s}_1) \right\},$$

where $\mathbf{b}^*(\mathbf{s}_1, t)$ is the buyer that $\mathbf{s}_1$ will match at t on the equilibrium path. We state the following theorem, whose proof trivially follows from the above considerations.

Theorem 45 *In presence of more buyers and one seller, $\mathbf{b}^*(\mathbf{s}_1, t)$ and $\mathbf{s}_1$'s equilibrium strategies are exactly the ones reported in Theorem 43 where $\mathbf{b}_1$ is substituted by $\mathbf{b}^*(\mathbf{s}_1, t)$ and equilibrium strategies of all the other $\mathbf{b}_i s$ are to make nonmatchable at the stage 1 and exit at stage 2.*

4.4 Two-Sided Competition: More Buyers and More Sellers

The study of the setting with more buyers and more sellers is not straightforward. This is due to the intrinsic complexity of the game: it is essentially a multistage game wherein $m + n$ agents concurrently act and the game changes at each stage. Nevertheless, for a large set of values of the parameters an efficient solution can be found. Indeed, for a large set of values of the parameters it is possible to limit the study of the agents' matching to the initial time point $t = 0$: from $t > 0$ all the agents will be matched and therefore agents' equilibrium strategies will be those described in Section 2. In what follows we provide such an algorithm and we experimentally evaluate when it is effective; in future works we will provide a solution for the values of the parameters such that the proposed algorithm fails.

The algorithm develops in three steps. We present them one by one.

Step 1. In this step agents' optimal offers in all the possible negotiations are computed. Formally, $x^*_{\mathbf{b}_i}(t, \mathbf{s}_j)$ and $x^*_{\mathbf{s}_j}(t, \mathbf{b}_i)$ for every $i \in \{1, \ldots, m\}$ and $j \in \{1, \ldots, n\}$ are computed. Their values are produced as stated in Section 2.

Step 2. In this step agents' preferences concerning the opponent to match are computed. Precisely, for every buyer $\mathbf{b}_i$ (and for every seller $\mathbf{s}_j$) it is necessary to sort the sellers (the buyers) from the one which gives $\mathbf{b}_i$ the maximum expected utility to the one which gives $\mathbf{b}_i$ the minimum expected utility. Formally, for the buyers we need to produce:

$$\begin{pmatrix} \mathbf{b}_1 : \mathbf{s}_2 \succ \mathbf{s}_3 \succ \mathbf{s}_1 \succ \mathbf{s}_5 \succ \mathbf{s}_6 \succ \ldots \\ \mathbf{b}_2 : \mathbf{s}_7 \succ \mathbf{s}_1 \succ \mathbf{s}_3 \succ \mathbf{s}_4 \succ \mathbf{s}_2 \succ \ldots \\ \ldots \qquad\qquad \ldots \\ \mathbf{b}_m : \mathbf{s}_7 \succ \mathbf{s}_5 \succ \mathbf{s}_2 \succ \mathbf{s}_1 \succ \mathbf{s}_6 \succ \ldots \end{pmatrix}$$

(this is to say that $\mathbf{b}_1$ prefers to match $\mathbf{s}_2$ than $\mathbf{s}_3$, prefers to match $\mathbf{s}_3$ than $\mathbf{s}_1$, and so on). The preferences of the sellers will be defined analogous. We recall that the preferences of a buyer $\mathbf{b}_i$ can be found by ordering $x^*_{\mathbf{b}_i}(0, \mathbf{s}_j) + x^*_{\mathbf{s}_j}(0, \mathbf{b}_i)$ for any $j \in \{1, \ldots, n\}$ from the minimum one to the maximum one. Analogously, the preferences of a seller $\mathbf{s}_j$ can be found by ordering $x^*_{\mathbf{b}_i}(0, \mathbf{s}_j) + x^*_{\mathbf{s}_j}(0, \mathbf{b}_i)$ for any $j \in \{1, \ldots, n\}$ from the maximum one to the minimum one.

Step 3. We iteratively apply the following procedure while it can be applied. If there exists a couple $(\mathbf{b}_i, \mathbf{s}_j)$ such that $\mathbf{s}_j$ is the most preferred seller for $\mathbf{b}_i$ and $\mathbf{b}_i$ is the most preferred buyer for $\mathbf{s}_j$, then:

- $\mathbf{b}_i$ and $\mathbf{s}_j$ match themselves and are removed from the matching problem,
- $\mathbf{b}_i$ is removed from the preferences of all the possible sellers present in the matching problem and, analogously, $\mathbf{s}_j$ is removed from the preferences of all the possible buyers present in the matching problem.

Given the result produced by the above iterated procedure, if all the buyers or all the sellers are matched, then an equilibrium strategy has been found. Otherwise, further analysis is required. The proof of optimality of the algorithm is trivial and is based on the iterated elimination of strictly dominated actions.

The proposed algorithm is efficient, since it requires:

- (Step 1) $2 \cdot m \cdot n$ backward inductions as those described in Section 2 to produce agents' optimal offers in all the possible negotiations,
- (Step 2) m sorts for producing buyers' preferences and n sorts for producing sellers' preferences,
- (Step 3) $\frac{1}{2} \min\{m^2, n^2\}$ searches for finding possible couples to match.

Summarily, the asymptotical computational complexity of the proposed algorithm is $O(m \cdot n)$.

We report an example of the use of the proposed algorithm. We consider a setting with three buyers $\mathbf{b}_1, \mathbf{b}_2, \mathbf{b}_3$ and three sellers $\mathbf{s}_1, \mathbf{s}_2, \mathbf{s}_3$. Buyers' parameters are: $RP_{\mathbf{b}_1} = RP_{\mathbf{b}_2} = RP_{\mathbf{b}_3} = 1$, $\delta_{\mathbf{b}_1} = 0.98$, $\delta_{\mathbf{b}_2} = 0.94$, $\delta_{\mathbf{b}_3} = 0.65$, $T_{\mathbf{b}_1} = 68$, $T_{\mathbf{b}_2} = 3$, $T_{\mathbf{b}_3} = 84$. Sellers' parameters are: $RP_{\mathbf{s}_1} = RP_{\mathbf{s}_2} = RP_{\mathbf{s}_3} = 0$, $\delta_{\mathbf{s}_1} = 0.77$, $\delta_{\mathbf{s}_2} = 0.89$, $\delta_{\mathbf{s}_3} = 0.73$, $T_{\mathbf{s}_1} = 91$, $T_{\mathbf{s}_2} = 71$, $T_{\mathbf{s}_3} = 19$. We report their preferences:

$$\begin{pmatrix} \mathbf{b}_1 : \mathbf{s}_1 \succ \mathbf{s}_3 \succ \mathbf{s}_2 \\ \mathbf{b}_2 : \mathbf{s}_3 \succ \mathbf{s}_1 \succ \mathbf{s}_2 \\ \mathbf{b}_3 : \mathbf{s}_3 \succ \mathbf{s}_1 \succ \mathbf{s}_2 \end{pmatrix} \quad , \quad \begin{pmatrix} \mathbf{s}_1 : \mathbf{b}_3 \succ \mathbf{b}_2 \succ \mathbf{b}_1 \\ \mathbf{s}_2 : \mathbf{b}_3 \succ \mathbf{b}_2 \succ \mathbf{b}_1 \\ \mathbf{s}_3 : \mathbf{b}_3 \succ \mathbf{b}_2 \succ \mathbf{b}_1 \end{pmatrix}$$

Since $\mathbf{b}_3$'s most preferred seller is $\mathbf{s}_3$ and $\mathbf{s}_3$'s most preferred seller is $\mathbf{b}_3$, then $\mathbf{b}_3$ and $\mathbf{s}_3$ match themselves and they are removed from other agents' preferences. We obtain:

$$\begin{pmatrix} \mathbf{b}_1 : \mathbf{s}_1 \succ \mathbf{s}_2 \\ \mathbf{b}_1 : \mathbf{s}_1 \succ \mathbf{s}_2 \end{pmatrix} \quad , \quad \begin{pmatrix} \mathbf{s}_1 : \mathbf{b}_2 \succ \mathbf{b}_1 \\ \mathbf{s}_2 : \mathbf{b}_2 \succ \mathbf{b}_1 \end{pmatrix}$$

Since $\mathbf{b}_2$'s most preferred seller is $\mathbf{s}_1$ and $\mathbf{s}_1$'s most preferred seller is $\mathbf{b}_2$, then $\mathbf{b}_2$ and $\mathbf{s}_1$ match themselves and they are removed from other agents' preferences. We obtain:

$$\begin{pmatrix} \mathbf{b}_1 : \mathbf{s}_2 \end{pmatrix} \quad , \quad \begin{pmatrix} \mathbf{s}_2 : \mathbf{b}_1 \end{pmatrix}$$

Finally, $\mathbf{b}_1$ and $\mathbf{s}_2$ match themselves. Therefore, the matched agents are: $(\mathbf{b}_1, \mathbf{s}_2)$, $(\mathbf{b}_2, \mathbf{s}_1)$, and $(\mathbf{b}_3, \mathbf{s}_3)$.

We report now an example where the application of our algorithm does not produce any equilibrium strategies. Buyers' parameters are: $RP_{\mathbf{b}_1} = RP_{\mathbf{b}_2} = RP_{\mathbf{b}_3} = 1$, $\delta_{\mathbf{b}_1} = 0.71$, $\delta_{\mathbf{b}_2} = 0.97$, $\delta_{\mathbf{b}_3} = 0.75$, $T_{\mathbf{b}_1} = 10$, $T_{\mathbf{b}_2} = 19$, $T_{\mathbf{b}_3} = 51$. Sellers' parameters are: $RP_{\mathbf{s}_1} = RP_{\mathbf{s}_2} = RP_{\mathbf{s}_3} = 0$, $\delta_{\mathbf{s}_1} = 0.92$, $\delta_{\mathbf{s}_2} = 0.91$, $\delta_{\mathbf{s}_3} = 0.98$, $T_{\mathbf{s}_1} = 43$, $T_{\mathbf{s}_2} = 4$, $T_{\mathbf{s}_3} = 87$. Agents' preferences are:

$$\begin{pmatrix} \mathbf{b}_1 : \mathbf{s}_2 \succ \mathbf{s}_1 \succ \mathbf{s}_3 \\ \mathbf{b}_2 : \mathbf{s}_1 \succ \mathbf{s}_2 \succ \mathbf{s}_3 \\ \mathbf{b}_3 : \mathbf{s}_2 \succ \mathbf{s}_1 \succ \mathbf{s}_3 \end{pmatrix} \quad , \quad \begin{pmatrix} \mathbf{s}_1 : \mathbf{b}_3 \succ \mathbf{b}_1 \succ \mathbf{b}_2 \\ \mathbf{s}_2 : \mathbf{b}_1 \succ \mathbf{b}_3 \succ \mathbf{b}_2 \\ \mathbf{s}_3 : \mathbf{b}_3 \succ \mathbf{b}_1 \succ \mathbf{b}_2 \end{pmatrix}$$

Notice that the procedure described in the Step 3 cannot be applied, since there is not any couple $(\mathbf{b}_i, \mathbf{s}_j)$ such that $\mathbf{b}_i$'s most preferred seller is $\mathbf{s}_j$ and $\mathbf{s}_j$'s most preferred buyer is $\mathbf{b}_i$.

We experimentally evaluate the effectiveness of our algorithm. We consider experimental settings characterized by a different number of agents, precisely, by different values for $\min\{m, n\}$s. For each value of $\min\{m, n\} \in \{1, \ldots, 25\}$ we have considered 10^5 different settings where agents' parameters are chosen with uniform probability distribution from the following intervals: $\delta_i \in (0, 1)$, $T_i \in [2, 100]$, $RP_{\mathbf{b}_i} = 1$, $RP_{\mathbf{s}_i} = 0$. In Tab. 2 we report the percentage of success of the proposed algorithm. The algorithm results very effective for $\min\{m, n\} \leq 6$.

Table 2. Experimental evaluation of the effectiveness of the proposed algorithm

$\min\{\mathbf{m}, \mathbf{n}\}$	success	$\min\{\mathbf{m}, \mathbf{n}\}$	success	$\min\{\mathbf{m}, \mathbf{n}\}$	success
2	$\sim 99.7\%$	6	$\sim 90.1\%$	10	$\sim 74.2\%$
3	$\sim 98.2\%$	7	$\sim 86.1\%$	15	$\sim 55.5\%$
4	$\sim 96.2\%$	8	$\sim 82.4\%$	20	$\sim 37.0\%$
5	$\sim 93.4\%$	9	$\sim 78.1\%$	25	$\sim 24.7\%$

5 Conclusions and Future Works

Automated bargaining is a prominent challenge for artificial intelligence, being bargaining the principal negotiation protocol. The study of bargaining is vast in literature both in bilateral settings and in market settings, but no work provides a model that satisfactorily captures electronic markets.

In this paper we propose an extension of the classic alternating-offers to capture the setting wherein there are more buyers and more sellers. The proposed model satisfactorily extends the alternating-offers protocol: in presence of a unique buyer and a unique seller, agents' equilibrium strategies are those in the original protocol.

Furthermore, we game theoretically study the proposed model. Precisely, we provide agents' equilibrium strategies in presence of one-sided competition and an algorithm that produces agents' equilibrium strategies in presence of two-sided competition for a large set of values of the parameters. Finally, we experimentally evaluate the effectiveness of the proposed algorithm.

Our intention is to refine our model to allow agents to rematch themselves also during the negotiation and to provide an algorithm able to produce agents' equilibrium strategies for all the values of the parameters.

References

1. Serrano, R.: Bargaining. In: The New Palgrave: a Dictionary of Economics, 2nd edn. McMillian, London (2008) (in press)
2. Rubinstein, A.: Perfect equilibrium in a bargaining model. Econometrica 50, 97–109 (1982)
3. Osborne, M.J., Rubinstein, A.: Bargaining and Markets. Academic Press, San Diego (1990)
4. Kraus, S.: Strategic Negotiation in Multiagent Environments. The MIT Press, Cambridge (2001)
5. Gatti, N., Amigoni, F.: A cooperative negotiation protocol for physiological model combination. In: Proceedings of AAMAS, New York, USA, pp. 656–663 (2004)
6. Di Giunta, F., Gatti, N.: Bargaining over multiple issues in finite horizon alternating-offers protocol. Annals of Mathematics in Artificial Intelligence 47, 251–271 (2006)
7. Gatti, N., Di Giunta, F., Marino, S.: Alternating-offers bargaining with one-sided uncertain deadlines: an efficient algorithm. Artificial Intelligence (2008) (in press)
8. Binmore, K., Shaked, A., Sutton, J.: An outside option expirement. The Quaterly Journal of Economics 104, 753–770 (1989)
9. Harsanyi, J.C., Selten, R.: A generalized Nash solution for two-person bargaining games with incomplete information. Management Science 18, 80–106 (1972)
10. Napel, S.: Bilateral Bargaining: Theory and Applications. Springer, Berlin (2002)
11. Jehiel, P., Moldovanu, P.: Cyclical delay in bargaining with externalities. Review of Economic Studies 62, 619–637 (1995)

Bidding Heuristics for Simultaneous Auctions: Lessons from TAC Travel

Amy Greenwald[1], Victor Naroditskiy[1], and Seong Jae Lee[2]

[1] Department of Computer Science, Brown University
{amy,vnarodit}@cs.brown.edu
[2] Department of Computer Science, University of Washington
seongjae@u.washington.edu

Abstract. We undertake an experimental study of heuristics designed for the Travel division of the Trading Agent Competition. Our primary goal is to analyze the performance of the sample average approximation (SAA) heuristic, which is approximately optimal in the decision-theoretic (DT) setting, in this game-theoretic (GT) setting. To this end, we conduct experiments in four settings, three DT and one GT. The relevant distinction between the DT and the GT settings is: in the DT settings, agents' strategies do not affect the distribution of prices. Because of this distinction, the DT experiments are easier to analyze than the GT experiments. Moreover, settings with normally distributed prices, and controlled noise, are easier to analyze than those with competitive equilibrium prices. In the studied domain, analysis of the DT settings with possibly noisy normally distributed prices informs our analysis of the richer DT and GT settings with competitive equilibrium prices. In future work, we plan to investigate whether this experimental methodology—namely, transferring knowledge gained in a DT setting with noisy signals to a GT setting—can be applied to analyze heuristics for playing other complex games.

1 Introduction

In the design of autonomous trading agents that buy and sell goods in electronic markets, a variety of interesting computational questions arise. One of the most fundamental is to determine how to bid on goods being auctioned off in separate markets when the agent's valuations for those goods are highly interdependent (i.e., complementary or substitutable). The Trading Agent Competition (TAC) Travel division was designed as a testbed in which to compare and contrast various approaches to this problem [1]. We partake in an empirical investigation of heuristics designed for bidding in the simultaneous auctions that characterize TAC in a simplified TAC-like setting.

At a high-level, the design of many successful TAC agents (for example, Walverine [2], RoxyBot (Greenwald and Boyan 2004 & 2005) and ATTac [3]) can be summarized as: Step 1: *predict*, i.e., build a model of the auctions' clearing prices; Step 2: *optimize*, i.e., solve for an (approximately) optimal set of bids,

W. Ketter et al. (Eds.): AMEC/TADA 2008, LNBIP 44, pp. 131–146, 2010.
© Springer-Verlag Berlin Heidelberg 2010

given this model. This paper is devoted to the study of bidding, that is, the optimization piece of this design. We assume that agents are given price predictions in the form of a black box from which they can sample a vector of predicted prices; such samples are called *scenarios*. Because finding an optimal solution to the bidding problem is not generally tractable, our study centers around a series of *heuristics* that construct bids based on approximations or simplifications. We subject these heuristics to experimental trials within a simplified version of the TAC domain that we find more amenable to experimental study than the full-blown TAC Travel game.

2   TAC Travel Game

In this section, we briefly summarize the TAC Travel market game. For more details, see http://www.sics.se/tac/.

A TAC Travel agent is a simulated travel agent whose task is to organize itineraries for a group of clients to travel to and from TACTown. The agent's objective is to procure "desirable" travel goods as inexpensively as possible. An agent desires goods (i.e., it earns utility for procuring them) to the extent that they comprise itineraries that satisfy its clients' preferences.

Travel goods are sold in simultaneous auctions:

- Flights are sold by the "TAC seller" in dynamic posted-pricing environments. No resale is permitted.
- Hotel reservations are also sold by the "TAC seller," in multi-unit ascending call markets. Specifically, 16 hotel reservations are sold in each hotel auction at the 16*th* highest price. No resale is permitted.
- Agents trade tickets to entertainment events among themselves in continuous double auctions.

Flights and hotel reservations are complementary goods: flights do not garner utility without complementary hotel reservations; nor do hotel reservations garner utility without complementary flights. Tickets to entertainment events, e.g., the Boston Red Sox and the Boston Symphony Orchestra, are substitutable.

Clients have preferred departure and arrival dates, and a penalty is subtracted from the agent's utility for allocating packages that do not match clients' preferences exactly. For example, a penalty of 200 (100 per day) is incurred when a client who wants to depart Monday and arrive on Tuesday is assigned a package with a Monday departure and a Thursday arrival. Clients also have hotel preferences, for the two type of hotels, "good" and "bad." A client's preference for staying at the good rather than the bad hotel is described by a *hotel bonus*, utility the agent accumulates when the client's assigned package includes the good hotel.

3   Bidding Heuristics

Our test suite consists of six marginal-utility-based and two sample average approximation heuristics. We present a brief description of these heuristics here.

Interested readers are referred to Wellman, Greenwald, and Stone ([4]) for more detailed explanations.

3.1 Marginal-Utility-Based Heuristics

In a second-price auction for a single good, it is optimal for an agent to simply bid its independent value on that good [5]. In simultaneous auctions for multiple goods, however, bidding is not so straightforward because it is unclear how to assign independent values to interdependent goods. Perfectly complementary goods (e.g., an inflight and outflight for a particular client) are worthless in isolation, and perfectly substitutable goods (e.g., rooms in different hotels for the same client on the same day) provide added value only in isolation. Still, an agent might be tempted to bid on each good its *marginal* utility (MU), that is, the incremental value of obtaining that good relative to the collection of goods it already owns or can buy. Many reasonable bidding heuristics (e.g., Greenwald and Boyan ([6], [7]), Stone *et al.* ([3])) incorporate some form of marginal utility bidding.

Definition 1. *Given a set of goods X, a valuation function $v : 2^X \to \mathbb{R}$, and bundle prices $q : 2^X \to \mathbb{R}$. The marginal utility $\mu(x, q)$ of good $x \in X$ is defined as:*

$$\mu(x) = \max_{Y \subseteq X \setminus \{x\}} [v(Y \cup \{x\}) - q(Y)] - \max_{Y \subseteq X \setminus \{x\}} [v(Y) - q(Y)]$$

Consistent with TAC Travel, we assume additive prices: that is, in the above equation, the bundle pricing function q returns the sum of the predicted prices of the goods in Y.

Our heuristics actually sample a set of scenarios, not a single vector of predicted prices. We consider two classes of marginal utility heuristics based on how they make use of the information in the scenarios.

Bidding Heuristics that Collapse Available Distributional Information. The following heuristics collapse all scenarios into a single vector of predicted prices, namely the average scenario, and then calculate the marginal utility of each good assuming the other goods can be purchased at the average prices.

StraightMU bids the marginal utility of each good.

TargetMU bids marginal utilities only on the goods in a target set of goods. The target set is one that an agent would optimally purchase at the average prices.

TargetMU* is similar to TargetMU, but calculates marginal utilities assuming only goods from the target set are available. This results in higher bids.

Bidding Heuristics that Exploit Available Distributional Information. The heuristics discussed thus far collapse the distributional information contained in the sample set of scenarios down to a point estimate, thereby operating on approximations of the expected clearing prices. The heuristics described next more fully exploit any available distributional information; they seek bids that are effective across multiple scenarios, not in just the average scenario.

AverageMU calculates the marginal utilities of all goods, once per scenario, and then bids the *average* MU of each good in each auction.

BidEvaluator evaluates K candidate bidding policies on a fixed set of E sample scenarios. The policy that earns the highest total score is selected. BidEvaluator generates its candidates by making successive calls to the TargetMU heuristic, each time sending it a different scenario to use as its predicted prices.

BidEvaluator* is identical to BidEvaluator, except that its candidate bidding policies are generated by calling TargetMU* instead of TargetMU.

3.2 Sample Average Approximation

The problem of bidding under uncertainty—how to bid given a distributional model of predicted prices—is a stochastic optimization problem. The objective is to select bids that maximize the expected value of the difference between the value of the goods the agent wins and the cost of those goods. Formally,

Definition 2 (Stochastic Bidding Problem). *Given a set of goods X, a (combinatorial) valuation function $v : 2^X \to \mathbb{R}$, and a distribution f over clearing prices $p \in \mathbb{R}^X$, the stochastic bidding problem is defined as:*

$$\max_{b \in \mathbb{R}^X} \mathbb{E}_{p \sim f} \left[v(\mathrm{Win}(b, p)) - \tilde{p}(\mathrm{Win}(b, p)) \right] \tag{1}$$

Here, $x \in \mathrm{Win}(b, p)$ if and only if $b(x) \geq p(x)$, and $\tilde{p} : 2^X \to \mathbb{R}$ is the *additive* extension of $p \in \mathbb{R}^X$, that is, the real-valued function on bundles defined as follows: $\tilde{p}(Y) = \sum_{x \in Y} p(x)$, for all $Y \subseteq X$.

Sample average approximation (SAA) is a standard way of approximating the solution to a stochastic optimization problem, like bidding under uncertainty. The idea behind SAA is simple: (i) generate a set of sample scenarios, and (ii) solve an approximation of the problem that incorporates only the sample scenarios.

Technically, the TAC Travel bidding problem, in which the goal is to maximize the difference between the value of allocating travel packages to clients and the costs of the goods procured to create those packages, is a stochastic program with integer recourse [8]. Using the theory of large deviations, Ahmed and Shapiro [9] establish the following: the probability that an optimal solution to the sample average approximation of a stochastic program with integer recourse is in fact an optimal solution to the original stochastic program approaches 1 exponentially fast as the number of scenarios $S \to \infty$. Given time and space constraints, however, it is not always possible to sample sufficiently many scenarios to make any reasonable guarantees about the quality of a solution to the sample average approximation.

Our default implementation of SAA which we call SAABottom always bids one of the sampled prices. However, given a set of scenarios, SAA is indifferent between bidding the highest sampled price or any amount above that price: in any case SAA believes it will win in all scenarios. Consequently, we do not know exactly how much SAA is willing to pay when it bids the highest sampled price. In the settings with imperfect price prediction or when SAA is given too few scenarios, it may be desirable to bid above the highest sampled price to increase the chances of winning. For this reason, we introduce a modified SAA heuristic— SAATop—in which bids equal to the highest sampled price are replaced with the "maximum" bid. In general, this bid is the most the agent is willing to pay. In our domain, this maximum is the sum of the utility bonus (300; see Footnote 2) and, for good hotels, the largest hotel bonus among the agent's clients'.

4 Experiments in TAC Travel-Like Auctions

We consider four experimental settings: normally distributed prices in two decision-theoretic settings, one with perfect and another with imperfect prediction; and competitive equilibrium (CE) prices in a decision-theoretic setting with perfect prediction and a game-theoretic setting with typically imperfect prediction.

Our experiments were conducted in a TAC Travel-like setting, in which nearly all the standard rules apply.[1] Most notably, we simplified the dynamics of the game. In TAC, flights and entertainment tickets are available continuously at time-varying prices, and hotel auctions close one at a time, providing opportunities for agents to revise their bids on other hotels. In this work, we focus on one-shot auctions. More specifically, we assume all hotels close after one round of bidding.

To reduce variance, we eliminated entertainment trading and simplified flight trading by fixing flight prices at zero.[2,3]

We built a simulator of the TAC server, which can easily be tailored to simulate numerous experimental designs. Our simulator is available for download at http://www.sics.se/tac/showagents.php.

Each trial in an experiment (i.e., each simulation run) proceeded in five steps:

1. The agents predict hotel clearing prices in the form of *scenarios* - samples from the predicted distribution of clearing prices.
   - In the settings where prices are normally distributed, the scenarios were sampled from given distributions of predicted prices.
   - In the settings characterized by competitive equilibrium prices, scenarios were generated by simulating simultaneous ascending auctions, as described in Lee *et al.* [8].

---

[1] For a detailed description of the TAC Travel rules, visit http://www.sics.se/tac

[2] Since we fixed flight prices at zero (instead of roughly 700 for round trip tickets), we adjusted the utility bonus for constructing a valid travel package down from 1000 to 300. That way, our simulation scores fall in the same range as real game scores.

[3] Initially, we ran experiments with flight prices fixed at 350, which is the value close to the average flight price in the TAC Travel game. However the resulting one-shot setting was not interesting as flight tickets represented a very high sunk cost and the dominant hotel bidding strategy was to bid very high on the hotels that would complement the flights in completing travel packages.

2. The agents construct bids using price information contained in the scenarios and submit them.

3. The simulator determines hotel clearing prices, and bids that are equal to or above those clearing prices are deemed winning bids.

   – In the *decision-theoretic* settings, the clearing prices were sampled from given distributions of clearing prices.
   – In the *game-theoretic* setting, each hotels' clearing price was set to the 16th highest bid on that hotel.

4. Agents pay clearing prices for the hotels they win. They use the hotels and free flight tickets to create packages for their clients, based on which they earn the corresponding utilities.

5. Each agent's final score is the difference between its utility and its cost.

The first two steps in the above sequence correspond to the prediction and optimization steps typical of autonomous bidding agents. To carry out step 2, the agents employ heuristics from a test suite that includes the eight bidding heuristics detailed in Wellman, *et al.*([4]), and summarized above.

Regarding price prediction in step 1, hotel price predictions were perfect in our first and third experimental setups and imperfect in our second and fourth. In the first two, hotel prices were predicted to be normally distributed; in the second two, hotel prices were predicted to be competitive equilibrium prices. Our first three experimental setups were decision-theoretic; the fourth was game-theoretic. In the second setup, we simply tweaked the normal distribution of predicted prices to generate a similar, but distinct, normal distribution of clearing prices. In the fourth setup, the game-theoretic setting, clearing prices were dictated by the outcome of 16th price auctions. All setups, with all settings of the parameters (μ, σ, and λ), were run for 1000 trials.

5   Decision-Theoretic Experiments with Perfect Distributional Prediction

Our first experimental setup is decision-theoretic, with prices determined exogenously. Each agent is endowed with perfect distributional information, so that it constructs its bids based on samples drawn from the true price distribution. Under these conditions, it is known that the SAA-based heuristics bid optimally in the limit as $S \to \infty$ [9]. The purpose of conducting experiments in this setting was twofold: (i) to evaluate the performance of the SAA-based heuristics with only finitely many scenarios; and (ii) to evaluate the performance of the MU-based heuristics relative to that of the SAA-based heuristics. We find that both the SAA-based heuristics and certain variants of the MU-based heuristics (primarily, TargetMU* and BidEvaluator*) perform well assuming low variance, but that the SAA-based heuristics and AverageMU outperform all the other heuristics assuming high variance.

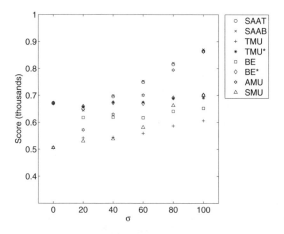

Fig. 1. Mean Scores. Decision-theoretic setting with perfect distributional prediction.

5.1 Setup

Hotel prices were drawn from normal distributions with mean values[4] $\bar{\mu} = (150, 150, 150, 150, 250, 250, 250, 250)$ constant across experiments and standard deviations $\sigma \in \{0, 20, 40, 60, 80, 100\}$ varying across experiments.

5.2 Results

Figure 1 depicts the mean scores earned by each agent in each experiment: i.e., for each setting of σ.

The SAA-based agents perform better than most of the agents as variance increases. They gain an advantage by submitting low bids on more goods than necessary in an attempt to win only the goods that are cheap. We refer to this strategy as *hedging*. We see that the SAA agents employ hedging because the number of bids they place increases, their average bids decrease, and the number of hotels they win remains constant as the variance increases. The number of low-priced hotels increases with the variance making hedging especially effective when variance is high.

Recall that target bidders (TargetMU, TargetMU*, BidEvaluator, and Bid-Evaluator*) bid only on goods in their target set, i.e. they do not hedge. Consequently, failing to win one of the requisite hotels results in not being able to complete a package (most packages are for one-night stays as extending the stay for an extra day is likely to be more expensive than incurring the penalty for deviating from client's preferences). TargetMU and BidEvaluator win fewer and fewer hotels as the variance increases, and hence complete fewer and fewer packages. At the same time the average cost of hotels they win decreases. The agents'

---

[4] In this, and all, hotel price vectors, the first four numbers refer to the price of the bad hotel on days 1 through 4, respectively, and the second four numbers refer to the price of the good hotel on days 1 through 4, respectively.

scores have a slight upward trend as the benefit from lower cost outweighs the loss from completing fewer packages.

BidEvaluator bids on more hotels than TargetMU when variance is 100. Recall that BidEvaluator chooses the best of K bidding policies. Bidding policies that bid on more hotels score higher because they hedge, implicitly. For example, a policy that bids to reserve two nights for a client may earn a higher score than a policy that bids to reserve one night as the reservation for two nights can be used to create two separate one-night packages if some of the other bids fail.

TargetMU* and BidEvaluator*, the main rivals of the SAA-based agents, do not perform well in this setting. Just like TargetMU and BidEvaluator, TargetMU* and BidEvaluator* bid only on target goods. When variance is low ($\sigma = 20$), bidding high on target good is a good strategy as evidenced by TargetMU*'s and BidEvaluator*'s good performance. As variance increases the agents fail to win some of the target goods. In fact when variance is 100, TargetMU* submits 5.8 bids but wins only 4.8 while BidEvaluator* submits 7.4 bids and wins only 5.2. The average cost of hotels that TargetMU* and BidEvaluator* do win is 50% higher than the prices the SAA-based agents pay per hotel.

Interestingly, AverageMU's strategy happens to be very close to hedging when variance is high. StraightMU submits a lot of bids too but unlike AverageMU does not perform well. StraightMU's bids are higher than AverageMU's resulting in more purchased hotels and higher average hotel cost. The increase in cost that StraightMU incurs compared to AverageMU is not compensated by the increase in utility that extra hotels bring.

In conclusion, the SAA-based agents and AverageMU with their hedging strategy outperform the other agents when variance is high.

6   Decision-Theoretic Experiments with Imperfect Distributional Prediction

In our second decision-theoretic experimental setup, the agents construct their bids based on samples drawn from a normal distribution that resembles, but is distinct from, the true distribution. Our intent here is to evaluate the agents' behavior in a controlled setting with imperfect predictions, in order to inform our analysis of their behavior in the game-theoretic setting, where predictions are again imperfect. We find that SAATop performs worse than TargetMU*, and BidEvaluator* at low variance, but outperforms most of the other agents at high variance.

6.1   Setup

In these experiments, the *predicted* price distributions were normal with mean values $\bar{\mu} = (150, 150, 150, 150, 250, 250, 250, 250)$, whereas the *clearing* price distributions were normal with mean values $\bar{\mu} + \lambda$. That is, the mean of each predicted distribution differed by λ from the true mean. For example, for $\lambda = -40$, predicted prices were sampled from normal distributions with $\bar{\mu} = (150, 150, 150, 150, 250,$

250, 250, 250), and clearing prices were sampled from normal distributions with $\bar{\mu} = (110, 110, 110, 110, 210, 210, 210, 210)$. Hence, negative values of λ implied "overprediction." Similarly, positive values of λ implied "underprediction." The λ parameter varied as follows: $\lambda \in \{-40, -30, -20, -10, 0, 10, 20, 30, 40\}$. We chose as standard deviations of the distributions a low setting ($\sigma = 20$) and a high setting ($\sigma = 80$).

In the low (and similarly in the high) deviation experiments the strategies of the agents did not change with λ because the agent received the same predictions for all values of λ. Experiments in this setting evaluate the strategies from the perfect prediction setting with $\sigma = 20$ and $\sigma = 80$ under different distributions of clearing prices as controlled by the values of λ.

6.2 Results

Low Variance: $\sigma = 20$. The results assuming low variance are shown in Figure 2(a). Recall from the perfect prediction experiments that the strategy of bidding high on the goods from a target set is as good as hedging when variance is low. In particular, TargetMU* and BidEvaluator* perform as well as the SAA-based agents. We will see that hedging is not a good strategy in the low-variance setting with imperfect prediction while bidding high on the goods in a target set works fairly well.

In an attempt to hedge, the SAA-based agents submit twice as many bids as TargetMU, TargetMU*, BidEvaluator, and BidEvaluator*. The strategy of the SAA-based agents is to bid low hoping to win approximately half the bids. Because predictions are not perfect, the SAA-based agents win too many hotels when prices are lower than expected and too few hotels when prices are higher than expected. Not surprisingly, SAATop, which bids higher than its counterpart, performs worse than SAABottom when prices are lower than expected and better than SAABottom when the opposite it true.

When there is a high degree of overprediction and variance is low, (e.g., when $\lambda = -40$ and $\sigma = 20$), clearing prices are very likely to be below predicted prices. Since TargetMU always bids at least the predicted price, it is likely to win all the hotels it expects to win in this setting, and hence performs well. Consequently, TargetMU*, BidEvaluator, and BidEvaluator* all perform well. In contrast, when prices are often lower than expected, AverageMU and StraightMU win too many goods and thus incur high unnecessary costs.

As λ increases from -40 to -10, AverageMU and StraightMU win fewer unnecessary hotels, which improves their scores. But once λ reaches 0, they fail to win enough hotels, and their utilities decrease as λ increases to 40. TargetMU and BidEvaluator encounter the same difficulty.

TargetMU* and BidEvaluator* bid higher than TargetMU and BidEvaluator; hence, underprediction affects the former pair less than the latter pair.

To summarize, in the low-variance setting TargetMU*'s and BidEvaluator*'s strategy of bidding high on a target set of goods is more robust to imperfect predictions than the strategy of the SAA-based agents that involves some hedging.

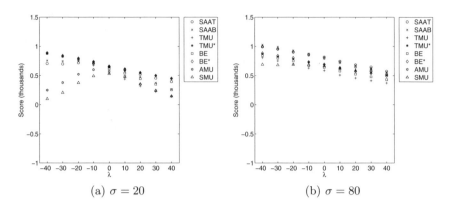

(a) $\sigma = 20$ (b) $\sigma = 80$

Fig. 2. Mean Scores. Imperfect prediction.

High Variance: $\sigma = 80$. The results assuming high variance are shown in Figure 2(b). As we observed in the experiments with perfect prediction and $\sigma = 80$, hedging allowed the SAA-based agents to dominate. We will see that hedging is effective in the high-variance setting even when predictions are not perfect.

The SAA-based agents submit over four times as many bids as TargetMU, TargetMU*, BidEvaluator, and BidEvaluator*. In contrast to the setting with low variance, high overprediction ($\lambda = -40$) does not cause the SAA-based agents to overspend on hotels. In the high-variance setting the SAA-based agents' bids are 40% lower than in the low-variance setting ($\sigma = 20$) and only one-third of the bids are winning bids.

Similarly, the SAA-based agents perform much better in the high underprediction ($\lambda = 40$) setting when variance is high than when variance is low. In the high-variance setting with underprediction the SAA-based agents win at least as many hotels as the high bidding TargetMU* and BidEvaluator* agents. Although the SAA-based agents bid half the price that TargetMU* and BidEvaluator* bid, a much higher number of bids that the SAA-based agents submit combined with high variance results in a similar number of winning bids.

Performance of the other agents is similar to their performance in the setting with perfect prediction. TargetMU, TargetMU*, BidEvaluator, and BidEvaluator* do not hedge and perform poorly in under and over prediction settings. Target bidders often fail to win some of the target hotels even in the overprediction setting. AverageMU submits a lot of low bids resulting in a well-hedged strategy and the scores that are as high as SAA's for some values of λ. As before, StraightMU wins too many hotels.

In contrast to the setting with low variance and imperfect predictions, the SAA-based agents' hedging strategy works well when there is high variance.

7   Experiments with Competitive Equilibrium Prices

In contrast with our first two experimental settings, in which the hotel clearing prices and their corresponding predictions are exogenously determined and hence independent of any game specifics, in our second two experimental settings, both hotel clearing prices and predictions are determined endogenously (i.e., based on features of each game instance). Specifically, following Walverine [2], hotel clearing prices and their corresponding predictions are taken to be approximate *competitive equilibrium* (CE) prices. CE prices are prices at which supply equals demand when all market participants act as price-taking profit maximizers [10]. CE prices need not exist, and likely do not in many of the games studied here. Still, we approximate CE prices as follows: in a market inhabited by its own eight clients and eight randomly sampled clients per competitor, each agent generates a scenario by simulating simultaneous ascending auctions (i.e., increasing prices by some small increment until supply exceeds demand; see Lee *et al.* [8] for details); the resulting prices form a scenario.

7.1   Setup

In this context, where hotel price predictions are (roughly) competitive equilibrium prices, we designed two sets of experiments: one decision-theoretic and one game-theoretic. In the former, hotel clearing prices are also the outcome of a simulation of simultaneous ascending auctions, but depend on the actual clients in each game, not some random sampling like the agents' predictions. (Our simulator is more informed than the individual agents.) In the latter, hotel clearing prices are determined by the bids the agents submit. As in TAC Travel, the clearing price is the 16th highest bid (or zero, if fewer than 16 bids are submitted). Note that hotel clearing prices and their respective predictions are not independent of one another in these experiments.

In these experiments games are played with a random number of agents drawn from a binomial distribution with $n = 32$ and $p = 0.5$, with the requisite number of agents sampled uniformly with replacement from the set of eight possible agent types. The agents first sample the number of competitors from the binomial distribution, and then generate scenarios assuming the sampled number of competitors, resampling that number to generate each new scenario.

7.2   Decision-Theoretic Experiments

Marginal frequency distributions of CE prices in these experiments have means (109, 126, 126, 107, 212, 227, 227, 210) and standard deviations (47, 37, 37, 46, 50, 41, 41, 49). Standard deviation in this setting is close to 40 making this setting similar to the one with perfect prediction and $\sigma = 40$. The mean hotel prices are approximately 20% lower in this CE setting but we do not expect the difference in mean hotel prices to have a strong effect on the ranking of the agents and attribute the differences in relative results to the different structure of prices: unlike the setting with normally distributed prices, CE prices are not independent.

SAATop, SAABottom, TargetMU*, and BidEvaluator* are among the best agents in this CE setting (see Figure 3(a)). However, StraightMU and especially AverageMU perform poorly. AverageMU and StraightMU submit more bids and win more hotels than the other agents, but cannot create as many packages as the top-scoring agents. This is because (i) CE prices of substitutable goods are similar, and (ii) marginal utilities of substitutable goods are similar. As a result, AverageMU and StraightMU bid almost the same amount on all substitutable goods and either win or lose all of them.

SAA-based agents employ some hedging but do not perform significantly better than the non-hedging heuristics TargetMU* and BidEvaluator*.

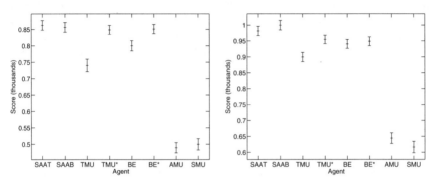

(a) DT setting with CE price prediction (b) GT setting with CE price prediction

Fig. 3. Mean scores and confidence intervals

7.3   Game-Theoretic Experiments

The predicted prices are the same as in the decision-theoretic experiments with CE prices and 32 agents: means (109, 126, 126, 107, 212, 227, 227, 210) and standard deviations (47, 37, 37, 46, 50, 41, 41, 49). Marginal frequency distributions of clearing prices have means (91, 98, 100, 91, 198, 186, 187, 197) and standard deviations (41, 33, 32, 40, 50, 56, 54, 50). L1-norm of the difference between mean price vectors is 197. Predicted prices are slightly higher (by about 20) than the clearing prices. This is similar to the decision-theoretic setting with overprediction ($\lambda = -20$) and medium deviation (between 20 and 80).

Indeed, we find that the results in this setting (see Figure 3(b)) are similar to the results in the decision-theoretic setting with imperfect prediction and high variance: $\lambda = -20$ and $\sigma = 80$ (see the ranking of agents for $\lambda = -20$ in Figure 2(b)). The ranking of non-SAA agents is almost the same in both settings. A notable exception is AverageMU, which performs much worse in the game-theoretic setting for the reasons described above. SAATop and SAABottom are the best agents in this setting, with SAABottom performing slightly better.

8   Summary and Discussion of Experimental Results

In our experiments, we evaluated the performance of various bidding heuristics in simultaneous auctions. Based on our findings, we summarize the performance of the heuristics analyzed as follows:

- SAATop and SAABottom perform well in all settings except for the setting with imperfect prediction and low variance. SAATop and SAABottom are especially effective in high-variance settings because they are able to take advantage of hedging opportunities.
- TargetMU and BidEvaluator are competitive only in the settings with low variance and high overprediction. BidEvaluator outperforms TargetMU in high-variance settings.
- TargetMU* and BidEvaluator* perform well in the settings with low variance.
- AverageMU performs well in the settings with independent prices.
- StraightMU performs worse than the other heuristics.

We can also make the following observations about the various bidding behaviors:

- SAABottom, SAATop, and AMU place low bids on many goods, intending to win whatever sells at cheap prices. These heuristics incur high penalties for not satisfying their clients' precise preferences.
- TargetMU, TargetMU*, BidEvaluator, and BidEvaluator* place higher bids but on fewer goods, namely those for which their clients have clear preferences. These heuristics incur lower penalties, but risk alienating some clients, by not allocating them any travel packages at all.[5]

The performance of SAA is known to approach optimality as the number of scenarios approaches ∞ in decision-theoretic settings. We investigated the viability of two SAA heuristics with only finitely-many scenarios in both decision-theoretic and game-theoretic settings. Our first and third experimental settings (with normally distributed and competitive equilibrium prices, assuming perfect price prediction) established the viability of these heuristics in decision-theoretic settings with only finitely-many scenarios. Our fourth experimental setting established the viability of these heuristics (again, with only finitely-many scenarios, but in addition) in a rich game-theoretic setting.

9   Related Work

The test suite considered here is far from exhaustive. In this section, we mention several heuristics that were not included in our study—some TAC-specific; some more general—and the reasons for their exclusion.

The creators of the ATTac agent [3] propose using AverageMU for TAC hotel bidding. ATTac also employs distributional information about hotel prices to

---

[5] No penalty is incurred when a client is not allocated any package at all. (Of course, no utility is awarded either.)

determine the benefit of postponing flight purchases until hotel prices are known; this additional functionality, while certainly of interest, is not applicable to the one-shot auction setting studied here.

WhiteBear's [11] TAC hotel bids are computed by taking a weighted average of the current price and the marginal utility of each hotel. The particular weights, which were fine-tuned based on historical competition data, varied with time. In a one-shot setting, WhiteBear's strategy essentially reduces to TargetMU: it is too risky to bid anything lower.

SouthamptonTAC [12] and Mertacor [13] focus on hotel price prediction, and do not thoroughly analyze bidding. SouthamptonTAC uses fuzzy reasoning to predict how hotel prices change during the game.

Unlike the heuristics studied in this paper, Walverine's [2] bidding strategy incorporates some game-theoretic reasoning. Specifically, Walverine analytically calculates the distribution of marginal utilities of the other agents' clients and bids a best-response to this distribution. The authors implicitly assume that the other agents bid marginal utilities (i.e., act decision-theoretically) and only their agent bids a best-response (i.e., acts game-theoretically). We learned from the study reported in this paper that SAA can be a successful bidding heuristic in certain markets. Following Walverine's line of thought, we can imagine bidding a best-response to a distribution of SAA bids. However, if this bidding strategy were successful, we would have to assume that other agents would act game-theoretically as well; that is, they would also play a best-response to a distribution of SAA bids. We may then seek a fixed point of this process. This line of inquiry could be fascinating, but any approach based on this insight of Walverine's warrants a detailed study of its own.

Aside from TAC Travel there is a rich literature on bidding in other settings. We reference a few papers here, highlighting some of the settings that have been studied. We are not aware of any papers that address the problem of bidding in multiple one-shot auctions for both complementary and substitutable goods. Gerding et al. ([14]) describes a strategy for bidding in simultaneous one-shot second-price auctions selling perfect substitutes. Byde, Priest, & Jennings ([15]) consider the decision-theoretic problem of bidding in multiple auctions with overlapping closing times. Their model treats all goods as indistinguishable (i.e., winning any n goods results in utility $v(n)$). Krishna & Rosenthal ([16]) characterize a symmetric equilibrium for the case of one-shot simultaneous auctions with indistinguishable complementary goods (i.e. $v(n) \geq nv(1)$).

10   Conclusion

The primary purpose of this work was to show that using as much distributional information as possible is an effective approach to bidding in TAC Travel-like one-shot simultaneous auctions. Most TAC Travel agents used point price predictions or employed little distributional information about prices in constructing their bids. Some of the difficulties with using distributional price predictions include the inaccuracy of and the high computational cost of optimizing with respect to distributional predictions. We showed experimentally that the SAA heuristic, which uses more distributional information than the other heuristics in our test suite, is one of the best heuristics in the GT setting.

The underlying research question motivating this line of inquiry was: how can we facilitate the search for heuristics that perform well against a variety of competing agents in complex games? Analyzing the performance of an individual agent in a game-theoretic setting is complicated because each agent's performance is affected by the strategies of the others, and can vary dramatically with the mix of participants. Others tackling this problem in the TAC Travel domain have employed more direct game-theoretic analysis techniques based on equilibrium computations (e.g., Vetsikas *et al.* [17] and Jordan, Kiekintveld, & Wellman [18]). In contrast, we first used systematic decision-theoretic analysis to help us understand some of the intrinsic properties of our bidding heuristics, before attempting any game-theoretic analysis. We found that certain properties of the heuristics that may have been hard to identify in game-theoretic settings, such as how they perform in conditions of over- vs. under-prediction, carried over from our DT to our GT settings.

In summary, the methodology advocated in this paper for analyzing game-theoretic heuristics is this: first, evaluate the heuristic in DT settings with perfect and imperfect predictions; and second, measure the accuracy of the agent's predictions in GT experiments and use the corresponding DT analysis to inform the analysis of the GT results. It remains to test this methodology in other complex games, such as TAC SCM [19].

Acknowledgments

This research was funded by NSF Grant #IIS-0133689 and the Samsung Foundation of Culture.

References

1. Wellman, M., Wurman, P., O'Malley, K., Bangera, R., Lin, S., Reeves, D., Walsh, W.: A Trading Agent Competition. IEEE Internet Computing (April 2001)
2. Cheng, S., Leung, E., Lochner, K., O'Malley, K., Reeves, D., Schvartzman, L., Wellman, M.: Walverine: A Walrasian trading agent. Decision Support Systems 39(2), 169–184 (2005)
3. Stone, P., Schapire, R., Littman, M., Csirik, J., McAllester, D.: Decision-theoretic bidding based on learned density models in simultaneous, interacting auctions. Journal of Artificial Intelligence Research 19, 209–242 (2003)
4. Wellman, M.P., Greenwald, A., Stone, P.: Autonomous Bidding Agents: Strategies and Lessons from the Trading Agent Competition. MIT Press, Cambridge (2007)
5. Vickrey, W.: Counterspeculation, auctions, and competitive sealed tenders. Journal of Finance 16, 8–37 (1961)
6. Greenwald, A., Boyan, J.: Bidding under uncertainty: Theory and experiments. In: Proceedings of the 20th Conference on Uncertainty in Artificial Intelligence, July 2004, pp. 209–216 (2004)

7. Greenwald, A., Boyan, J.: Bidding algorithms for simultaneous auctions: A case study. Journal of Autonomous Agents and Multiagent Systems 10(1), 67–89 (2005)
8. Lee, S., Greenwald, A., Naroditskiy, V.: Roxybot-06: An $(SAA)^2$ TAC travel agent. In: Proceedings of the 20th International Joint Conference on Artificial Intelligence, January 2007, pp. 1378–1383 (2007)
9. Ahmed, S., Shapiro, A.: The sample average approximation method for stochastic programs with integer recourse (2002) Optimization Online, http://www.optimization-online.org
10. Mas-Colell, A., Whinston, M., Green, J.: Microeconomic Theory. Oxford University Press, New York (1995)
11. Vetsikas, I.A., Selman, B.: A principled study of the design tradeoffs for autonomous trading agents. In: AAMAS 2003: Proceedings of the second international joint conference on Autonomous agents and multiagent systems, pp. 473–480. ACM, New York (2003)
12. He, M., Jennings, N.R.: Southamptontac: An adaptive autonomous trading agent. ACM Trans. Interet Technol. 3(3), 218–235 (2003)
13. Toulis, P., Kehagias, D., Mitkas, P.: Mertacor: A successful autonomous trading agent. In: Fifth International Joint Conference on Autonomous Agents and Multiagent Systems, Hakodate, pp. 1191–1198 (2006)
14. Gerding, E., Dash, R., Yuen, D., Jennings, N.R.: Optimal bidding strategies for simultaneous vickrey auctions with perfect substitutes. In: 8th Int. Workshop on Game Theoretic and Decision Theoretic Agents, pp. 10–17 (2006) (lib/utils:month1_112586)
15. Byde, A., Preist, C., Jennings, N.R.: Decision procedures for multiple auctions. In: AAMAS 2002: Proceedings of the first international joint conference on Autonomous agents and multiagent systems, pp. 613–620. ACM, New York (2002)
16. Krishna, V., Rosenthal, R.W.: Simultaneous auctions with synergies. Games and Economic Behavior 17(1), 1–31 (1996), http://ideas.repec.org/a/eee/gamebe/v17y1996i1p1-31.html
17. Vetsikas, I.A., Selman, B.: Bayes-nash equilibria for mth price auctions with multiple closing times. SIGecom Exch. 6(2), 27–36 (2007)
18. Jordan, P.R., Kiekintveld, C., Wellman, M.P.: Empirical game-theoretic analysis of the tac supply chain game. In: AAMAS 2007: Proceedings of the 6th international joint conference on Autonomous agents and multiagent systems, pp. 1–8. ACM, New York (2007)
19. Arunachalam, R., Sadeh, N.M.: The supply chain trading agent competition. Electronic Commerce Research and Applications 4(1), 66–84 (2005)

Applications of Classifying Bidding Strategies for the CAT Tournament

Mark L. Gruman and Manjunath Narayana

Department of Computer Science, University of Massachusetts, 140 Governors Drive
Amherst, MA, 01003, USA
{mgruman,narayana}@cs.umass.edu

Abstract. In the CAT Tournament, specialists facilitate transactions between buyers and sellers with the intention of maximizing profit from commission and other fees. Each specialist must find a well-balanced strategy that allows it to entice buyers and sellers to trade in its market while also retaining the buyers and sellers that are currently subscribed to it. Classification techniques can be used to determine the distribution of bidding strategies used by all traders subscribed to a particular specialist. Our experiments showed that Hidden Markov Model classification yielded the best results. The distribution of strategies, along with other competition-related factors, can be used to determine the optimal action in any given game state. Experimental data shows that the GD and ZIP bidding strategies are more volatile than the RE and ZIC strategies. An MDP framework for determining optimal actions given an accurate distribution of bidding strategies is proposed as a motivator for future work.

1 Introduction

The field of Catallactics, or the science of exchanges, has received significant attention in the Artificial Intelligence community over the past few years, in large part, due to increasing use of e-commerce environments such online auctions and ticket vendors. In particular, significant attention has been given to designing efficient markets in which traders of numerous roles and preferences interact and exchange goods while utilizing various bidding strategies and trading tactics. The CAT Tournament [1], an offshoot of the original Trading Agents Competition introduced in 2007, is a contest in which markets (hereon referred to as "specialists") attempt to lure buyers and sellers (hereon collectively referred to as "traders") to their respective trading platforms in hopes of maximizing profit. Unlike the original TAC Classic and TAC SMC competitions in which specialists fulfilled stationary requests, CAT specialists must respond to a variety of bidding techniques employed by the traders who also wish to maximize their own profits; this dynamic environment serves as the main motivation for developing adaptive markets that actively respond to the traders' ever-changing preferences.

Successful specialist design requires a balanced decision-making strategy that entices new traders to subscribe to the specialist while also retaining existing traders. One method of developing such a strategy involves creating a model for every trader and determining how each action affects each model. This approach is highly infeasible,

W. Ketter et al. (Eds.): AMEC/TADA 2008, LNBIP 44, pp. 147–160, 2010.
© Springer-Verlag Berlin Heidelberg 2010

however, because the specialist does not receive any information regarding the traders other than which ones are currently subscribed to it; all incoming bids are masked before they reach the specialist, so the specialist is unable to definitively link each bid with a particular trader. Creating a model for each trader is also highly ineffective given that there may be hundreds of traders interacting with one another. Processing hundreds of models can take a significant amount of time on even the most powerful systems and may require more system memory than is available.

One important feature of the CAT Tournament is that all traders use strictly one of four previously-defined bidding strategies. In this paper we describe how classification techniques can be used to exploit the fact that traders must use one of four bidding strategies, reducing the number of models required to accurately represent all traders to just four. We provide experimental results indicating how certain actions affect the trader pool, especially groups of traders utilizing the same bidding strategy. We also discuss how these group models can be used to train the specialist, allowing it make decisions quickly during the competition.

The paper first provides a brief description of each bidding strategy in Section 2. The benefits of classifying traders according to bidding strategies are described in detail in Section 3, along with a comprehensive analysis of various classification techniques that have been applied to this problem and their final results. Section 4 briefly describes how classification (in conjunction with other game factors) can be used to determine the optimal action the specialist should take at any particular point in the competition. Experimental results are presented in Section 5, followed by a brief conclusion and a discussion of possible future work in Section 6.

2 Bidding Strategies

All traders in the CAT Tournament are required to utilize one of four bidding strategies. A brief description of each strategy is provided here, but the reader is urged to consult the original publications (see references [2]-[5]) that describe the strategies in detail.

A trader using the Double Auction strategy [3] (henceforth called GD) keeps track of the number of bids accepted and rejected by the market at a particular price. Subsequent values for the bids are chosen depending on the probability of acceptance of a bid, given the past history. Utilizing the Extensive Form Game strategy [5] (hereon referred to as RE), a trader alters its future bid values based on the profits that were observed for the previous bids. The Zero Information-Constrained (ZI-C) strategy [4] involves generating random bids constrained between a maximum and minimum value. A buyer using the ZI-C strategy will never bid more than what it believes a good is worth. Likewise, a seller will never sell a good for less than the amount it cost the seller to obtain the good. Finally, if a trader uses the Zero Information, Plus (ZIP) strategy [2], it utilizes the same trading techniques as a trader that employs ZI-C, but it also updates the constraints based on feedback from the market. Thus, each process (except when using the ZI-C strategy) receives feedback from the market in various forms and updates itself to generate new bids.

3   Classifying Traders by Bidding Strategies

In the CAT Tournament, all traders must employ one of four previously-defined bidding strategies when placing bids with their respective specialist. With this stipulation, it is reasonable to assume that all traders utilizing the same bidding strategy will behave similarly (at least more so than the other traders). Likewise, any action taken by the specialist, such as raising or lowering a particular fee, will most likely have a similar affect on all traders utilizing the same bidding strategy. These assumptions allow the specialist to reason about how its actions may affect an entire group of traders rather than individuals, turning the trader-modeling problem into a classification problem. We discuss the validity of our assumption in the Experimental Results section (5).

For simplicity, we consider only the bids that the specialist has received from its traders, and disregard the information available from other markets. Unfortunately, the collected data cannot be used for classification in its rawest form because bids are masked before they reach the specialist, making it virtually impossible to determine from which trader each bid originated. As a result, a set of collected data was manually unmasked in order to train and then test various classifiers.

At this point we need to point out that, based on the assumption that traders act as groups, it is sufficient for the classifier to predict the proportional utilization of each bidding strategy rather than identify the bidding strategy used by each individual trader. This relaxation becomes crucial during the actual competition when all of the bids are again masked and the specialist is unable to determine the origin of each bid it receives.

Bid sequences were collected for 400 traders (100 traders for each strategy), with their identities unmasked. We decided that focusing on the selling trader sequences alone would suffice to evaluate the efficacy of the classification strategy. In all, 2076 bid sequences were generated by the system. Two-thirds (1384) of these samples were randomly chosen to be the training set and one-third of the data (692) was used for testing.

We describe our data collection methods in Section 3.1 and then examine two classification techniques in detail, focusing our attention on SVM Classification in Section 3.2 and HMM Classification in Section 3.3. In Section 3.4 we briefly discuss other classification techniques that were considered but not explored in detail.

3.1   Data Collection

CAT, each trader makes a bid to the market and continues to update it until another trader in the same market accepts the bid price and a transaction takes place. We call each string of updated bids from the same trader a "bid sequence". Sample bid sequences can be seen in Fig. 1. Given the competitive nature of the market with several traders attempting to make the transaction, a buyer's bid could be accepted by a seller at any point during the bid process. This means that the number of bids a trader has to make before successfully concluding a transaction is not constant. As a result, the number of bids in each bid sequence can vary significantly. There is no upper bound on the length of the sequence. The number of bids in the sequence can range from 1 to any large number depending on the state of the market and the strategies of other traders in that market. We witnessed a number of occasions in which bid sequences contained more than 200 bids. The problem is further complicated when we consider multiple traders using different strategies.

```
Seller_GD_1- 84.0, 90.4, 102.9
Seller_RE_1- 93.6
Seller_GD_3- 153.9, 140.5, 75.6, 90.3
Seller_ZIP_1- 100.2, 98.7, 89.6, 77.6, 109.4
Seller_ZIP_4- 59.0, 85.2, 82.7, 81.3, 73.4
Seller_ZIC_3- 34.5, 56.7, 78.9
Seller_GD_3- 152.8, 132,6
...
```

Fig. 1. Illustration of bid sequences from a sample market with multiple traders employing different bidding strategies

The traders' bidding data was collected through numerous simulations of a typical CAT competition[1]. Although there were no problems collecting a sufficient amount of data (one could always run more simulations), the "raw" data collected could not immediately be used for classification purposes for a number of reasons. The most significant obstacle of data classification was dealing with anonymized data. By "anonymized" we mean that the true origin of each bid was masked. This occurred per the specification of the CAT Competition Protocol, in which bids shouted by traders first reached the server, which replaced the identity of the bid source with a unique bid identifier used only for that particular sequence of bids. Once a transaction completed, the bid identifier was discarded and a new bid identifier was assigned to the next sequence of bids from the same trader. As a result, all bids were masked by the time they reached the specialist. Thus, the specialist could determine neither the true identity of each bid, nor which bid sequences originated from the same trader.

The random order in which the bids arrived also further complicated the process of determining the true origin of each bid. Fortunately, the CAT source code (freely available to all CAT Competition participants and researchers) gives users access to all functional modules that make up the competition. With these additional resources, and a number of code modifications, we were able to obtain the required data in its "unmasked" form, allowing them to identify the true source of each bid that the specialist received. This data was collected under the assumption that it would be used for training only, since the identity of each bid would not be available to the specialist during an actual competition.

3.2 Classification Using a Support Vector Machine

Support Vector Machines are a set of popular classification algorithms that strive to simultaneously minimize classification error and maximize the margin of separation of data [7].

In order to perform classification using the SVM, collected data was first converted to the appropriate data format. Each sequence of bids was represented by a unique

---

[1] Simulations were run using the TAC Market Design Competition Platform[6], which was obtained at https://sourceforge.net/projects/jcat

vector, and each bid in the sequence became a feature in the corresponding vector. Feature numbers were assigned incrementally, so a bid sequence made up of n bids was represented by a vector of features 1 through n. Each vector was assigned a classification as follows: a bid sequence coming from a trader using the GD strategy was classified as class 1, RE as class 2, ZIP as class 3, and ZIC as class 4. An example of the data can be seen in Fig. 2.

SVM training and classification was performed using LibSVM® v2.85 [8]. Prediction results using SVM classification varied greatly, depending largely on the type of kernel that was used for training. Training on the sigmoid kernel (with default gamma and coefficient values) yielded the worst results, predicting only 28.2% of the testing set correctly (only 3% better than completely random prediction). Training under the linear and polynomial kernels also yielded rather poor results, predicting only 32.8% and 38.4% of the testing data correctly, respectively. The sigmoid kernel, however, produced much better results, predicting 53.8% of the testing data correctly under default parameters and 59.7% of the data correctly when gamma was set to 0.8. An observation was also made that the GD and ZI-C strategies were predicted with a high degree of accuracy, while data from the ZIP and RE strategies was more difficult to classify.

```
1   1 : 83.02029493660217
1   1 : 84.91796358721331
1   1 : 113.72054114472121    2 : 116.14283320959657    3 : 116
1   1 : 84.9176358721331
...
2   1 : 112.84017410967499
2   1 : 192.3076814096421     2 : 111.3076814096421
...
3   1 : 89.74849000047514
3   1 : 109.12522211910922
3   1 : 80.72191004970509
3   1 : 139.5462076581298     2 : 107.85463726359954
...
4   1 : 95.08454458555207
4   1 : 91.39030987862498
4   1 : 94.43402012111619
```

Fig. 2. Bid sequence data converted to SVM format. The number of bids in each sequence varied and was heavily dependent on the bidding strategy utilized by each bidding trader.

3.3 Classification Using a Hidden Markov Model

Hidden Markov Models are graphical models that can be used to model the underlying process that generates a given set of data [9]. They are most widely used for classifying time-series data, (e.g. speech processing [10]).

HMM-based classification showed a small improvement over the SVM-based method that was used earlier, supporting our expectation that a Hidden Markov Model would most effectively model the variables involved in the bidding process. Several HMM runs were executed with different values for the parameters (number of hidden states and mixture components). A summary of the results can be seen in Fig. 3. The HMM models took between 10 and 68 minutes to train depending on the number of states and mixture components. In contrast, SVM training ranged between only a few seconds and 2-3 minutes. Nevertheless, the accuracy for the HMM method was always greater than 52%, and we were able to achieve about 62% accuracy by tuning the parameters (number of hidden states = 10, number of mixture components = 10).

A small experiment was also carried out to explore the efficacy of feature reduction of the observed dataset in the HMM classification framework. We could not use standard reduction methods like PCA because the dataset included instances of varying feature lengths (treating each bid as a single feature). Most samples had only one feature, while some had as many as 200. Experiments showed that when only two features were used, the HMM accuracy fell to 49%, while using only the first 10 features improved upon earlier best results slightly. Thus, we concluded that a moderate reduction in the number of features could result in improved performance while also maintaining the integrity of the observed data.

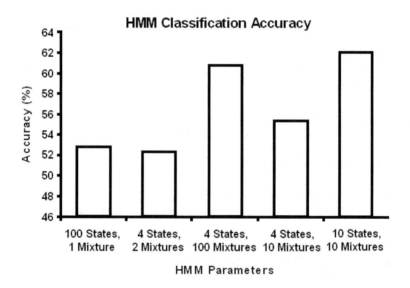

Fig. 3. HMM Classification results for varying parameters

3.4 Alternative Classification Techniques

A number of other interesting methods were explored for improving the results of the HMM. We tried to fit a Conditional Random Fields (CRF) model to the data, using the *CRF Toolbox for MATLAB®* source code provided by Professor Kevin Murphy (U. of B.C.). The model failed to converge in many cases, however, and resulted in accuracy that was not much better than random performance.

Since SVM is the most popular and successful classification method in most applications, we decided to also try the time-dependent Fourier kernel [11]. We expected that the power of SVM when combined with some time information provided by the Fourier kernel would show significant improvement in the classification accuracies. A Fourier kernel was calculated for all the instances in the training and testing data set, as required by the LibSVM framework for implementing user-defined kernels in LibSVM. Accuracy of between 28% and 42% was observed for different cases of the Fourier kernel, suggesting that it was not an improvement over the other kernel functions of the SVM framework.

We decided that the pyramid kernel [12], given its ability to classify datasets that have a varying number of features, would be used in future work.

4   Utilizing Classification to Determine Optimal Action Policies

An accurate model of CAT is required for the specialist to make sound decisions throughout the competition. The specialist is privy to a large amount of data, most notably every bid it receives from its traders, but it is not immediately clear how this data should be represented in the game model. Clearly, modeling every individual bid is not only impractical but also very likely infeasible and probably unnecessary. The classification techniques we discussed in the previous section allow us to model all bids using a simple yet highly-descriptive distribution. We can then use this distribution, along with a number of other observable factors, to uniquely and correctly identify the *state* of the competition and take the *action* that is deemed optimal for that state. The characteristics required to identify a CAT state are described in Table 1.

The distribution of bidding strategy combinations was represented by a predetermined number in the range of 0 to 24, because there are 24 (4!) unique orders in which the bidding strategies can be listed. Then, utilizing the classification results from Section 3, the bidding strategies were ordered in a sequence starting with the most popular and ending with the least popular. Finally, the sequence was matched with the pre-defined list to obtain the unique number representing that particular sequence of strategies.

In addition to the distribution of bidding strategies, the specialist should consider a number of other observable factors such as Position, Trader Count, and Current Fees. All of these factors may be subject to a wide range of values or may not be bounded at all, so a reduction function must be applied to relegate the number of total possible states to a finite and practical quantity. For example, it may be sufficient to categorize Trader Count based on a particular range of total traders (e.g. 0-10% of all traders, 10-20%, etc...). Likewise, the Current Fees factor can be classified in relation to some numerical constants determined to be "threshold boundaries" for certain groups of traders.

The actions each specialist can take can be limited to raising, lowering, or maintaining each of the five fees the specialist charges each trader. However, because four of the five fees do not have an upper bound, it does not make sense to enumerate the actions based on raw values (of which there are infinitely many). Similar to the Trader Count factor used to define the state of the CAT Tournament, raw actions must also be mapped to produce a finite and enumerable set of distinct actions. One such mapping involves simply determining whether each fee has been raised, lowered, or unmodified, resulting in 3^5, or 243 unique actions. We describe our implementation of this framework in section 5.4.

Table 1. Summary of the CAT state components and their respective value ranges

Component	Description	Range of Values
Distribution	Bidding strategy combinations ...	$0-24$
Position	Numerical score position	$0-N^2$
Trader Count	Number of subscribed traders	$0-T^3$
Current Fees	Hash value of the fees	$0-F^4$

5 Experimental Results

A set of experimental test runs was executed to determine if certain actions had a more profound effect on specific groups of traders; they yielded a number of interesting properties for various bidding strategies. We also describe our attempt to determine optimal bidding policies using a Markov Decision Process (MDP) framework outlined earlier.

We first describe the environment in which our experiments were executed, as well as the algorithm that was implemented to adjust fees throughout the experiments.

5.1 Testing Environment

All non-clustering experiments were run on a Compaq C712NR laptop with the following specifications:

> Intel® Pentium® Dual-core CPU T2310 @ 1.46GHz
> 1 GB DDRAM, 789 MHz
> Windows XP with Service Pack 2
> Java™ SE Runtime Environment (build 1.6.0_05-b13)

All CAT agents (server, specialists, and traders) were run on the same machine. The server and traders were run using the *tournament.params* parameter file provided with the CAT source code. Important features included:

> 400 total traders (100 for each bidding strategy)
> 200 buyers, 200 sellers (8 groups of 50 traders total)
> Game length of 4000 days (usually terminated earlier)
> Day length of 20 rounds
> Round length of 1000 milliseconds

All experiments were run with a total of 5 specialists. To simulate a realistic tournament environment, publicly available binaries from the 2007 CAT Tournament[5] were used as specialist adversaries, specifically *CrocodileAgent*, *jackaroo*, *PersianCat*, and *TaxTec*.

---

[2] N refers to the number of specialists competing in the CAT tournament.

[3] T refers to the number of traders that are subscribed to the specialist in the CAT Tournament.

[4] F refers to the maximum hash value used to uniquely identify the fees charged by the specialist. This value is directly dependent on the number of categories used for each fee.

[5] Binaries of 2007 CAT Tournament specialists were obtained from
http://www.sics.se/tac/showagents.php

5.2 Fee Adjustments

Following the discussion in the previous section, fees were randomly adjusted in one of three ways:

1) increase a fee by a factor of 2
2) decrease a fee by a factor of 2
3) retain an existing fee

The likelihood of all outcomes was set to the same frequency (1/3). Our fee-adjustment algorithm ensured that the profit fee would not surpass 100% (per the specification of the CAT protocol) and set an arbitrary amount for a fee when it was being increased from 0, since increasing 0 by a factor of two again results in 0.

Finally, a special "stabilization" algorithm was implemented for a subset of the experiments. Specifically, the algorithm maximized the specialist's chances of regaining traders if the number of subscribed traders reached 0. In this case, all fees were immediately reduced to 0 and maintained at that level until at least 10% of the trader pool was again subscribed to the specialist.

Algorithm for Non-Stabilizing Fee Increases

```
funct IncreaseFee(fee):
  if (increase_fee)
    if (fee > 0)
      fee = fee * 2.0;
      if (fee > 1.0 && isProfitFee(fee))
        fee = 1.0;
    else
      if (fee.type == profitFee)
        fee = 0.1;
      else
        fee = 1.0;
```

5.3 Experiments

A number of experiments were run and a large amount of data was collected. We separate the results we deemed most interesting into the following categories: largest increases in traders, largest decreases in traders, and largest discrepancy in trader strategies.

Largest Increases in Trader Count. Unsurprisingly, some of the largest increases in trader count came during the first day of a stabilization sequence when all fees were reset to 0. The increase in traders ranged from 9 to 24 traders. The traders that immediately subscribed to the stabilizing specialist represented all of the bidding strategies fairly equally, although the total number of recently-joined sellers was often higher than the total number of recently-joined buyers.

More surprisingly, a continued state of stabilization did not yield a constant increase in traders. In one case it took 356 trading days before the stabilizing specialist had regained 10 percent of the total trader pool (although it had regained 9% of the trader pool in 191 days). This result, presented in Fig. 4, conveyed that once traders had settled upon a particular specialist a significant decrease in fees of another specialist was not sufficient in tearing the traders away from their host, and only action taken by the host specialist resulted in traders looking for another specialist.

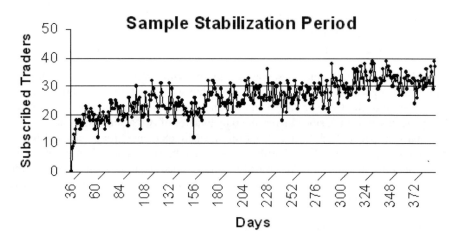

Fig. 4. Stabilization sequence which lasted 356 days

Largest Decreases in Trader Count. Analogous to the largest increases, the most significant decreases in trader count occurred when multiple fees increased simultaneously, sometimes bringing the specialist's trader count to zero and initiating a stabilization sequence.

Interestingly, an increase in multiple fees almost always resulted in a significant decrease in trader count regardless of whether other fees had decreased or remained the same. Additionally, the data suggested that trader count decreased when multiple fees increase regardless of the actual amount by which the fees rose. For example, three fees doubling from 1.0 to 2.0 during one day resulted in a decrease in trader count with the same magnitude as that of three fees doubling from 16 to 32. A small link appeared to exist between a decrease in the registration and information fees and a decrease in the buyers using GD bidding and sellers using RE bidding.

Largest Discrepancy in Bidding Strategies. After modifying the provided CAT source code, we were able to identify the bidding strategies of all traders placing bids through our specialist. This allowed us to analyze the distribution of strategies at any point during the CAT competition and yielded some interesting results. Here we note that this information is not available during the actual competition when bids are masked, so the results we have gathered should be used only to identify general properties of the bidding strategies.

Our first observation was that traders employing the GD and ZIP bidding strategies were generally more volatile than traders who were utilizing the RE and ZIC bidding strategies. For example, during a sequence of days in which the total count of traders decreased we observed that the percentage of total traders utilizing the ZIP strategy nearly doubled while the percentage of total traders utilizing the GD strategy decreased by nearly a factor of 2 (see Fig. 5).

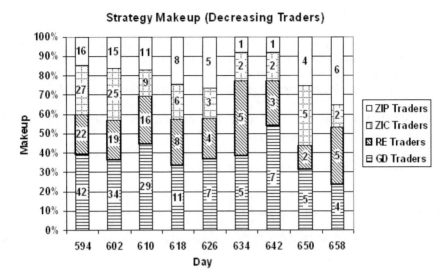

Fig. 5. Bidding strategy makeup during a sequence of decreasing traders

In the same experiment, we also observed the representation of each bidding strategy during a sequence of days in which the total number of traders gradually increased. Under this scenario, the percentage of total traders utilizing the ZIP strategy decreased by a factor of 2 while the proportion of traders utilizing the GD strategy nearly doubled (see Fig. 6). Although the proportion of traders employing the other two strategies also changed during the same sequences, the changes were not reciprocal of one another when comparing the sequences.

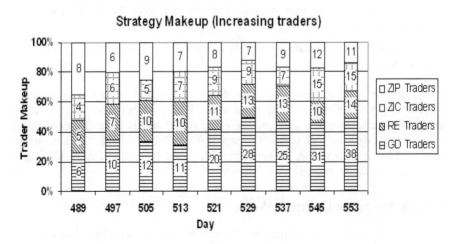

Fig. 6. Bidding strategy makeup during a sequence of increasing traders

5.4 Determining Optimal Actions Using an MDP

Very early in our testing cycle we observed that CAT states possess the Markov Property, suggesting that a Markov Decision Process (MDP) framework could be used to determine the optimal action for each state. Thus, we attempted to address the decision-making problem presented in section 4 with the following MDP definition:

CAT MDP Definition. Let $< S, A, R, P >$ represent the MDP decision-making problem in the CAT tournament, where:

S is a CAT state, further decomposed into 4 criterion:

Distribution ::= S_1, S_2, S_3, S_4, represents the strategies utilized by the subscribed traders in decreasing order of popularity.

Position ::= <FIRST, MIDDLE, LAST>, refers to the specialist's overall score when compared with other specialists' scores.

Traders ::= <0-10%, 10-20%, 20-30%, 30%+>, represents the percentage of all traders subscribed to our specialist.

Fees ::= <Flat Fees | Profit Fee>, where
  Flat::=<0, 0–1, 1–20, 20–100, 100–1000, 1000+>
  Profit ::= <0, 0-0.25, 0.25-0.5, 0.5-0.75, 0.75-1, 1>

A is a CAT action, represented by the tuple $<f_1, f_2, f_3, f_4, f_5>$ where $f_x ::=$ <raise, lower, keep> represents an action for each of the five fees.

R is the reward function for each CAT state. Since the ultimate goal in CAT is to maximize profit, we defined the reward of each state to be the profit earned during the most recent day of trading.

P is the transition probability matrix for every pair of states. Matrix values were experimentally obtained.

After a number of experiments[6] we realized that our state definition was not sufficient in accurately representing the CAT game state. We based this conclusion on the observation that the reward of a given state often varied greatly (often by thousands of points), suggesting that our states were not sufficiently unique. It was not immediately obvious what additional criteria could be used to better identify CAT game states and remains a top priority for future work.

6 Conclusion and Future Work

We present a number of techniques for classifying traders according to their bidding strategies and show that a Hidden Markov Model yields the best results. Our

---

[6] Our implementation of the MDP framework utilized source code written for the AIMA[13] textbook and can be obtained from http://code.google.com/p/aima-java

experimental data presents a number of conclusions regarding fees and how they affect bidding strategies. Most notably, we demonstrate that traders utilizing the GD and ZIP strategies are more volatile than those employing the RE a ZIC strategies. We also note that multiple fee increases generally lead to a loss of traders. Finally, we show evidence supporting the claim that traders are hesitant about switching, regardless of their strategies.

We also proposed a model for discovering optimal action policies while also exploiting the strategy-specific properties presented here. Although our framework appears to support the Markov Property (suggesting that MDP-related algorithms would do well in determining optimal action policies), the criteria we chose were not sufficient to uniquely identify CAT game states. Establishing which criteria should be used to identify CAT states remains an interesting and unsolved problem. Additional experiments should also be performed to determine if bidding strategies can be further exploited. Especially interesting is the interrelationship of the various bidding properties and whether or not certain actions affect the strategies in a similar fashion.

Acknowledgements. First and foremost, we would like to thank Professor Shlomo Zilberstein for his support of this project over the past two years, including regular meetings regarding research progress and advice regarding methodology. We would also like to thank Professor Sridhar Mahadevan for providing us with an opportunity to discuss our work and how it relates to Machine Learning, and for providing us with a MATLAB® implementation of the Expectation-Maximization Algorithm using a Hidden Markov Model. Finally, we would also like to thank Professor Kevin Murphy for his CRF Toolbox source code, which allowed us to evaluate the effectiveness of using a Conditional Random Fields model to classify traders.

References

1. Gerding, E., McBurney, P., Niu, J., Parsons, S., Phelps, S.: Overview of CAT: A Market Design Competition. Technical Report ULCS-07-006. Department of Computer Science, University of Liverpool. Liverpool, UK (2007),
   http://www.csc.liv.ac.uk/research/techreports/tr2007/tr07006abs.html
2. Cliff, D.: Minimal-intelligence agents for bargaining behaviors in market-based environments. Technical Report HP–97–91, Hewlett Packard Laboratories, Bristol, England (1997)
3. Gjerstad, S., Dickhaut, J.: Price Formation in Double Auctions. Games and Economic Behavior 22, 1–29 (1998)
4. Gode, D.K., Sunder, S.: Allocative efficiency of markets with zero-intelligence traders: Markets as a partial substitute for individual rationality. The Journal of Political Economy 101(1), 119–137 (1993)
5. Roth, A.E., Erev, I.: Learning in extensive-form games: Experimental data and simple dynamic models in the intermediate term. Games and Economic Behavior 8, 164–212 (1995)
6. Niu, J., Cai, K., Parsons, S., Gerding, E., McBurney, P., Moyaux, T., Phelps, S., Shield, D.: JCAT: A platform for the TAC Market Design Competition. In: Proceedings of the Seventh International Conference on Autonomous Agents and Multi-Agent Systems (AAMAS 2008), Estoril, Portugal (May 2008)

7. Burges, C.J.C.: A Tutorial on Support Vector Machines for Pattern Recognition. Data Mining and Knowledge Discovery 2, 121–167 (1998)
8. Chang, C.-C., Lin, C.-J.: LIBSVM: a library for support vector machines (2001), Software available at `http://www.csie.ntu.edu.tw/~cjlin/libsvm`
9. Bilmes, J.A.: What HMMs can do. IEICE Transactions on Information and Systems E89-D(3), 869–891 (2006)
10. Rabiner, L.R.: A Tutorial on Hidden Markov Models and Selected Applications in Speech Recognition. In: Proceedings of the IEEE International Conference, vol. 77(2), pp. 257–286 (February 1989)
11. Ruping, S.: SVM kernels for time series analysis (Technical Report), Department of Computer Science. University of Dortmund, Dortmund, Germany (2001)
12. Grauman, K., Darrell, T.: The Pyramid Match kernel: discriminative classification with sets of image features. In: Proceedings of the IEEE International Conference on Computer Vision (ICCV), Beijing, China (October 2005)
13. Russell, S., Norvig, P.: Artificial Intelligence: A Modern Approach. Prentice Hall Series in Artificial Intelligence, Englewood Cliffs, New Jersey (1995)

Coordinating Decisions in a Supply-Chain Trading Agent

Wolfgang Ketter[1], John Collins[1,2], and Maria Gini[1,2,⋆]

[1] Dept of DIS, RSM Erasmus University, Rotterdam, NL
[2] Dept of CSE, University of Minnesota, Minneapolis, MN, USA

Abstract. An autonomous trading agent is a complex piece of software that must operate in a competitive economic environment. We identify the problem of decision coordination as a crucial element in the design of an agent for TAC SCM, and we review the published literature on agent design to discover a wide variety of approaches to this problem. We believe that the existence of such variety is an indication that much is yet to be learned about designing such agents.

1 Introduction

Supply-Chain Management is an especially challenging domain for a rational decision-maker. Such an agent must not only operate simultaneously in multiple markets (a customer market and a supplier market), but it must coordinate its market activities with each other and with internal processes such as production scheduling and inventory management in a way that maximizes its utility across an extended time horizon.

Organized competitions can be an effective way to drive research and understanding in complex domains, free of the complexities and risks of operating in open, real-world environments. Artificial economic environments typically abstract certain interesting features of the real world, such as markets and competitors, demand-based prices and cost of capital, and omit others, such as human resources, secondary markets, taxes, and seasonal demand. The Trading Agent Competition for Supply-Chain Management [1] (TAC SCM) is based on an economic simulation in which competing autonomous agents operate in a simple supply-chain scenario, purchasing components, managing a factory and warehouse, and selling finished products to customers.

TAC SCM has been an active competition since 2003, and the design of the game has been stable since 2005. More than 50 different teams have participated, and a number of papers have been published that describe agent designs, agent and game analyses, and specific methods for modeling the markets and decision processes in the simulation.

TAC SCM is an interesting challenge for a number of reasons. Different groups have approached the problem from a variety of perspectives, depending on the individual interests and backgrounds of the participants. For example, a team that is primarily interested in developing and testing machine-learning techniques will have a very different approach to the problem than a team that is primarily interested in developing methods to solve constrained optimization problems under uncertainty. To better understand this

---

⋆ Supported in part by the National Science Foundation under award NSF/IIS-0414466.

W. Ketter et al. (Eds.): AMEC/TADA 2008, LNBIP 44, pp. 161–174, 2010.
© Springer-Verlag Berlin Heidelberg 2010

variety, we conducted an informal survey of many of the active teams in 2007. In this paper, we explore in some depth and attempt to classify the variety of approaches we have observed to one of the special challenges in designing a successful agent for TAC SCM, the problem of coordinating the various decision processes.

2   Overview of the TAC SCM Game

In a TAC SCM game, each of the competing agents plays the part of a manufacturer of personal computers. Figure 1 gives a schematic overview of the TAC SCM game. Agents compete with each other in a procurement market for computer components, and in a sales market for customers. A game runs for 220 simulated days over about an hour of real time. Each agent starts with no inventory and an empty bank account. The agent with the largest bank account at the end of the game is the winner.

Customers express demand each day by issuing a set of Request for Quotes (RFQs) for finished computers. Each RFQ specifies the type of computer, a quantity, a due date, a reserve price, and a penalty for late delivery. Each agent may choose to bid on any subset of the day's RFQs. For each RFQ, the bid with the lowest price will be accepted, as long as that price is at or below the customer's reserve price. Once a bid

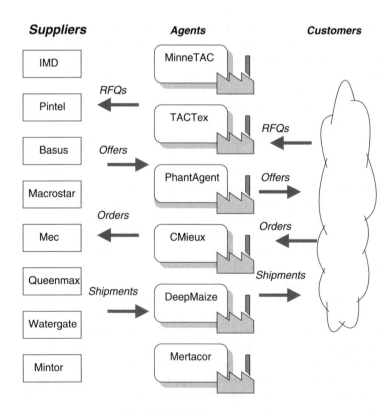

Fig. 1. TAC SCM game scenario

is accepted, the agent is obligated to ship the requested products by the due date, or it must pay the stated penalty for each day the shipment is late. Agents do not see the bids of other agents, but aggregate market statistics are supplied to the agents periodically. The customer market is segmented into a low-cost segment with five products, a mid-range segment with six products, and a premium segment with five products. Customer demand in each segment varies independently through the course of the game by a random walk with a superimposed Poisson distribution.

2.1 Agent Decision Processes

Agents assemble computers from parts, which must be purchased from suppliers. When agents wish to procure parts, they issue RFQs to individual suppliers, and suppliers respond with bids that specify price and availability. If the agent decides to accept a supplier's offer, then the supplier will ship the ordered parts on or after the due date. Late shipments are possible because supplier capacity varies from day to day by a mean-reverting random walk. Supplier prices are based on the ratio of demand to current uncommitted capacity, so agents have to decide when to place their orders, for what amounts, what due dates, and at what minimum price.

Once an agent has the necessary parts to assemble computers, it must schedule production in its finite-capacity production facility. Each computer model requires a specific set of parts, and a specified number of assembly cycles. Assembled computers are added to the agent's finished-goods inventory, and may be shipped to customers to satisfy outstanding orders.

An agent operating in the TAC SCM scenario must make the following four basic decisions during each simulated "day" in a competition:

1. decide what parts to purchase, from whom, and when to have them delivered (Procurement).
2. schedule its manufacturing facility (Production).
3. decide which customer RFQs to respond to, and set bid prices (Sales).
4. ship completed orders to customers (Fulfillment).

These decisions are supported by models of the sales and procurement markets, and by models of the agent's own production facility and inventory situation. The details of these models and decision processes are the primary subjects of research for participants in TAC SCM. These models may be populated with historical data from previous games, and with observations in the current game. During a game, agents can observe market reactions to their own actions (bids accepted or not, price and quantity data in supplier offers), and a very limited set of market summary data. In-game summary information is limited to daily high and low order prices for each product in the customer market, and summary reports every 20 days that give average prices and aggregate quantities. Many important factors, such as current capacity and outstanding commitments of suppliers, and sales volumes and price distributions in the customer market, are not visible to the agents.

2.2   Game Balance

The design of TAC SCM was carefully tuned over the first three years to make the competition interesting and challenging. The most obvious opportunities for strategic manipulation [2,3] have been eliminated. Agents must manage their reputations with respect to each supplier, to discourage agents from making large requests and then turning down the resulting offers. Suppliers reserve approximately half of their total capacity at the beginning of the game for future demand, which makes it very difficult to "corner" the market for some component type.

The parameters of the game scenario are set to ensure that decision coordination among procurement and sales is reasonably challenging. Figure 2 shows the overall balance between supply and demand. It is a histogram of the daily customer RFQ count over 200 games, about 40,000 observations. Superimposed on the histogram are the mean customer demand, the aggregate capacity of the six agent factories, and the expected supplier capacity. The key message from this balance is that expected customer demand is somewhat below the expected ability of the market to supply that demand. This means that an agent can expect to buy enough parts to keep its factory busy, but a strategy that simply tries to keep the factory busy all the time is likely to result in a large unsold inventory at the end of an average game[1]. On the other hand, there are some games in which the agents cannot supply all the demand, and the variability of the game can lead to serious imbalances between customer demand for specific products and the availability of parts to build them.

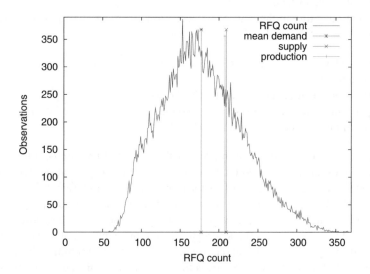

Fig. 2. Game balance. Mean customer demand is below the production capacity of all the agents, and below the expected availability of parts in the supplier market.

---

[1] This balance was first introduced in the 2005 competition. Price wars were a large problem in the early rounds of that competition until the full-production agents were eliminated.

3   Agent Design and the Decision Coordination Problem

Kiekintveld et al. [4] identify three key issues that a successful TAC SCM agent must address: dealing with substantial *uncertainty* in a highly *dynamic* economic environment, in competition with other self-interested agents whose behavior is naturally *strategic*. To this list we would add two other issues: making *coordinated* decisions across multiple domains in order to maximize payoff over time, and operating effectively in an *oligopoly* market. Because of the relatively small number of players in the customer and supplier markets, both are best characterized as oligopoly markets, and so many of the simplifying assumptions that can be used effectively in large markets do not hold. One such assumption is that the decisions of individual players have negligible impact on the observable market behavior. In contrast, competitive TAC SCM agents cannot act simply as "price-takers" in these markets - their decisions can move the markets decisively, and failure to account for this reaction can cause significant deviations from predicted outcomes.

The complexity of the problems an agent must solve to be competitive in TAC SCM has produced a number of interesting design approaches. To understand the spectrum of agent designs, we conducted a survey of the research community via the TAC SCM discussion email list in the period May-September 2007. Some common themes were an emphasis on modularity, use of constrained optimization techniques, machine learning, dealing with uncertainty, and a focus on coordination of decisions among procurement, production, sales, and fulfilment. Detailed results of the survey are presented in [5].

Two of the four agent decision problems, procurement and sales, are dominated by the variability of the game scenario and are strongly affected by the actions of other agents, while the production-scheduling and fulfillment decisions are internal to the agent and less affected by the inherent variability in the game. Because of this, some agent designs simply fold fulfillment into the sales problem, and production scheduling is sometimes also bundled into sales, especially for agents that use a make-to-order production strategy.

Simply stated, a solution to coordination problem will maximize (expected) profit over an entire game, subject to availability of individual part types in the supplier market, demand in the customer market, and capacity of the agent's factory. Of course, prices and availability in the supplier market are at least partly determined by the behavior of other agents in the simulation. In addition, prices in the customer market are largely determined by the behavior of the other agents, since competition almost always keeps prices well below customer reserve prices. This problem is commonly viewed as one of enabling independent decision processes to coordinate their actions while minimizing the need to share representation and implementation details.

As we shall see, many approaches to the coordination problem have been tried, and there is little evidence from tournament standings that any of these approaches dominates the others. In fact, a study by Jordan et al. [6] has shown that no single dominant strategy has yet been found, and our analysis shows that the top three agents in the Jordan study, namely TacTex, DeepMaize, and PhantAgent, use different coordination mechanisms. We do know that the "push" strategy that was popular in the 2003 and 2004 competitions (for example, Benisch et al. [7]) is not effective, because the factory can produce more than what can be sold at a profit, at least in expectation. This approach attempts to purchase enough parts early in the game to keep factory utilization high for the entire game, thereby eliminating procurement from the coordination problem.

In the following sections, we explore the variety of coordination approaches that we have observed among published agent designs and the respondents to the 2007 survey. We note that none of them have tried to solve the general problem in its entirety, presumably because the variability inherent in the simulation and the difficulty of predicting the behaviors of other agents have so far defeated all attempts to do so. Therefore, what we see is that each design has chosen a more manageable approach, one that simplifies the problem through approximations, through heuristics, and through focus on much shorter time horizons than the entire game.

3.1 Predicted Sales Volume

Because the balance of supply, demand, and production capacity in the simulation design has defeated a simple "push" approach to coordination, the next obvious choice would seem to be adoption of a "pull" approach, in which sales activities pull finished goods through the factory, which in turn pulls in components through the procurement market.

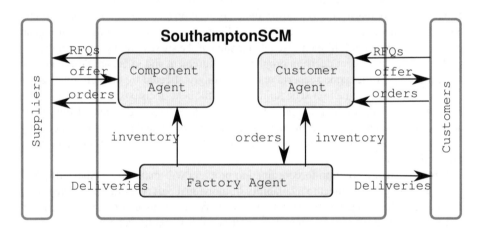

Fig. 3. SouthamptonSCM: Coordination primarily by the Customer Agent

A good example of this approach is SouthamptonSCM [8]. This agent was a finalist in the 2004 competition, and placed second in 2005. Figure 3 is a schematic representation of this design. In SouthamptonSCM, a Customer Agent uses fuzzy reasoning to compute offer prices, based on inventory level, customer demand, and time in the game[2]. Priority is given to the products with the highest expected per-unit profit. The Component Agent buys a portion of its components with long lead-times, because prices tend to be lower with longer lead times. The remaining component inventory is

---

[2] A separate rule set is used near the end of the game, because of the need to exhaust inventory and because prices tend to be much more volatile late in the game.

purchased with shorter lead times, in response to observed customer demand and to depletion of inventory by sales to customers. The Factory Agent primarily builds outstanding customer orders, and if it has spare capacity and available parts, it builds up a modest inventory of finished goods.

The MinneTAC agent [9,10], shown in Figure 4, can be configured in a number of different ways, but the configuration used in the 2007 and 2008 competitions solves a linear program each day to maximize expected profit over a 20-day horizon, subject to constraints on production capacity, customer demand, and anticipated inventory. The output of the linear program is "sales quotas" for each product for each of the next 20 days. The current-day quota is used by the Sales Manager to set prices in the customer market, and future-day quotas are used by the Supplier Manager to drive procurement. A slightly different configuration of MinneTAC was a finalist in the 2005 and 2006 competitions.

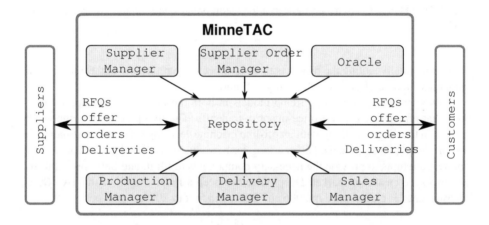

Fig. 4. MinneTAC: Coordination through the Repository, details depend on configuration

As we can see from Figure 4, MinneTAC uses a very different design approach from the other agents we examine here. The Repository acts as a "blackboard", and the various components interact only through the Repository. The Oracle component is a wrapper for a large number of small modules, called "Evaluators", that can be strung together as specified in a configuration file to do the necessary analysis and prediction tasks requested by the decision components. The actual coordination among decision components happens because they share some of those Evaluators. Specifically, both the Sales Manager and the Supplier Manager use the sales quotas produced by one of the Evaluators.

3.2 Future Production Schedule

DeepMaize [4] coordinates its decisions through a principled approach called "value-based decomposition". In this approach, a long-term production schedule is constructed

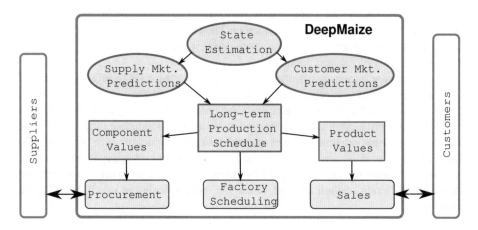

Fig. 5. DeepMaize: Coordination through a long-term production schedule, using value-based decomposition

by incrementally adding the products that are expected to return the highest profit. The general scheme is shown schematically in Figure 5.

This approach depends on pricing models in both the customer and supplier markets that effectively capture price-quantity tradeoffs. The two prediction components shown in the diagram, along with an off-line machine-learning process, are responsible for producing those models. Given a long-term production schedule, the Procurement module attempts to provide the necessary components to fill it, and Sales uses it to set prices in the customer market. DeepMaize has been a finalist in all of the TAC SCM tournaments. It placed third in 2006 and 2007, and first in 2008.

3.3 Inventory Management

Three published agent designs appear to focus on an inventory model to coordinate decisions. Mertacor [11,12] is the clearest example. As we see in Figure 6, an "Inventory Manager" component is the central element in this design. Mertacor uses an "Assemble to Order" approach, which is recommended in the literature on inventory management for situations where assembly times are significantly shorter than procurement lead times. The Inventory Manager attempts to maintain component stocks above a minimum threshold, subject to committed and expected sales, and to committed deliveries from suppliers. Mertacor placed third in the 2005 competition.

PhantAgent [13] is another design that appears to focus on inventory management, although as we see in Figure 7, the inventory management function is conceptually combined with the procurement function in a Component Module. The goal of the Component Module is to maintain expected stocks of each component type within narrow bounds throughout the game. It computes expected stocks for each component for each day until the end of the game, and formulates new supplier orders to make up any deficits. PhantAgent placed second in 2006, and first in the 2007 competition.

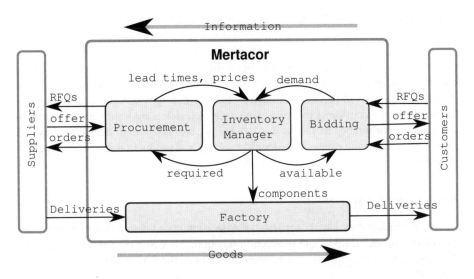

Fig. 6. Mertacor: Coordination through the Inventory Manager

For each component c, and for each day d from the current day until the end of the game, the expected stock is computed as

$$I_{c,d} = I_{c,d-1} + incoming_{c,d} - usage_{c,d}$$

where $I_{c,d}$ is the expected inventory of component c on day d, $incoming_{c,d}$ is the quantities of committed supplier orders, and $usage_{c,d}$ is the expected usage of component c on day d.

PhantAgent is interesting in another way. It deals with the inherent complexity and uncertainty of the TAC SCM environment, and the resulting strategic inter-dependencies between the different agent modules, using heuristic approximations rather than

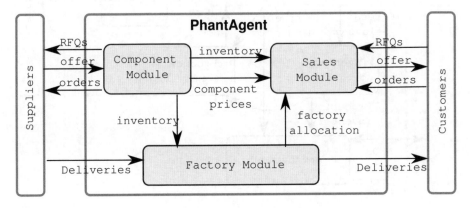

Fig. 7. PhantAgent: Coordination is by inventory control, originating in the Procurement module

optimization algorithms. The team's assessment is that finding optimal solutions to the different sub-problems does not always lead to the best overall performance.

Another agent whose decision coordination mechanism seems focused on inventory control is CrocodileAgent [14,15]. The agent drives procurement to maintain expected component inventory stocks within defined minimum and maximum bounds. Similarly, Production operates to maintain a finished goods inventory within pre-defined bounds. Sales then bids on customer requests using a simple pricing algorithm, in an attempt to sell products, profitably, as fast as they are being produced. When demand is low, the profitability constraint causes inventory to back up, and production and procurement to slow down.

3.4   Central Strategy Module

An agent that has very clearly separated the decision coordination issues from the details of procurement, sales, and production scheduling is CMieux [16], a finalist in the 2007 and 2008 competitions. A schematic diagram of the CMieux design is shown in Figure 8.

The Strategy module sets overall goals for the remainder of the system, such as the portion of expected demand to target, and the portion of the production schedule (ATP, the products Available to Promise) that should be sold to customers (DTP, products Desired to Promise). The Forecast module observes the markets and makes predictions about demand, prices, and delays in supplier shipments. The Inventory Projector combines that with current inventories and expected supplier deliveries to generate inventory projections over time. Procurement uses the projected inventory along with an

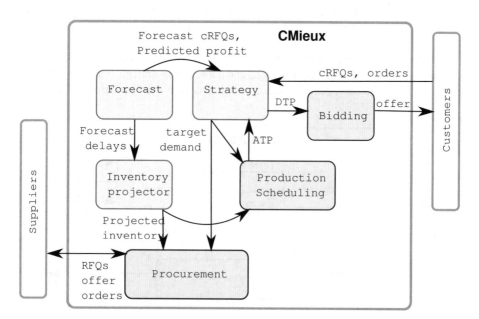

Fig. 8. CMieux: Coordination by a separate Strategy module

optimistic version of the production schedule (what Production would expect to build if there were no inventory constraints) to decide what to order from suppliers, and supplies Inventory Projector with actual supplier orders.

3.5   Separate Supply and Demand Models

The design of TacTex [17] is quite different from the others we have reviewed, in the sense that it does not try to centralize decision coordination at all. Instead, it employs a Supply Manager that interacts with suppliers and models the supply market, and a Demand manager that interacts with customers and models the customer market. Coordination is achieved by communication between these two models. TacTex has been a very strong competitor, placing first in 2005 and 2006, and second in 2007.

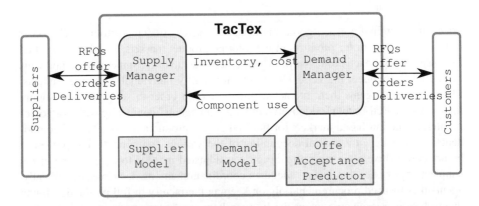

Fig. 9. TacTex: Coordination is by communication of inventory, cost, and projected usage data between the Supply Manager and the Demand Manager

In this design, the Supply Manager attempts to minimize the cost of procuring the components requested by the Demand Manager, and provides in return an inventory projection including current inventory and expected future deliveries, along with re-placement cost estimates for each component type. The Demand Manager, in turn, seeks to maximize the agent's profits from sales, subject to constraints from the customer market, its own production capacity, and the information provided by the Supply Manager.

3.6   Internal Markets

RedAgent [18] is a unique approach to agent design. It won the first year's competition in 2003, but did not do well in 2004 and was never updated after the rule change in 2005.

As we can see from Figure 10, RedAgent manages the flow of components from suppliers through production and into sales and fulfillment of customer orders through a series of internal markets. The Bidder observes its inventory status and the current

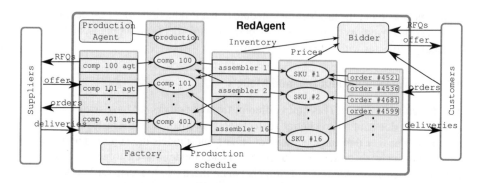

Fig. 10. RedAgent: Coordination by a sequence of internal markets

prices in its internal finished-goods markets, and makes offers to customers. Customer orders then compete for products in the internal product markets, which are supplied by assemblers for each product type. Those assemblers in turn compete for components in internal component markets, which are supplied by individual component agents. The component agents then interact with suppliers in order to set prices and supply their markets. RedAgent used loosely-coupled "sub-agents" competing with each other in internal auction-based markets for finished goods, production capacity, and components. This achieved a radical decoupling of the various components, but proved to be not competitive after the game design was adjusted in 2005 to defeat some of the simplest approaches that lacked adequate coordination among decisions. Specifically, agents that focused procurement only on keeping the factory in full production found themselves overproducing when the balance between factory capacity and expected customer demand was adjusted.

4   Conclusions and Future Work

We have presented a brief overview of agent design ideas and architectures for TAC SCM, using information both from a survey of agent development teams and from published results. The overall survey outcome shows that there are common themes emerging from the different research groups on how to design a successful supply-chain trading agent. A clear challenge that each agent design must meet is the need to coordinate its internal processes (production scheduling) with action in procurement and customer markets. We have observed a variety of approaches to the decision coordination problem, including the use of sales to "pull" products and supplies through the system, coordination through internal models of inventory and prices, assigning current and future value to inventory and production resources, and the use of an explicit top-level strategy component that coordinates the lower-level decision processes. The fact that after several years of competition there is still much to be learned, suggest that the recipe for a full competent supply-chain trading agent is still an unsolved problem, even for an abstract, constrained environment like TAC SCM.

Many of these agents are available in either binary or source form through the TAC SCM Agent Repository at http://www.sics.se/tac/showagents.php.

References

1. Collins, J., Arunachalam, R., Sadeh, N., Ericsson, J., Finne, N., Janson, S.: The Supply Chain Management Game for the 2006 Trading Agent Competition. Technical Report CMU-ISRI-05-132, Carnegie Mellon University, Pittsburgh, PA (2005)
2. Ketter, W., Kryzhnyaya, E., Damer, S., McMillen, C., Agovic, A., Collins, J., Gini, M.: Analysis and design of supply-driven strategies in TAC-SCM. In: Workshop: Trading Agent Design and Analysis at the Third Int'l. Conf. on Autonomous Agents and Multi-Agent Systems, New York, pp. 44–51 (2004)
3. Wellman, M.P., Estelle, J., Singh, S., Vorobeychik, Y., Kiekintveld, C., Soni, V.: Strategic interactions in a supply chain game. Computational Intelligence 21(1), 1–26 (2005)
4. Kiekintveld, C., Miller, J., Jordan, P.R., Wellman, M.P.: Controlling a Supply Chain Agent Using Value-Based Decomposition. In: Proc. of 7th ACM Conf. on Electronic Commerce, Ann Arbor, USA, pp. 208–217 (2006)
5. Collins, J., Ketter, W., Gini, M.: Flexible decision control in an autonomous trading agent. Electronic Commerce Research and Applications 8(2), 91–105 (2009)
6. Jordan, P.R., Kiekintveld, C., Wellman, M.P.: Empirical game-theoretic analysis of the tac supply chain game. In: Proc. of the Sixth Int'l. Conf. on Autonomous Agents and Multi-Agent Systems, pp. 1188–1195 (2007)
7. Benisch, M., Greenwald, A., Grypari, I., Lederman, R., Naroditskiy, V., Tschantz, M.: Botticelli: A supply chain management agent designed to optimize under uncertainty. ACM Trans. on Comp. Logic 4(3), 29–37 (2004)
8. He, M., Rogers, A., Luo, X., Jennings, N.R.: Designing a successful trading agent for supply chain management. In: Proc. of the Fifth Int'l. Conf. on Autonomous Agents and Multi-Agent Systems, pp. 1159–1166 (2006)
9. Collins, J., Ketter, W., Gini, M.: Flexible decision support in a dynamic business network. In: Verwest, P., van Liere, D., Zheng, L. (eds.) The Network Experience – New Value from Smart Business Networks, pp. 233–246. Springer, Heidelberg (2008)
10. Collins, J., Ketter, W., Gini, M., Agovic, A.: Software architecture of the MinneTAC supply-chain trading agent. Technical Report 08-031, University of Minnesota, Department of Computer Science and Engineering, Minneapolis, MN (2008)
11. Chatzidimitriou, K.C., Symeonidis, A.L., Kontogounis, I., Mitkas, P.A.: Agent Mertacor: A robust design for dealing with uncertainty and variation in SCM environments. Expert Systems with Applications 35(3), 591–603 (2008)
12. Kontogounis, I., Chatzidimitriou, K., Symeonidis, A., Mitkas, P.: A Robust Agent Design for Dynamic SCM Environments. In: Antoniou, G., Potamias, G., Spyropoulos, C., Plexousakis, D. (eds.) SETN 2006. LNCS (LNAI), vol. 3955, pp. 127–136. Springer, Heidelberg (2006)
13. Stan, M., Stan, B., Florea, A.M.: A Dynamic Strategy Agent for Supply Chain Management. In: Eighth International Symposium on Symbolic and Numeric Algorithms for Scientific Computing, pp. 227–232 (2006)
14. Podobnik, V., Petric, A., Jezic, G.: The crocodileagent: Research for efficient agent-based cross-enterprise processes. In: Meersman, R., Tari, Z., Herrero, P. (eds.) OTM 2006 Workshops. LNCS, vol. 4277, pp. 752–762. Springer, Heidelberg (2006)
15. Petric, A., Podobnik, V., Jezic, G.: The CrocodileAgent: Designing a robust trading agent for volatile e-market conditions. In: Nguyen, N.T., Grzech, A., Howlett, R.J., Jain, L.C. (eds.) KES-AMSTA 2007. LNCS (LNAI), vol. 4496, pp. 597–606. Springer, Heidelberg (2007)

16. Benisch, M., Sardinha, A., Andrews, J., Sadeh, N.: CMieux: adaptive strategies for competitive supply chain trading. In: Proc. of 8th Int'l. Conf. on Electronic Commerce, pp. 47–58. ACM Press, New York (2006)
17. Pardoe, D., Stone, P.: An autonomous agent for supply chain management. In: Adomavicius, G., Gupta, A. (eds.) Handbooks in Information Systems Series: Business Computing. Elsevier, Amsterdam (2007)
18. Keller, P.W., Duguay, F.O., Precup, D.: Redagent - winner of the TAC SCM 2003. SIGecom Exchanges 4(3), 1–8 (2004)

The 2007 TAC SCM Prediction Challenge

David Pardoe and Peter Stone

Department of Computer Sciences
The University of Texas at Austin
{dpardoe,pstone}@cs.utexas.edu

Abstract. The TAC SCM Prediction Challenge presents an opportunity for agents designed for the full TAC SCM game to compete solely on their ability to make predictions. Participants are presented with situations from actual TAC SCM games and are evaluated on their prediction accuracy in four categories: current and future computer prices, and current and future component prices. This paper introduces the Prediction Challenge and presents the results from 2007 along with an analysis of how the predictions of the participants compare to each other.

1 Introduction

The Trading Agent Competition Supply Chain Management scenario (TAC SCM) [1] provides a unique testbed for studying and prototyping supply chain management agents by providing a competitive environment in which independently created agents can be tested against each other in an open academic setting. In order to be competitive, an agent must be able to successfully perform a number of interrelated tasks. While this fact contributes to the complexity and realism of the scenario, it can also make it difficult to determine the relative effectiveness of agent components in isolation. To address this issue, in 2007 two challenges were designed to be run in addition to the full SCM game, each designed to measure an agent's performance on one specific task: a Procurement Challenge, and a Prediction Challenge. This paper focuses on the Prediction Challenge. The contributions of this paper are the specification of this new challenge (designed by the authors), the presentation of the 2007 results, and an analysis of how the predictions of the challenge participants compare to each other.[1] In addition, a brief description of the prediction methods used by the challenge participants and others is provided.

2 The Prediction Challenge

As the Prediction Challenge is closely tied to the full TAC SCM game, we begin by providing a short summary of the full game. Full details may be found in the official specifications [1]. In a TAC SCM game, six agents compete as computer

---

[1] Software, results, and the complete specifications are available from the Prediction Challenge website: http://www.cs.utexas.edu/~TacTex/PredictionChallenge

W. Ketter et al. (Eds.): AMEC/TADA 2008, LNBIP 44, pp. 175–189, 2010.
© Springer-Verlag Berlin Heidelberg 2010

manufacturers. Agents must purchase components (CPUs, motherboards, hard drives, and memory, each coming in multiple varieties) from suppliers and sell the assembled computers (coming in 16 configurations) to customers. Both component and computer sales take place through a process involving requests for quotes (RFQs): the buyer sends the seller an RFQ with details such as quantity and due date, the seller responds with a price, and the buyer accepts or declines the offer. Each type of component and computer is assigned a base price that serves as a point of reference, but prices can fluctuate significantly during a game due to factors such as variable customer demand, supplier capacity, and the actions of the agents themselves. Agents are unable to see the prices at which other agents are buying components and selling computers. A game lasts for 220 simulated days, and in each round of the competition, a group of agents competes in a number of games, usually 16.

While the methods used by different SCM agents to manage the supply chain vary considerably, many of these agents share a similar design at a high level - they divide the full problem into a number of smaller tasks and then solve these tasks using decision theoretic approaches based on maximizing utility given various predictions about the economy. The success of an agent thus depends on both the accuracy of the many kinds of predictions it makes and the manner in which these predictions are used, making it difficult to assign credit to individual agent components. To give a concrete example, suppose that based on available statistics from past games and the current one, agent A predicts that it will be able to sell one type of computer for $2000 on day 45, and agent B predicts that it will be able to sell that computer for $1900. They then make component purchases, plan manufacturing, and commit to customer orders based on these and other predictions. Ultimately, agent A wins. Is it safe to draw conclusions about the accuracy of these predictions based on this outcome? No.

The goal of the Prediction Challenge is to allow a head to head comparison of agents' prediction accuracy without concern for how these predictions are used. In the example above, if we had recorded the predictions and then observed on day 45 that the specific type of computer sold for an average price of $1870, we could say that agent B made a more accurate prediction. This is exactly what takes place in the Prediction Challenge. There are many quantities for which agents may make predictions, such as customer demand, the probability that a particular offer to a customer will be accepted, and supplier capacities. However, the Prediction Challenge focuses only on those predictions that can be expressed in the form of a price, namely component prices and computer prices. As agents need to be able to make predictions about future prices as well as current prices in order to plan effectively, the accuracy of predictions for both current and future prices is measured. There are thus four prediction categories in the Prediction Challenge: current and future computer prices, and current and future component prices.

Instead of making predictions about live TAC SCM games in which they are participating, participants in the challenge make predictions on behalf of another agent called the SCMPredictionAgent (or PAgent for short). (For clarity, we will refer to the manufacturing agents that participate in SCM games as *agents*, and the prediction agents participating in the Prediction Challenge as *participants*.) Before the competition, the organizers of the challenge run a number of games in which PAgent competes against other agents. The identities of these other agents and the resulting game logs are not made available to participants until after the competition. During the competition, participants connect to a game server which re-plays these games from the game logs. For each day of each game, participants receive the exact messages sent to PAgent (incoming messages), as well as the messages it sent to the game server in response (outgoing messages) - exactly the same information that would be available to an agent during a live game. In addition to these incoming and outgoing messages, each participant is also given a set of predictions that must be made before the information for the following day will be sent.

There are a number of benefits to running the competition using logs from completed games instead of using live games. First, there is no restriction on the number of participants that may compete head to head at one time. Second, each participant will receive exactly the same information about the state of each game and will be asked to make the same predictions. Finally, in live games there would be an incentive for participants to behave differently than in normal TAC SCM games, such as by manipulating prices in order to make past predictions come true.

Although predictions could be made on behalf of any agent from a completed game, the use of a single agent (PAgent) for which source code is available simplifies the task of participants by helping them to understand exactly what behavior to expect from the agent. PAgent was designed to be as simple as possible and to behave in a consistent and predictable manner while still exhibiting reasonable behavior. (PAgent was developed by the authors and is an extension of their TacTex Starter Agent[2] , which is in turn a simplified version of their TacTex agent [2] made available for educational purposes.)

The exact predictions that are made by each participant are as follows:

- **Current computer prices:** The price at which each RFQ sent from customers on the current day will be ordered (i.e., the lowest price that will be offered by any manufacturer for that RFQ). These predictions are required on all but the first day and the last two days of each game, when few or no computers are sold. If the RFQ does not result in an order, the prediction will be ignored when accuracy is evaluated. Therefore, participants do not need to be concerned with whether an order will result, only what the price will be if there is an order.
- **Future computer prices:** For each of the 16 types of computers, the median price at which it will sell 20 days in the future. These predictions are required on all but the last 22 days of each game (thus the last day *on* which current computer price predictions is required is the last day *for* which future computer price predictions are required). If no computers of a certain

---

[2] http://www.cs.utexas.edu/~TacTex/starterAgent

type are sold, the prediction for that type will be ignored when accuracy is evaluated.

- **Current component prices:** The price that will be offered for each RFQ sent by the PAgent to a supplier on the current day. The PAgent sends RFQs to suppliers on all but the last 10 days of each game. If an RFQ results in no offer (due to the reserve price) or an offer (or offers) with modified quantity or due date, the prediction for that RFQ will be ignored when accuracy is evaluated.
- **Future component prices:** The price that will be offered for each of a number of provided RFQs that will be sent by the PAgent to suppliers in 20 days. For each of the 16 pairs of a supplier and a component that it supplies, a zero-quantity RFQ is provided that will be sent by the PAgent in 20 days with a due date chosen at random between 5 and 30 (or the number of days remaining, if less than 30) days after the date the RFQ is sent. Because the PAgent sends no RFQs during the last 10 days of a game, predictions for future RFQs do not need to be made during the last 30 days of the game.

To test the ability of participants to make predictions for games with various competitors, each participant is required to make predictions for 3 sets of games. In each set, the PAgent will have run against a different group of five competitors chosen at random from the TAC agent repository.[3] Each set contains 16 games, meaning that participants have a chance to improve their predictions through repeated experience with the same group of competitors. Participants make predictions for one game at a time, and must complete the predictions for one game day before receiving information for the next day. Unlike the standard SCM game, participants do not need to compete simultaneously, so they may connect to the game server at any time and make predictions at their own pace. There is, however, an eight hour time limit.

Performance is evaluated separately for each of the four prediction categories. Root mean squared error is used as the scoring metric, and all errors are measured as a fraction of the base price of the computer/component. Participants are ranked in each category, and the overall winner is the agent with the highest average rank over all four categories.

3   Prediction Methods

Four participants competed in the 2007 Prediction Challenge: Botticelli (Brown University), DeepMaize (University of Michigan), Kshitij (Indian Institute of Technology Kharagpur), and TacTex (The University of Texas at Austin). Tac-Tex and DeepMaize finished second and third, respectively, in the full 2007 SCM competition, and Botticelli was one of 12 semifinalists. This section provides brief descriptions of the prediction methods used by the top two participants, which have been published in full elsewhere, along with an overview of other prediction methods that have been used by TAC SCM agents. The methods used by Botticelli and Kshitij have not been published or made known to the authors.

---

[3] https://www.sics.se/tac/showagents.php

DeepMaize [3] makes predictions for current and future computer prices using a k-nearest neighbors algorithm. For each prediction to be made, similar situations from a data set of previous games are identified, and the prediction is based on the prices observed in those situations. Predictions can be made about both the probability of winning an order at a given price and the expected winning price. Situations are chosen and weighted using Euclidean distance between a set of state features such as the date, estimated levels of supplier capacity and customer demand, and observed computer prices. Each neighbor is chosen from a different past game to provide sufficient diversity. DeepMaize uses two separate data sets, one from past TAC SCM tournament data and one from self-play, and updates the weighting of each set online based on past accuracy.

TacTex [2] tracks computer prices using a particle filter. For each of the 16 types of computer, TacTex maintains a filter that represents a distribution over possible sales prices (to be precise, the lowest price that will be offered by *another* agent in response to an RFQ for that type of computer). Each particle represents a Gaussian with a certain mean and variance and has a weight indicating its relative likelihood. The distribution over sales prices represented by the filter is the weighted sum of these Gaussians. Each day, a new set of particles is generated from the old. For each new particle to be generated, an old particle is selected at random based on weight, and the new particle's estimate of mean and variance are set to those of the old particle plus small changes, drawn randomly from the distribution of day-to-day changes seen in a data set of past games. The new particles are then reweighted, with the weight of each particle set to the probability of the previous day's price-related observations occurring according to the distribution represented. As with DeepMaize, TacTex uses the distributions generated by these filters during the full TAC SCM game to estimate the probability of winning an order given a certain offer price. In the Prediction Challenge, for each computer RFQ TacTex predicts that the sales price will be the mean of the distribution for that computer, or the price offered by the PAgent if that is lower.

To make predictions for future computer prices, TacTex uses the additive regression algorithm from the WEKA machine learning package [4]. Additive regression is an iterative method in which at each step a decision stump is fit to the residual of the previous step, and the sum of the output of the stumps is taken as the output of the model. Using a large number of games including a variety of agent groups from the TAC agent repository (and including the PAgent in each game), TacTex creates a training data set in which each instance represents a future computer price prediction that would have been made and is labeled with the difference between the actual median price for a computer and the price that would have been predicted by the particle filter 20 days previously. Each instance consists of 31 features that represent data available to the agent during the game and are similar to those used by DeepMaize in its k-nearest neighbors approach. During the Prediction Challenge, TacTex makes predictions for each type of computer's future price by adding the change predicted by its learned additive regression model to its prediction of the current computer price.

DeepMaize tracks component prices by recording the prices offered by each supplier over a number of recent days (five days in the full SCM competition, but only one day in the Prediction Challenge). The price for a component request with a given due date can then be predicted by taking the recorded price for that due date, if one exists, or by linearly interpolating between prices offered on different due dates if not. To improve the resulting predictions, DeepMaize also uses the reduced error pruning tree from WEKA, a form of decision tree, to learn the difference between actual observed prices in a data set of past games and the predictions of the linear interpolation method. This use of regression is similar to the method used by TacTex to predict changes in future component prices; however, instead of only learning to make predictions for the change in prices over 20 days, DeepMaize also includes features that allow it to specify the number of days in the future for which the change should be predicted. As a result, DeepMaize can used its learned model to predict both the corrections needed to the linear interpolation method for the current component price predictions, and the changes in prices expected for the future component price predictions.

TacTex makes predictions about current component prices by attempting to directly estimate the available production capacity of each supplier on each future day. The prices offered by suppliers are determined entirely by the fraction of their capacity that is free before the requested due date, so each offer can be used to determine the free capacity over a certain range. If two offers with different due dates are available, the fraction of the supplier's capacity that is committed in the period between the first and second date can be determined by subtracting the total capacity committed before the first date from that committed before the second. With enough offers over many days, TacTex can maintain a reasonable estimate of the fraction of capacity committed by a supplier on any single day, and use this estimate to make price predictions.

TacTex makes future component price predictions using the same method it uses for future computer price predictions. Additive regression is used to learn a model that can predict the difference between current predictions and the prices that will exist in 20 days.

In addition to the prediction methods used by these participants, a number of techniques used in previous TAC SCM agents have been documented, primarily for predicting current computer prices. A previous version of DeepMaize used equilibrium analysis to make predictions about the future state of the market, from which information such as future prices could be extracted [5]. CMieux [6] makes predictions about computer prices using a form of modified regression tree called a distribution tree that learns to predict a distribution over winning prices using data from past games. For current component prices, CMieux predicts the price that will be offered for an RFQ with a given due date by using a nearest neighbors approach that considers recent offers with similar due dates. Foreseer [7] uses a form of online learning to learn multipliers indicating the impact of various RFQ properties on current computer prices. A previous version of Botticelli [8] used a heuristic in which linear regression is performed on recent computer prices to predict a distribution over winning prices.

4   Results and Analysis

In this section, we present the results of the Prediction Challenge and then analyze the data in a number of ways.

4.1   Results

Tables 1-4 show the prediction accuracy of each participant in each prediction category in terms of RMS error. Table 5 shows the overall place and average rank of each participant. Table 6 shows the five agents against which the PAgent competed in each of the three sets of 16 games. The winning participant, DeepMaize, had the lowest error on both current and future component price predictions, while TacTex had the lowest error on both current and future computer price predictions. For each category, the difference between the top agent and other agents is statistically significant with at least 98% confidence according to paired t-tests comparing the RMS errors for each of the 48 games. A few observations can be made from these results.

First, in each prediction category, the difference between the best and third best RMS error was fairly small, at most 12%. This fact suggests that the prediction methods used by the top three participants are all reasonably effective, and that there may be limited room for improvement. At the same time, the magnitudes of these errors are significant, suggesting that making predictions in TAC SCM is inherently difficult. To give perspective to these results, the agents in the final round of the 2007 TAC SCM competition had average profit margins between 1% and 7.5%, so prediction errors of these (similar) magnitudes could conceivably have a significant impact on agent performance.

Also, for both computers and component prices, the ranking of participants is the same for both current and future predictions. This is perhaps not surprising, as it seems reasonable that a participant able to make better short term predictions would have an advantage in making long term predictions. As expected, errors for future price predictions are much higher than errors for current price predictions, roughly by a factor of two.

4.2   Average Daily Errors

We begin our analysis by looking at how prediction errors vary across time. Figures 1-4 show the average RMS errors in each prediction category over all 48 games for each game day. (To improve visibility only the top three participants are shown; Kshitij's errors are consistently higher without displaying notably different patterns.) The most obvious feature of these graphs is that errors are usually very high at the beginning and end of games. Making predictions at the beginning of games can be difficult because there is little or no information about previous prices, and because prices can change rapidly as agents place large component orders (driving component prices up) and begin selling computers as components arrive (driving computer prices down). Computer prices are often unpredictable at the ends of games when agents are trying to sell off

Table 1. Current computer prices

Name	Error
1. TacTex	.0455
2. DeepMaize	.0468
3. Botticeli	.0471
4. Kshitij	.0487

Table 2. Future computer prices

Name	Error
1. TacTex	.0916
2. DeepMaize	.0959
3. Botticeli	.1024
4. Kshitij	.1109

Table 3. Current component prices

Name	Error
1. DeepMaize	.0392
2. Botticeli	.0417
3. TacTex	.0428
4. Kshitij	.1333

Table 4. Future component prices

Name	Error
1. DeepMaize	.0943
2. Botticeli	.0970
3. TacTex	.1034
4. Kshitij	.1389

Table 5. Overall placing and average rank of each participant

Place	Name	Avg. rank
1	DeepMaize	1.5
2	TacTex	2
3	Botticelli	2.5
4	Kshitij	4

Table 6. Agents in each of the three sets of games

Set	Agents
A	Maxon06, MinneTAC05, DeepMaize05, Foreseer05, PhantAgent06
B	GoBlueOval05, GeminiJK05, RationalSCM05, PhantAgent05, TacTex06
C	PhantAgent06, Maxon06, RationalSCM05, Tiancalli06, PhantAgent05

Table 7. RMS errors over the first 20 days, last 20 days, and middle portion of the prediction interval for each category (lowest error in bold)

Name	Current computer			Future computer			Current component			Future component		
	start	mid	end	start	mid	end	start	mid	end	start	mid	end
DeepMaize	**.0562**	.0403	**.0947**	**.0965**	.0913	.1356	**.0484**	.0341	.0810	**.0920**	**.0951**	**.0936**
TacTex	.0771	**.0342**	.1026	.1473	**.0774**	**.1262**	.0868	**.0313**	**.0797**	.1219	.0992	.1210
Botticelli	.0665	.0381	.0984	.1240	.0952	.1408	.0505	.0365	.0858	.0965	.0975	.0969

their remaining inventory – for each computer type, prices may suddenly become very high or low depending on inventory levels and thus competition. TacTex appears to suffer the most from errors at the start and end of games, especially when predicting component prices, while DeepMaize has particularly low errors in initial component price predictions and is roughly the same as Botticelli elsewhere. Occasional large errors such as these can be very damaging to a participant's overall performance due to the fact that RMS error, and not mean absolute error, is used in scoring.

In some cases, sudden error spikes can be attributed to the behavior of a specific agent. The spike in current component price errors on day 201 (and thus in future component price errors on day 181) occurs only in the games in Set A and is caused by MinneTAC05 sending large requests for components on that date but not accepting the resulting offers, presumably with the goal of driving up prices for other agents. It is interesting to note that Botticelli and TacTex recovered completely (returned to the previous low error level) in two days, while DeepMaize recovered in three days, suggesting that such spikes will only confuse agents for a short period of time.

The timing of the distinct jumps in late-game current computer price prediction errors observable in Figure 1 can also be traced to specific agents. The jump at day 202 occurs only in games from set C and is caused by Tiancalli06 suddenly dropping the prices it offers, while the jump at day 209 occurs only in games from set B and is caused by GeminiJK05 doing the same. The final rise over the last few days appears to be caused by widely varying (often very high) prices resulting from reduced competition to sell certain types of computers.

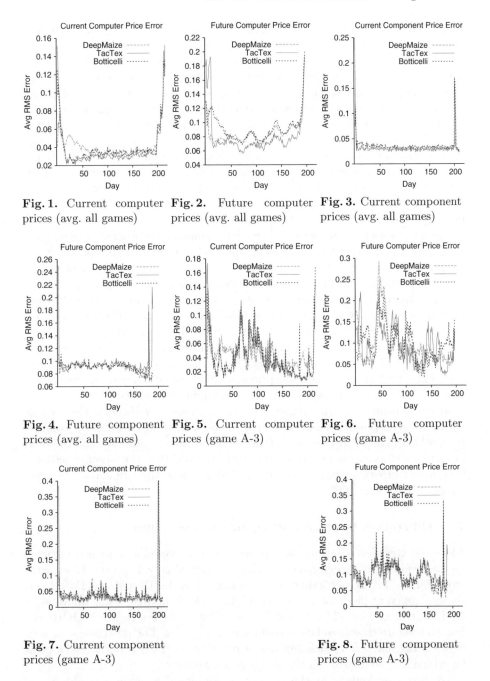

Fig. 1. Current computer prices (avg. all games)

Fig. 2. Future computer prices (avg. all games)

Fig. 3. Current component prices (avg. all games)

Fig. 4. Future component prices (avg. all games)

Fig. 5. Current computer prices (game A-3)

Fig. 6. Future computer prices (game A-3)

Fig. 7. Current component prices (game A-3)

Fig. 8. Future component prices (game A-3)

Compared to the starting and ending errors, average prediction errors during the middle of games tend to be much lower, and they are more consistent both over time and between participants. Still, there are some notable patterns. Tac-Tex consistently has slightly lower errors for current computer price and current component price predictions and significantly lower errors for future computer price predictions, but errors for future component price predictions are generally a little higher than those of Botticelli or DeepMaize. DeepMaize suffers early on from higher errors for current computer price predictions, while Botticelli likewise has higher errors for future computer price predictions at the start of games, but otherwise the two participants have extremely similar patterns of errors.

The level of errors for current component prices remains nearly constant throughout games, while errors for future computer prices undergo notable swings for reasons that are unclear. These swings appear to some degree when each of the three sets of games is considered alone, although the swings occur at different times and scales for each set. While somewhat consistent, errors for current computer prices tend to be lower in the early parts of games for TacTex and Botticelli (probably due to the fact that competition tends to remain strong across all computer types while agents work through the components ordered at the start of each game), and errors for future component prices drop near the ends of games for Botticelli and DeepMaize (probably due to the fact that component orders, and thus changes in supplier prices, tend to dwindle during this period).

It is important to note that these observations do not necessarily hold when individual games are analyzed. Figures 5-8 show the daily RMS errors for a single representative game, game 3 from Set A. The most striking difference is the fact that for both current and future computer price predictions, errors vary considerably between the participants. Errors also show more variance across time, except for current computer prices, where there are only occasional spikes that are likely caused by unusually heavy component requests.

In the remainder of this paper, we ignore errors over the first and last 20 days for which predictions are required for each prediction category. Doing so removes the highly variable effects (start and end game conditions, and the spike in component price errors caused by MinneTAC05) that can obscure patterns that would otherwise be visible. Table 7 shows how the elimination of these errors affects the results.

4.3   Differences between Participants across Games

To get a better view of how prediction error varies across games, we now compare the performance of participants on each game individually. Figures 9-12 show the errors for TacTex in each game plotted against those for DeepMaize. Each figure shows a different prediction category. Figures 13-16 show the same information for Botticelli and DeepMaize, and Figures 17-20 compare TacTex to Botticelli. For each figure, the correlation coefficient r is given. The dotted line in each figure is the line $y = x$, meaning that a point below the line represents a game for which the participant on the y-axis had lower error.

We begin by looking at the current computer price predictions. Figure 17 shows that the errors of TaxTex and Botticelli are highly correlated, with Botticelli's errors being higher than TacTex's by a similar amount in each game. Comparing either participant to DeepMaize (Figures 9 and 13) paints a different picture. While there is still a strong correlation between errors, it appears that as the difficulty of making predictions in a game increases, the performance of DeepMaize increases relative to the performance of the others, to the point that DeepMaize has the lowest errors of any participant on the most difficult games. One possible explanation for this result is that the prediction methods of other participants (the particle filter in the case of TacTex) are highly tuned for "typical" games and thus suffer as computer prices behave more atypically, while DeepMaize's use of a kNN-based predictor allows it to better handle unusual situations by matching them with similar situations from its data set. This prediction category is the only one in which such a phenomenon occurs, and this fact is particularly interesting because it makes it difficult to state that one participant's method of prediction is best (in expectation) under all circumstances. An agent with access to the prediction methods of all participants might choose to use TacTex's method in most cases but to use DeepMaize's method in certain games where prediction appeared particularly difficult.

Errors for future computer prices (Figures 10, 14, and 18) exhibit a different pattern. Here there is some correlation between the errors of DeepMaize and Botticelli, but very little between the errors of either of these two participants and those of TacTex. In fact, for Set C, the errors of TacTex appear completely unrelated to those of the other two participants. This low correlation suggests that the difficulties experienced by DeepMaize and Botticelli are not related to a particular set of games or common to all games, but have to do with particular situations that can occur in all three sets of games and that TacTex is able to handle correctly. In the case of DeepMaize, these situations may be different from those encountered in the data set used by the kNN-based predictor, or the distance metric used by the predictor may be unable to distinguish these situations from unrelated ones in the data set. The fact that DeepMaize and Botticelli have a higher degree of correlation suggests that they may have difficulties under some of the same circumstances.

The pattern of errors for current component prices (Figures 11, 15, and 19) is much clearer. Here there is a high degree of correlation between the errors of different participants, with the errors of one participant differing from those of another by a fairly consistent amount. It should be noted that the reason why TacTex has the lowest errors here, but the third lowest error in Table 3, is the exclusion of the beginning of each game, where TacTex had very high errors.

While not as highly correlated as the errors in current component prices, the errors for future component price predictions (Figures 12, 16, and 20) show a somewhat similar pattern.

In addition to making comparisons between the participants, we can also compare the difficulty of making predictions for each of the three sets of games. For computer prices, it appears to be easier to make predictions for Set B, especially current predictions, while Set A tends to have higher future prediction errors. On the other hand, predicting component prices appears to be more difficult for Set B, especially current component prices. The reasons for these differences between sets are not clear, unlike the error spikes in Figures 1 and 3 that could be traced to specific agent behaviors. Better understanding these differences would

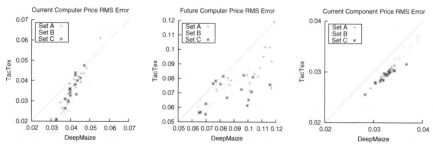

Fig. 9. Current computer prices (TT / DM, $r=.92$)

Fig. 10. Future computer prices (TT / DM, $r=.70$)

Fig. 11. Current component prices (TT / DM, $r=.97$)

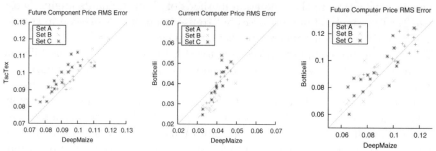

Fig. 12. Future component prices (TT / DM, $r=.87$)

Fig. 13. Current computer prices (Bot. / DM, $r=.87$)

Fig. 14. Future computer prices (Bot. / DM, $r=.85$)

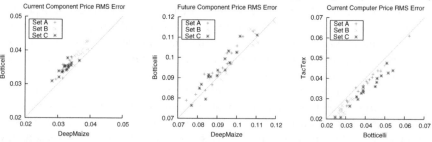

Fig. 15. Current component prices (Bot. / DM, $r=.93$)

Fig. 16. Future component prices (Bot. / DM, $r=.95$)

Fig. 17. Current computer prices (TT / Bot., $r=.97$)

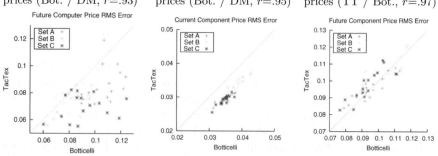

Fig. 18. Future computer prices (TT / Bot., $r=.49$)

Fig. 19. Current component prices (TT / Bot., $r=.94$)

Fig. 20. Future component prices (TT / Bot., $r=.87$)

likely be useful in designing improved predictors that can handle a wider variety of agent behaviors.

It is interesting to note that the patterns observed above (such as correlations between errors and which participant had the lowest errors) generally appear to hold equally well for all three sets of games. Given that the prediction methods used often require the user to choose a data set composed of past game results, it would not be surprising for a participant to make particularly accurate predictions on games that are most similar to the games in the chosen data set, and for certain participants to favor certain sets of games as a result, but this does not appear to have happened.

4.4   Differences between Participants across Days

To make comparisons at a finer level of detail, we can also plot the errors of each agent on a daily basis, rather than for each game. Figures 21-26 show a subset of the comparisons from Figures 9-20 at this level. Again, RMS error is measured, and the first and last 20 days of errors are omitted. These figures largely serve to shed further light on the observations that have been made previously. Unlike the previous set of figures, no indication is given about the set of games from which each point plotted came, but plotting each set separately reveals very similarly shaped distributions for each set.

Figure 23 shows that the daily errors for the current computer predictions of TacTex and Botticelli are highly correlated, as would be expected from Figure 17. The correlation between TacTex and DeepMaize is much weaker, as seen in Figure 21 (the plot of Botticelli and DeepMaize is nearly the same). As noted before, Figures 9 and 13 show that the performance of DeepMaize tends to improve relative to the other participants as the predictions become more challenging. While a distribution of the same shape (high correlation but a high slope) in Figure 23 would cause this outcome, instead it appears that there are some predictions for which DeepMaize has similar errors (those along the line $y = x$), along with a cluster of predictions (along the bottom-left) for which DeepMaize has higher errors. It may be the case that there are certain relatively easy predictions with which DeepMaize has difficulty, and that these easy predictions occur less often in the more challenging games. Many of the points in this cluster are from the early parts of games where DeepMaize has higher errors (see Figure 1), but not all – even with the first 70 days omitted from the plot, the cluster is still visible.

Based on Figures 10 and 14, we would expect DeepMaize's daily future computer price prediction errors to be weakly correlated with those of TacTex and somewhat correlated with those of Botticelli, and Figures 22 and 24 confirm this expectation (the plot of TacTex and Botticelli is similar to Figure 22). Looking at Figure 2, in which Botticelli and DeepMaize have nearly identical average daily errors, it is perhaps surprising that their correlation here is not higher.

Figures 25 and 26 show the daily errors for the current and future component price predictions of DeepMaize and TacTex (plots for Botticelli are similar). These errors are highly correlated, as they were in Figures 11 and 12. Figure 25

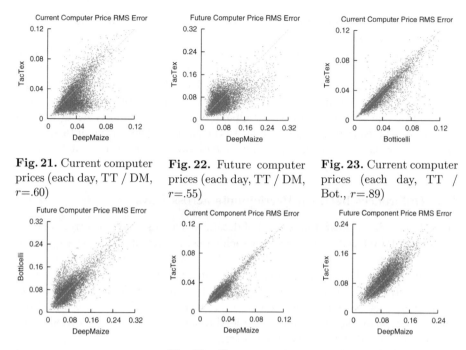

Fig. 21. Current computer prices (each day, TT / DM, r=.60)

Fig. 22. Future computer prices (each day, TT / DM, r=.55)

Fig. 23. Current computer prices (each day, TT / Bot., r=.89)

Fig. 24. Future computer prices (each day, Bot. / DM, r=.77)

Fig. 25. Current component prices (each day, TT / DM, r=.90)

Fig. 26. Future component prices (each day, TT / DM, r=.85)

illustrates that the pattern observed for a single game in Figure 7 (mostly low errors around 0.03, with occasional spikes that affect all participants similarly) is true in general. Similarly, the pattern seen in one game in Figure 8 (errors more evenly distributed over a wide range but still highly correlated between participants) appears in Figure 26.

One additional observation that can be made is that while a participant may show consistently lower errors at the full-game level (for instance, TacTex in Figures 10 and 11), there may still be a large number of days on which it has higher errors (Figures 22 and 25). This observation may indicate that there is still room for the participant to improve, or it may simply be a result of the stochastic nature of the game (that is, for each situation in which predictions are made, there may actually be a wide distribution over possible outcomes depending on random game factors such as demand fluctuations). Both possibilities are likely true to some degree.

5   Conclusion

We have introduced the TAC SCM Prediction Challenge and analyzed the results of the 2007 competition. Our analysis showed that different prediction methods can achieve similar prediction accuracy and that errors are frequently, but not always, correlated. At the same time, some participants are clearly stronger than others in certain areas. TacTex regularly had lower errors in three of the four prediction categories during the middle of each game, but suffered from high errors at the start and end of games. The winner, DeepMaize, was fairly effective in all aspects of the challenge.

There are many additional ways in which the results of the competition could be analyzed. We have focused on giving a high-level comparison of the prediction accuracy of the participants, but it would also be possible to continue this analysis at a finer level, such as by comparing accuracy on predictions for individual RFQs or by trying to identify the specific conditions under which one agent outperformed another. Such analysis could be useful in helping participants to identify the shortcomings of their prediction methods and to make future improvements.

Acknowledgments

We would like to thank the SICS team for developing the TAC SCM game server, all teams that have contributed to the agent repository, and the participants in the Prediction Challenge. This research was supported in part by NSF CAREER award IIS-0237699.

References

1. Collins, J., Arunachalam, R., Sadeh, N., Eriksson, J., Finne, N., Janson, S.: The Supply Chain Management game for the 2007 Trading Agent Competition. Technical report (2006), https://www.sics.se/tac/tac07scmspec.pdf
2. Pardoe, D., Stone, P.: An autonomous agent for supply chain management. In: Adomavicius, G., Gupta, A. (eds.) Handbooks in Information Systems Series: Business Computing. Elsevier, Amsterdam (2008)
3. Kiekintveld, C., Miller, J., Jordan, P.R., Callender, L.F., Wellman, M.P.: Forecasting market prices in a supply chain game. Submitted to Electronic Commerce Research Applications (2008)
4. Witten, I.H., Frank, E.: Data Mining: Practical Machine Learning Tools and Techniques with Java Implementations. Morgan Kaufmann, San Francisco (1999)
5. Kiekintveld, C., Wellman, M., Singh, S., Estelle, J., Vorobeychik, Y., Soni, V., Rudary, M.: Distributed feedback control for decision making on supply chains. In: Fourteenth International Conference on Automated Planning and Scheduling (2004)
6. Benisch, M., Sardinha, A., Andrews, J., Sadeh, N.: Cmieux: Adaptive strategies for competitive supply chain trading. In: Eighth International Conference on Electronic Commerce (2006)
7. Burke, D.A., Brown, K.N., Hnich, B., Tarim, A.: Learning market prices for a real-time supply chain management trading agent. In: AAMAS 2006 Workshop on Trading Agent Design and Analysis/Agent Mediated Electronic Commerce (2006)
8. Benisch, M., Greenwald, A., Grypari, I., Lederman, R., Naroditskiy, V., Tschantz, M.: Botticelli: A supply chain management agent. In: Third International Joint Conference on Autonomous Agents and Multiagent Systems (AAMAS), vol. 3, pp. 1174–1181 (2004)

Author Index

Printing: Mercedes-Druck, Berlin
Binding: Stein+Lehmann, Berlin